Totality Inside Out

Totality Inside Out

Rethinking Crisis and
Conflict under Capital

KEVIN FLOYD, JEN HEDLER PHILLIS,
AND SARIKA CHANDRA, EDITORS

Fordham University Press
NEW YORK   2022

Royalties earned from the sales of this book will be donated to the Marxist Literary Group.

Copyright © 2022 Fordham University Press

All rights reserved. No part of this publication may be reproduced, stored in a retrieval system, or transmitted in any form or by any means—electronic, mechanical, photocopy, recording, or any other—except for brief quotations in printed reviews, without the prior permission of the publisher.

Fordham University Press has no responsibility for the persistence or accuracy of URLs for external or third-party Internet websites referred to in this publication and does not guarantee that any content on such websites is, or will remain, accurate or appropriate.

Fordham University Press also publishes its books in a variety of electronic formats. Some content that appears in print may not be available in electronic books.

Visit us online at www.fordhampress.com.

Library of Congress Cataloging-in-Publication Data available online at https://catalog.loc.gov.

Printed in the United States of America

24 23 22   5 4 3 2 1

First edition

for Kevin Floyd

Contents

	Introduction: Totality Inside Out KEVIN FLOYD, WITH BRENT RYAN BELLAMY, SARAH BROUILLETTE, SARIKA CHANDRA, CHRIS CHEN, AND JEN HEDLER PHILLIS	1
1	Let the Dead Bury the Dead: Race, Gender, and Class Composition in the U.S. after 1965 TIM KREINER	29
2	(Un)making Value: Reading Social Reproduction through the Question of Totality MARINA VISHMIDT AND ZOE SUTHERLAND	67
3	Tripartheid: How Global White Supremacy Triumphs through Neoliberalism ARTHUR SCARRITT	91
4	Remapping the Race/Class Problematic SARIKA CHANDRA AND CHRIS CHEN	135
5	On Artistic Autonomy as a Bourgeois Fetish SARAH BROUILLETTE AND JOSHUA CLOVER	192
6	Ecology with Totality: The Case of Morton's *Hyperobjects* and Klein's *This Changes Everything* BRENT RYAN BELLAMY	211
	Acknowledgments	237
	List of Contributors	239
	Index	243

Totality Inside Out

Introduction: Totality Inside Out

KEVIN FLOYD, WITH BRENT RYAN BELLAMY,
SARAH BROUILLETTE, SARIKA CHANDRA,
CHRIS CHEN, AND JEN HEDLER PHILLIS

This volume breaks new ground by theorizing capitalist social relations as part of an integrated, unified, and contradictory totality. Through sustained engagement with recent developments in contemporary Marxist scholarship, it aims for a more expansive analysis of capitalism that uncovers interlinked sites of contemporary political conflict over racial and economic justice, materialist feminist and queer critique, climate change, and aesthetic value. How these categories might refer to the processes that systematically reproduce an internally divided social whole, we believe, is the urgent political question of our time. The essays included in this collection conceive of capitalism as a unitary and relentlessly totalizing historical and global socioeconomic system that has progressively reshaped a range of seemingly disconnected systems over time: systems of oppression, to be sure, but also systems of value and the global ecological system. These essays also maintain that Marxist and non-Marxist ambitions to describe the relationship between economic exploitation and these distinctive systems share a desire to illuminate the contours of a social whole and to reveal the imbrication of histories of political struggle organized around a wide-ranging set of categories (ranging from aesthetic value to the environment, along with those of race, class, gender, sexuality, and ability): they all aspire toward totality.

The specific form of totality that capitalism organizes, as Susan Ferguson has argued, cannot be arrived at by simply assembling additive lists of oppressions or by reducing the material specificity of these oppressions to underlying class relations.[1] Rather, such relations of domination and subordination are "reciprocally determined, or co-constituted" through a logic of accumulation that is not simply one terrain of social conflict among others but a unitary system of enforced social comparison that materially reproduces otherwise seemingly incommensurable forms of oppression in integral relation to each other.[2] Ferguson argues:

> To speak of a social whole dominated by the *capitalist* dynamic—a capitalist social formation—is not to say that the economic wage-labour relationship unilaterally *causes* racial or gender oppression. All social relations are integral to a complex social formation, which is broadly organised in accordance with capital's drive for accumulation and profit.[3]

Such an expanded view of capitalism as a logic not only of production, but of integrative social reproduction, helps to account for how the material imperative of accumulation has structurally shaped violent ongoing colonial, settler-colonial, and imperial histories and the historical trajectory of a range of contemporary emancipatory social movements.

The social whole that capitalism assembles is systematically reproduced through a self-expanding system of enforced social cohesion and competitive exploitation, extraction, and dispossession with increasingly ecocidal consequences. Such consequences are not simply a historical accident but rather a systemic feature of continuous accumulation and capitalist growth. Underscoring the necessity for an integrative analysis of contemporary political struggles, *Totality Inside Out*'s reimagining of older conceptions of the concept of totality challenges materialist analyses that have rigorously maintained the separation between exploitation and other seemingly discrete or ontologically separable forms of oppression. These essays emerge from the need for a broad reframing of capitalism as what Nancy Fraser has called "an institutionalized social order" that is reducible neither to the sphere of the economic (narrowly understood as exploitation at the point of production) nor to tallies of extrinsically related categories of identity.[4] The concept of the social whole reimagined in this collection is not axiomatic or presupposed as a ready-made solution to historical divisions. Rather, the essays implicitly and explicitly pose totality as an open question that cannot be theorized without a robust investigation into the linkages between different spheres of structured social activity.

As one of its major interventions, *Totality Inside Out* delivers a sharp critique of the now-traditional divide between the critique of political economy and so-called identity politics. By reexamining the conceptual premises that continue to sunder the former from the latter, the articles contained in this collection broadly contend that our basic categories of analysis must be rethought in order to avoid reestablishing false divisions between the history of capitalism and comparative racial and gender formation. Materialist critiques of the politics of identity have often reinforced this split by ignoring the particularity of the U.S. working class as a political identity in itself while radically underestimating the force of whiteness as a consequential form of interest group "solidarity" that has frequently overridden hard-won interracial connections forged between the enslaved, dispossessed indigenous populations, and working people across racial divisions. Feminist, critical race, ethnic studies, and disability studies scholars have long maintained that orthodox Marxist analyses fail to adequately account for the specific forms of domination experienced by people of color, women, queer subjects, and populations designated "disabled." However, the absence of a deeper engagement with the basic categories of capitalist political economy and the determinants of capitalist crises in works that have largely ignored recent developments in contemporary Marxist scholarship have not taken up the opportunity to scrutinize how oppressions are not only interlinked through but historically altered by their imbrication within capitalist structures.

The essays in the collection engage with recent Marxist work such as social reproduction theory, class composition approaches, and materialist energy critique, new approaches that possess the potential to reorient and dramatically expand older, orthodox Marxist accounts of race, gender, sexuality, and class itself as social locations and principles of social organization. As the essays that follow bear out, recognizing that political economy and subject formation, economics and identity, accumulation and climate catastrophe are co-constituting can help us to avoid reproducing deadlocked debates over causal primacy, or culture and political economy, and instead explore how capitalist imperatives might knit together racist, misogynistic, heteronormative, ableist, imperialist, and environmentally destructive social relations.

This collection is unified by its aspiration to remap a specifically capitalist social whole in a manner that diverges from orthodox readings from the historical-materialist tradition that have long identified the category of totality with the socioeconomic sphere. This narrow view is inherited from the theorist arguably most responsible for totality's place in the theory and practice of Marxism: György Lukács. As it is in the pages that follow, totality thinking for Lukács was an *intention*, an *aspiration*. Likewise, just as the essays in this collection do, Lukács understood totality as a practical matter that cannot be separated from the question of struggle.[5] But, for Lukács, neither this aspiration nor this struggle can be enacted by anyone: the proletarian is the only subject structurally and systemically positioned to have this potential because its self-knowledge coincides with knowledge of the social per se. That is, as soon as the proletarian knows itself—as soon as it comprehends the truth of its structural position within the capitalist social formation—it also knows the truth of the broader capitalist process. And so reification:

> The quantification of objects, their subordination to abstract mental categories makes its appearance in the life of the worker immediately as a process of abstraction of which he is the victim, and which cuts him off from his labour-power, forcing him to sell it on the market as a commodity, belonging to him. And by selling this, his only commodity, he integrates it (and himself: for his commodity is inseparable from his physical existence) into a specialised process that has been rationalised and mechanised, a process that he discovers already existing, complete and able to function without him and in which he is no more than a cipher reduced to an abstract quantity, a mechanised and rationalised tool.[6]

The worker therefore "perceives the split in his being preserved in the brutal form of what is in its whole tendency a slavery without limits."[7] But it is then this very fact that "forces him to surpass the immediacy of his condition" and ultimately implies the "destruction of those confusing categories of reflection which had deformed true objectivity into a posture of merely immediate, passive, contemplation."[8] It is crucial to note that Lukács's operative definition of *proletariat* does not include surplus populations, those expelled from the production process altogether, or dispossessed indigenous groups.[9] Here, this privileged standpoint is defined by the subjectivation of labor: the exploited, surplus-value–producing seller of labor power. Lukács's account of totality, that is, is rigorously corroborated with a standpoint immanent to capitalist social relations themselves.

Why would this totalizing aspiration want to distinguish this specific political subject? Because the social is here understood as essentially and exclusively socioeconomic—we might say the socioeconomic is reducible to point-of-production surplus-value extraction. Lukács's account of "the phenomenon of reification" famously extends Marx's theory of commodity fetishism to the whole of society, to "all the dimensions of social activity": "the structure of commodity relations [can] be made to yield a model of all the objective forms of bourgeois society together with all the subjective forms corresponding to them."[10] The standpoint of the proletariat is a privileged *social* standpoint precisely to the extent—and on this

Lukács insists—that the commodity form is the key to the social organization of life in contemporary capitalist societies more broadly. For Lukács, capitalist society rationalizes all spheres of life, and it is the commodity form that logically grounds this total process. This is the sense in which totality is inseparable from a standpoint immanent to capitalist social relations: it necessarily implies a radical/revolutionary subject, a subject with a critical, totalizing epistemological capacity. Indeed, the proletariat's singular potential to reconcile all contradictions of the social as such can hardly be more emphatic than in Lukács's notorious identification of the proletariat as history's "identical subject-object."[11]

And indeed, this identification of the specific social forms wrought by capital with the social as such continues in the work of key practitioners of totality thinking whose work engages centrally with the terms of Lukács's argument, though they take their distance from his faith in the proletarian identical subject-object. If, for example, reification, like commodity fetishism, is, for Lukács, a veil concealing an organic, unified social totality mediated by labor, contemporary critical theorist Moishe Postone in a sense maintains the opposite: that capital itself constitutes a blind, unconscious, totalizing social subject.[12] For Postone, capital is a system of social relations that dominates concrete persons by subjecting them to abstract, objective forms of routinized, obligatory practice; here, the system of capital dominates impersonally, compelling determinate forms of social activity (not the least of which, for Postone, is labor itself). Marx's categories, as Postone puts it, "refer to structured forms of practice that are simultaneously forms of subjectivity and objectivity."[13] In this account, labor is already an abstract compulsory form of social activity, dependent on the valorization of capital while remaining the necessary catalyst of that same process. Capital's organization of labor through the measure of abstract value implies the system's own ontological priority, its power to compel the very forms of social activity on which it depends. Labor becomes a reified, instrumental form of social action; it becomes practical activity no longer performed in order to produce, but in order to acquire what is produced by others. It becomes the very practice of self-valorizing value. From this perspective, if we want to say that capital is dead labor, we also have to say that labor is living capital.

Crucially, this means for Postone that totality is not an ontological unity veiled and fragmented by capital, but that capital itself—as in Adorno's ongoing account of capital as the totalized violence of an "exchange society"—is an objectively totalizing system of impersonal domination. Totality, here, is not something to be restored, but a web of violent domination to be abolished. If for Lukács, as for Hegel, we might say that the true is the whole, for Postone, as for Adorno, the whole is the false.[14] But even here again, as in Lukács, social domination is identified with socioeconomic domination. In Lukács, Adorno, and Postone, the practice of totality thinking universalizes value relations.

A concept as abstract and old-fashioned as totality may appear at first to be entirely disconnected from the material and very contemporary forms of oppression that we experience under capitalism today. But the universalization of the socioeconomic realm that sits at the center of orthodox totality thinking carries through to the false universalism that marked much of twentieth-century anti-capitalist politics, which, like Lukács, identified the industrial working class as the only subject capable of challenging capitalism's domination. Uncovering this history reveals a secret at the heart of the conflict between Marxist and feminist, anti-racist, and queer critiques of contemporary life: those political movements that emerged in the late sixties to organize on behalf of categories of race, gender, sexuality, and ability did so in response to the identarian standpoint politics embedded in the classical workers' movement. As Salar Mohandesi reminds us in a recent essay, so-called identity politics arose against the notion that "the specific political demands of a particular kind of skilled, male, and often white industrial worker in the capitalist heartland could stand in for the struggles of everyone else, allegedly producing a kind of unity from above."[15] To put it more plainly (and perhaps provocatively), what contemporary critics now call "identity politics" originated in order to set itself apart from an earlier form of identity politics, one that centered on white male industrial workers to the exclusion of all other oppressed people. Point-of-production politics was itself a form of disavowed identity politics that has been slow to recognize its own material specificity and the limits of its emancipatory vision based on the universalization of the position of the industrial worker. Such specification, we maintain, does not negate the strategic importance of such subjects and the historically changing racial and gendered composition of this class of workers for projects of anti-systemic social transformation.

Such an analysis helps us grasp the conditions under which documents like the 1977 manifesto "A Black Feminist Statement," produced by the black lesbian feminist Combahee River Collective, was produced. It also raises questions about the extent to which identity politics have become, as numerous contemporary critics seem to suggest, a mere tactical or strategic error one could simply choose to stop making. We may begin with this important passage from "A Black Feminist Statement":

> We realize that the liberation of all oppressed peoples necessitates the destruction of the political-economic systems of capitalism and imperialism as well as patriarchy. We are socialists because we believe that work must be organized for the collective benefit of those who do the work and create the products, and not for the profit of the bosses. Material resources must be equally distributed among those who create these resources. We are not convinced, however, that a socialist revolution that is not also a feminist and antiracist revolution will guarantee our liberation.[16]

What concerns provoked the skepticism expressed by that famous final sentence? It follows immediately upon an account of socialist revolution defined by the redistribution of the products of labor among workers. On one hand, then, anti-capitalism is here a political given, and the statement represents an effort to enrich what such a politics might mean, to think the problem of how to integrate anti-racist, anti-sexist, anti-homophobic analysis within an unmissably anti-capitalist political horizon. On the other, the passage suggests the way in which anti-capitalist revolution has been defined by *point-of-production politics*: a worker standpoint, and indeed arguably (in this famously influential articulation of identity politics) a worker *identity*. And the privilege accorded to this point-of-production standpoint is, needless to say, a problem: "We need to articulate the real class situation of persons who are not merely raceless, sexless workers, but for whom racial and sexual oppression are significant determinants in their working/economic lives."[17]

Also worth noting in the Combahee statement is the speed with which the question of workers' identities is followed by another: "We must also question whether lesbian separatism is an adequate and progressive political analysis and strategy, even for those who practice it, since it so completely denies any but the sexual sources of women's oppression, negating the facts of class and race."[18] Can we not make a claim about "raceless, sexless" workers that is analogous to this claim about lesbian separatism "negating the facts of class and race"? The privileges required to identify as a "raceless, sexless" worker have included, historically, of course, the very racial and gender privileges that tend to make race and gender invisible to the subject so privileged: whiteness and maleness. Notwithstanding the well-documented contributions to the workers' movement from women and people of color, the reasons worker identity has historically tended to be white and male are not hard to discern: because privileging one aspect of identity is much easier if you experience privilege in other dimensions. Therefore, the Combahee statement—this early, pivotal articulation of identity politics—responds to and, however implicitly, critiques another massively consequential form of identity politics that has rarely been identified as such: the historical workers' movement, which posited a crucial worker identity that tended routinely to presuppose whiteness and maleness.

In the workers' movement, as the authors of "A History of Separation" have provocatively and cogently argued, proletarianization—which refers most rigorously to a process, to a dynamic relation of exploitation that revolution would make obsolete, a relation to be *negated*—congealed over time into an identity to be *affirmed*.[19] The workers' movement insisted that a necessary step toward the overthrow of capitalism was the establishment of workers' power, specifically political power: the securing of specific rights and recognition from the state would become "essential weapons in the coming class war."[20] So unions and parties constructed a working-class identity "as a key feature of their organizing efforts," which "succeeded in convincing workers to suspend their interests as isolated sellers in a competitive labor market, and instead to act out of a commitment to the collective project of the labor movement."[21] This suspension of competition necessarily also required the suspension of other dimensions of their identities, including racial, national, and ethnic differences, that were to be eclipsed by their collective identity as workers. "A History of Separation" goes on:

> Within the labor movement, workers claimed that the class identity they promoted and affirmed really was *universal* in character. It supposedly subsumed all workers, regardless of their specific qualities: as mothers, as recent immigrants, as oppressed nationalities, as unmarried men (and at the outermost limit: as disabled, as homosexuals, and so on).[22]

This particularity-as-universality was constituted through a series of exclusions that made "non class identities . . . inessential traits which divided workers against one another."[23] As a result, "the horizontal struggle between political groups, organized around different identities, was perceived [from inside the workers' movement] as a vertical struggle between a depth category—the class essence—and a variety of surface categories."[24] Small wonder, then, that the homogenization that seemed to be taking place in the factory was always partial and that only a small portion of the proletariat ever identified with the workers' movement, with many proletarians continuing to align along the lines of race, nation, or gender, for example.[25] This context helps explain the Combahee Collective's concerns about whether the anti-capitalist revolution will also be anti-sexist and anti-racist: responding to a radical, proletarian, point-of-production standpoint defined in part by the invisibilized privileges of whiteness and maleness, the Combahee statement raises the problem of how heterosexism and racism are materially reproduced under capitalism at and beyond the point of production.

This history helps us see that what the term "identity politics" describes has always been a problem of totality, and this in multiple senses. Identity politics in its post-sixties form is a historical product, a side effect, of a specific, limited form of universalism: the point-of-production aspiration toward totality, the universalizing anti-capitalist standpoint that has traditionally taken the form of a worker standpoint. As Timothy Kreiner draws out in his contribution, "Let the Dead Bury the Dead: Race, Gender, and Class Composition in the U.S. after 1965," the earliest examples of radical movements organized around race and class were motivated by the exclusions that the point-of-production standpoint demanded. Identity politics was a direct response, in this sense, to a false universalism, a universalism that was itself a form of identity politics that pretended not to be. The transformation of these early identity-politics groups from radical to centrist, from opponents to enforcers of the status quo, took place because of ongoing organizational challenges and debates. As Kreiner demonstrates, understanding this complex history enables today's socialists, communists, and revolutionaries to recognize how radical forms of identity politics, like the arguments found in the Combahee statement, would enrich anti-capitalist politics rather than making peace with the current political economic order.

Marina Vishmidt and Zoe Sutherland pose a similar question in their contribution to this volume, "(Un)making Value: Reading Social Reproduction through the Question of Totality," but they begin from the side of identity politics. They argue that the concept of totality can intervene in long-standing debates in and around Marxist feminism, which are troubled by their own conflicts over universality and particularism, inclusion and exclusion. Attending not only to scholarly articulations of materialist feminism and intersectionality, Vishmidt and Sutherland turn also to recent feminist actions, including the International Women's Strike, the Polish strike against abortion, and the Argentinian Ni Una Menos strike against male violence, to argue for an approach to feminist theorizing and organizing that mobilizes already-existing grassroots movements without subsuming their diverse demands under a falsely universal category of "woman."

As the politics of identity transformed from revolutionary movements to organizations entirely compatible with the maintenance of capitalism, the labor movement followed suit, largely thanks to changes in specific social and material conditions, which have all but disappeared. As Robert Brenner has shown, in the crucial years between 1965 and 1973—the very years, it is worth underlining, when these early identity formations began to coalesce—the U.S. manufacturing rate of profit began a fall from which it has not recovered, "suddenly [projecting the world] from boom to crisis."[26] The secular collapse of growth and productivity since the seventies, along with hollowing out of the industrial sector, has undercut the material basis for point-of-production identity politics globally. Industrial workers, as "A History of Separation" suggests, "no longer appear the vanguard of a class in the process of becoming revolutionary," so much so that, "if the historical workers' movement is today alien to us, it is because the *form* of the capital labor relation that sustained the workers' movement no longer obtains."[27]

This alienation is perhaps nowhere more visible than in those moments where collaboration between labor and capital have intensified in recent decades. When organized workers take an action to keep a plant from closing, for example, "capital and labor find themselves now in collaboration to preserve capital's self-reproduction, to preserve the labor relation along with the firm's viability. . . . Caught in the affirmation trap, labor ceases to be the antithesis of capital."[28] Thus, the very critique leveled against those contemporary forms of identity politics that *would* make peace with the current social order—such as those espoused by Hillary Clinton's 2016 presidential campaign—can be leveled at the workers' movement since about 1973. Identity politics in its familiar, toothless contemporary form, as a politics that demands recognition by the state and representational inclusion within the current social order (rather than a radical questioning of that order), has at least one of its crucial precursors in the workers' movement.

And consider, as another dimension of this inseparability of the totality problem from the identity problem, the discourse of intersectionality. As Susan Ferguson notes, intersectional formulations of feminism "risk reproducing" what it sets "out to critique: a fragmented and textualised conception of reality."[29] It does not adequately explain "why and how oppressions interact in the ways that they do, and why they change across broad historical periods in the ways that they do."[30] The general focus on specifying the *subject* of politics tends to eclipse the larger systems of domination so that, according to Mohandesi, "partisans of this kind of intersectional identity politics almost always revert to composing breathless catalogues of injustice when trying to explain what they oppose—the colonial white supremacist heteronormative patriarchy, or something to that effect" because such lists are "the only way to present the object of social struggle."[31] On the one hand, then, identity politics, as a presupposition of the discourse of intersectionality, tends to imply a set of differing (and "interlocking") systems of oppression ultimately disarticulated from each other, in relation to which political agents can only build coalitions out of groups that are themselves coalitional and riven by internal divisions. The result is ontological atomism, as David McNally argues, where each of these systems of oppression is identified as "autonomous" rather than constituted through and through by other determinations.[32] But in this atomism we can make out the aspiration toward totality, even if it means that naming "the object of social struggle" has to take the form of a "breathless catalogue." An expression like "colonial white supremacist heteronormative patriarchy" clearly represents—in addition to whatever additional work it is doing—an aspiration toward totality, an effort to "name the system." The challenge we face—and that this collection tackles—is transforming this "breathless catalogue" into an account of how capitalism materially binds these systems of oppressions so that they are reproduced together. Despite sustained attention to the question of totality, both the workers' movement and "neoliberal" forms of anti-racist, feminist, and queer politics have not only accepted but often actively defended these systems, accepting the capitalist logic of accumulation and abstract value production as desirable measures of social progress. The underlying mechanisms that simultaneously produce persistent low or slow growth within the United States and other high-income countries, persistently low demand for labor relative to supply even in developing countries, and abstract catalogues of disconnected and formally analogous oppressions have remained undertheorized within contemporary scholarship, which has treated these as extrinisically related social phenomena or framed them as combinatory predicates of identity.

The essays in this collection attempt to bring these discourses together and, in so doing, to understand totality from the outside in. In this, *Totality Inside Out* enters into conversation with recent work on the specifically capitalist logic of social reproduction: those processes that serve to reproduce capital—or, more specifically, that without which capital cannot long survive. Nancy Fraser has called these the "background conditions of possibility" of the surplus-value producing capital-labor relation that are radically reshaped by that relation.[33] From this perspective, we can discern how gender and race make the white worker identity possible and how examining the outside of what has been traditionally considered the non-marketized domain of the "socioeconomic"—reproductive labor, surplus populations, environmentalism, and even aesthetic criticism—gives us a new view of totality. Rather than center itself on the now largely pro-capitalist white male industrial worker, this collection views totality from the outside in, attending to the identities and ideas historically understood to be secondary to the primary functioning of capitalism.

Increasingly prominent contemporary conversations around the question of social reproduction have once again highlighted what Marxist-feminism and the so-called domestic labor debates long ago highlighted: the inescapably gendered dimensions of the reproduction of the capital/labor relation. The contemporary critical discourse that examines processes of social reproduction, for example, as Susan Ferguson puts it:

> ... insists that our understanding of capitalism is incomplete if we treat it as simply an economic system involving workers and owners, and fail to examine the ways in which wider social reproduction of the system—that is, the daily and generational reproductive labor that occurs in households, schools, hospitals, prisons, and so on—sustains the drive for accumulation.[34]

This theoretical expansion of the concept of social reproduction highlights the way in which domestic, traditionally gendered household labor is typically understood as the site of labor power's generational reproduction and racialization. If labor power is the very source of surplus value, domestic household labor is the very source of labor power in a range of free and unfree forms. This traditionally gendered form of labor comprises a set of activities on which the reproduction of the capital-labor relation depends, and it has been subject to partial commodification. It is also, as Tithi Bhattacharya puts it, "naturalized into nonexistence": this is labor that is unwaged and—for that very reason—not generally socially recognized as labor at all.[35] Indeed, *Capital* would appear to reinscribe this naturalization, this refusal of recognition, focused as it is on capital's abstract laws of motion; it introduces the pivotal concept of labor power, maintaining that the capitalist "must be lucky enough" to find on the market a commodity capable of producing more value than that commodity costs to reproduce, and moves right past the question of where such an unusual commodity could come from.[36]

Indeed, this labor differs from shop-floor activity in that it does not itself produce value. The "production and reproduction of the special commodity at the heart of capitalism"—labor-power—is itself "noncapitalist."[37] The value of the commodity labor power, for Marx, is determined by the value of the means of subsistence it requires, means of subsistence that themselves are obviously commodified and internal to the circuit of value, but defining the value of labor power in this way also indicates that domestic household labor, the labor that transforms those means of subsistence into labor-power in the first place, adds no new value to that commodity. That is, the "naturalization" of this labor into "nonexistence" has, as at least one of its preconditions, an established, historically sedimented dissociation of reproductive labor from the value circuit.[38] The structurally separated reproductive and the value-creating productive spheres, according to Cinzia Arruzza, retain specific characteristics yet "are necessarily combined as concrete moments of an articulated totality."[39] She cautions against reading the "relation between production and reproduction in a mechanistic or deterministic manner," emphasizing that "there is no automatic or direct 'reflection' between the different moments of this totality . . . or between one particular moment and the totality as a whole."[40] Instead, questions of social reproduction, for Arruzza, enable inquiry into the relationship among the various spheres, such as welfare state policies, market/nonmarket-mediated domestic/care work, and formal/informal racialized migrant labor.

From this perspective, thinking capitalist totality can no longer identify the "formal economy" with the social as Lukács, Postone, and Adorno did. If capital remains an objectively totalizing social process, we can no longer understand this process exclusively in terms of the wage relation; we must also attend to the question of capitalism's systemic reproduction. To shift focus in such a way—from the production and circulation of value to the social reproduction of the capital-labor relation itself—is to restage the totality problem quite radically: insisting on the importance of including race, gender, and sexuality within a unitary framework and rejecting the logic of earlier dual-systems approaches. (But this also involves restaging the question of totality itself, demanding an answer to the question of what exactly a unitary framework would mean.) Theorizing gender, for instance, would understand the family form as central to capital's reproduction, even though it is "outside" the formal economy.[41] "The capitalist gender-order is thus structurally founded not on a transhistorical patriarchy or separate domestic mode of production, but on the social articulation between the capitalist mode of production and working-class households, which are fundamental to the production and reproduction of labor power."[42] This logic would reject notions of a separate domestic mode of production, for example, or a mere holdover from a previous mode of production.[43]

So the gendered reproductive sphere, not subject to the law of value and for that reason not subject to what Postone has influentially identified as the impersonal domination of the market, is a sphere in which more potentially openly conflictual and violent forms of domination are operative.[44] The reproduction of capital, understood through the prism of gender, turns centrally on this question of value and of what must be excluded from the circuit of value if the reproduction of the capital-labor relation is to be secured over the long term. This understanding of gender and reproductive labor doesn't deny that capitalism has a long history of undermining the family, encouraging cheaper female labor to enter the terrain of wage labor: "Compulsory work for the capitalist usurped the place, not only of the children's play, but also of independent labor at home, within customary limits, for the family itself."[45] Indeed, Lise Vogel makes the crucial dialectical point that the gendering of reproductive labor can be understood in terms of capital's most basic social contradictions, that capital is always either potentially or actually caught between two incompatible tendencies: to naturalize womanhood as that which reproduces labor power, and thereby dissociate womanhood from the circuit of value, or to draw women into the circuit of value in the form of relatively inexpensive labor power.[46] Such a dynamic of creating and recreating of the boundary between formally free subjects of waged exploitation and expropriable and expendable populations subject to direct domination also marks historical processes of racialization realized through the direct expropriation of land, enslavement, imperial warfare, immigration restrictions, penal state violence, and the creation of surplus populations.

Indeed, as Chris Chen demonstrates in "The Limit Point of Capitalist Equality," undertheorizing the mediation between racial structures and capitalist reproduction risks reinforcing a system of explanation that attributes the causes of racial oppression to the attributes of racial subjects. We need, then, to scrutinize how racial identity is the "consequence and not the cause" of a set of social processes and antagonisms that racial categories do not explain.[47] Just as class is most rigorously understood as a dynamic relation that has tended historically to congeal into an affirmable identity—the proletariat, to the extent that this term has any positive content, is the pure effect of an unrelentingly negative, antagonistic relation, and in this respect simply "the negation of this society"[48]—anti-racist social movements in the U.S. post–civil rights era have tended similarly to congeal into counterinsurgent racial liberal ideals of cultural inclusion, collapsing the concept of race into pluralist and increasingly ethnonationalist discourses of cultural difference, in order to manage more antagonistic and anti-systemic forms of opposition to racial domination.[49]

Racialization, moreover, mediates—in addition to everything else it does—the social reproduction of capital. The formation of racial and ethnic boundaries structures this reproduction in part through its effects on the socialization of wage labor. As Chen argues, naturalizing "a system of wage differentials, wealth stratification, and occupational and spatial segregation," racialization facilitates the familiar tactic of "divide and rule," thereby fueling capital's inherent tendency toward the devaluation of wage labor more generally.[50] At the same time, the consolidation and ongoing cohesion of a white cross-class identity within the United States and a resurgent white nationalism that speaks in the language of cultural difference and demographic preservation have arguably remained the most politically consequential instance of what critics decry as the anti-solidaristic character of "identity politics" within the postwar period. References to wealth stratification and spatial segregation already begin to suggest additional processes of expulsion and expropriation outside the wage relation proper: racialization has legitimated not only wage differentials but just as crucially the exclusion of specific populations from wage labor altogether—though hardly from capitalism itself. Race has thus in the present become a signifier of degrees of vulnerability to falling below the threshold of wage exploitation into the domain of what Neferti Tadiar has called "remaindered life" or "the time of social reproduction that lies beyond contemporary modes of exploitation of life as living labor" and subject to violent state management.[51]

Additionally, historians have tended in recent years to move away from the claim that the Atlantic slave system represented a precapitalist phenomenon external and historically prior to industrialization, however uneven such stages are understood to be. Instead, recent scholarship has emphasized instead the historically specific forms of commodity circulation and profitability within which the Atlantic slave system operated. As Peter James Hudson has pointed out, the new history of capitalism scholarship on slavery has sometimes avoided the question of how to theorize the role that race, racism, and white supremacy have played in the slave trade while ignoring the pathbreaking analysis provided by figures like Eric Williams and W. E. B. Du Bois.[52] Essays in this volume draw inspiration from a body of scholarship that has traced the historical emergence of blackness as a racial category of European origin as importantly marking a foundational racial distinction between the production of surplus value via wage labor from those forms of domination and expropriation that lay beyond the wage nexus but are nevertheless inscribed within capitalist social relations.[53]

Arthur Scarritt's contribution to this collection, "Tripartheid: How Global White Supremacy Triumphs through Neoliberalism," offers a new perspective on this historical dialectic. Moving between the United States and Peru and synthesizing the history of colonization, industrialization, and neoliberalization in each nation, he argues that white supremacy is a global phenomenon, one enacted by rentiers in order to maintain their class status. As he writes, this history "reveals the defining core of racial hierarchy as the political maintenance of an aristocratic social order commanded by a global rentier elite," enlarging the scope of traditional Marxist theories of racialization, which tend to understand it in terms of economic exploitation only. Instead, he argues that these elites have created and maintained, despite a brief period of pushback in the mid–twentieth century, "a highly costly system whose investments were not driven by maximizing economic returns but by keeping an elite class in power no matter the cost."[54] Crucially, the maintenance of this system depends on a shifting balance of inclusion and exclusion that pits identity groups against each other to claim the crumbs that fall from the elites' overflowing tables.

This historical dialectic of inclusion/exclusion within processes of formally "free" capitalist exploitation encompasses, moreover, not only racialized forms of unfree labor—slavery, indentured servitude, coolie labor, debt peonage—but also the securing of land and other natural resources through racialized processes of settler-colonial depopulation. The inclusion/exclusion dialectic, in other words, is necessarily mediated by the state's imposition of direct domination and expropriation that takes on a variety of modern forms, "such as prison labor, transnational sex trafficking, corporate land grabs, and foreclosures on predatory debt" that are all materially interconnected through the accumulation process.[55] This mediation has taken the form of "state-sanctioned or extralegal production and exploitation of group-differentiated vulnerability to premature death."[56] Multiple scholars have observed that the violent state management of surplus populations and pools of "surplus" labor created by "large-scale processes of dispossession have dramatically swelled the size of the global labour reserve."[57] Excluded from wage labor altogether but still reliant on commodity circulation for their own subsistence and reproduction, as Chen points out, "such populations are expendable but nonetheless trapped within the capital relation, because their existence is defined by a generalized commodity economy which does not recognize their capacity to labor," whether hidden in informal and illegal economies or existing beyond the boundaries of national citizenship.[58]

Here, we might propose, is racialization's contemporary centrality to the reproduction of the capital-labor relation: this population has to be violently managed and policed to neutralize insurgency as the material reproduction of proletarian life becomes increasingly volatile and contingent. Ruth Wilson Gilmore's examination of the contemporary state's managing of this potentially insurrectionary surplus humanity remains exemplary; she argues that "the relative surplus population [is] the problem for which prison became the state's solution."[59] In this respect, the abstract social process called capital—self-valorizing value, self-expanding value in motion—the inherent tendency of which is to shed labor power and thereby the very source of surplus value, of capital, itself—continually recreates a thoroughly racialized *outside* in order to secure the ongoing conditions of its own reproduction. Whether race is constitutive of the abstract, ideal-typical social logic of the process of *capital accumulation*, a subject of perennial scholastic debates, it has undeniably been constitutive of the historical socialization of *capitalism*.

Nikhil Singh has highlighted the importance, in mapping the system of capital, of accounting for those processes that serve to reproduce the capital relation but that are themselves external to the process of valorization per se. Underscoring the way in which the racial stigma that arises in support of chattel slavery "makes a specific and enduring contribution to developing what might be termed the material, ideological, and affective infrastructures of appropriation and dispossession that are indispensable to capitalism as a set of distinctive productive relationships," Singh emphasizes the dependence of "a narrow sphere of productive relations" on "a more expansive sphere of appropriation in which cheap human and extrahuman nature are taken up by commodity production."[60] And here again, as in the case of the gendered dimensions of capital's reproduction, to which we referred earlier, violence supplements impersonal socioeconomic forms of exploitation and exchange. "Embodied in the figures of the slave, the migrant worker, the household worker, the chronically unemployed, and the like, appropriation encompasses zones of both privatized and publicly sanctioned coercion and ethicopolitical devaluation that are inseparable from capitalist processes of valorization."[61] *Inseparable from*, and also *external to*, racialized capitalism "reproduces, as part of its logic, divisions between (re)productive humanity and disposable humanity," and indeed these "external" zones of insecurity "negate the idea that the value form successfully encompasses an entire way of life."[62]

So processes of racialization operate in the service of the reproduction of capital—while also being utterly outside the very logic of a Lukácsian aspiration toward totality, given the sheer rigor with which Lukács's account of totality is routed through the standpoint of the proletariat that, for him, is necessarily the standpoint of waged labor. Contemporary Afropessimist theorist Frank Wilderson, for example, is not wrong when he insists that the privileged subject of Marxism has been "a subaltern who is approached by variable capital—a wage" after a thoroughgoing process of dispossession.[63] But again, the affirmable worker identity into which Lukács's rigorously negative proletarian standpoint has congealed is itself constituted through and through by race: through "race," black chattel slavery in the United States constituted "free" labor as white, and whiteness as what Cheryl Harris has called "racially contingent forms of property and property rights" legally consolidated in the right to enslave and dispossess.[64] Building on Harris's analysis, Brenna Bhandar interrogates how "racial subjects and modern property laws are produced through one another in the colonial context."[65]

Understanding the role of capitalism in systematically reproducing internally racially divided social formations would have to remain attentive to, for example, modes of dispossession and capitalist reproduction *outside* of the wage relation. At the same time, such an account would also need to historicize how such processes have racially segmented formal labor markets. Even when consigned to disposability and what sociologist Orlando Patterson has called "social death," racialized populations are very much inside the historical logic whereby capital's inherent contradictions must be mitigated, the logic of capitalism's ongoing social and historical reproduction.[66] Without a more developed account of the relationship between racialization and capitalist value formation, Marxist critiques of "identity politics" typically hinge on defining race in terms of ideology, culture, or patterns of group inequality. In "Remapping the Race/Class Problematic," Sarika Chandra and Chris Chen intervene in contemporary U.S. scholarly and activist debates over the theoretical relationship between race and capitalism—including debates over whether racism or "economic anxiety" drives twenty-first-century white nationalist politics or over the internally fractured class politics of contemporary anti-racist movements. Such debates often reproduce a reified opposition between race and class as identities or forms of identification intrinsically associated with competing or complementary political objectives. The authors argue that scholarship on these questions reveals a number of persistent theoretical impasses generated by the often-discrepant ways that critics define race, class, and capitalism. Building on the recent work of Michael Dawson, Nancy Fraser, and others, the essay moves beyond the concept of identity to retheorize race not as an intrinsic property of individuals and groups but as a politically contested signifier emerging from the historical interplay of racial domination and changing experiences of what Dawson calls "linked fate." At the same time, the essay argues that politically heterogeneous and historically shifting experiences of racialized "linked fate" are embedded within a field of value relations and capitalist value as a medium of social cohesion on a global scale, systematically reproduced through co-constitutive, recursive, and specifically capitalist processes of exploitation, expropriation, and expulsion. Drawing on contemporary Marxist theory that insists on the historical specificity of how such core capitalist mechanisms of accumulation organize class relations, the authors argue that representations of class limited to empirical measures of income and wealth inequality or to socioeconomic status identities defined by implicitly or explicitly racialized cultural signifiers hinder theorists' attempts to adequately map the material structure of racial group formation within developed capitalist economies.

To be sure, cordoning race—not to mention gender, sexuality, and other identity categories—off from the socioeconomic is not exclusive to analyses of the history, development, and maintenance of capitalism. Indeed, it has become central to the recent revival of faith in the power of the aesthetic. In this tendency, art is worthy of acclaim to the extent that it at once knows and avoids the limitations that come with inhabiting any particular identity as point of view. It must instead come from no site, as it were—hence the name of the leading platform of this neo-Romantic approach to art: *nonsite*. The scholarship associated with this tendency suggests that to focus on identity is to distract from the real problems of capitalism and class—as if it were possible to separate out, as distinct categories, class relations, race, gender, and so on. Therefore, the best expressions of the aesthetic offer strong critiques of capitalism precisely by refusing identity-political claims. The artists worthy of distinction are praised for revealing capitalism's "objective" relations rather than its subjective effects, as though there is self-evidently separable subjectivity—"effects" that are trivially, merely, experiential. This is not an account from the perspective of totality.

Faith in autonomy is determined by the truth of heteronomy—and in multiple ways. From the earliest moments of the philosophy of art, the ideal of the autonomous artwork, imagined as an expression of the artist's genius, was tied to the development of a market for artistic expression large enough to support professional art careers. Individual genius was protected by the ideal of the autonomous work and could thus serve to back claims to copyright and fair remuneration. Once art was indexed so thoroughly to commerce, its distinction from the commercial sphere became a favored quality. "Real" artists needed a way to explain why the general public made the wrong choices when it patronized more popular works.[67] In this respect the ideal of aesthetic autonomy has long been the art world's generative, materially significant self-conception, its insufficient self-presentation as non-capitalist, autonomous, and so on. This history of aestheticist thought continues stubbornly into the present, in the insistence on art's ideal autonomy and the power of the artist to resist being coerced by the art market. The same aestheticism subtends faith in the exceptional political purchase of literature and art, its special ability to grasp and explain the world to people who would otherwise fail to see it clearly.

The appeal of this mode of thought is hard to fathom, however, when one considers the social worlds of cultural production and consumption—how access to supposedly enlightening aesthetic experiences tends to be, in practical terms, a real challenge for anyone except art-world initiates. Involvement in art worlds has always been organized around exclusions and controlled inclusions; it has enforced, patrolled, and been organized by identity categories (think of art's exoticism, tokenism, marketing of "otherness," recuperation of radical critique, and so on). The production of elite aesthetic culture is inseparable from entrenched social conditions of exclusion determined by whiteness and by inheritance of wealth, especially at gatekeeping, agenting, curatorial, and editorial levels. Prospective industry personnel need to be in the position to undertake unpaid internships while living in expensive cities; they need degrees from prestigious schools, which have become only harder to access because of rising tuitions; and they need to possess the right sort of signals of cultural competence associated with a literary disposition.[68] The extremes of wealth and poverty that characterize the contemporary moment make it yet harder for art fields to meaningfully alter any of these conditions—they are instead condemned merely to explore them endlessly via "institutional critique."

We prefer to emphasize that the discourse of the aesthetic is, in fact, wholly inseparable from the totality of social relations. We thus argue against designating elite cultural forms, like art-gallery works, as especially important and wondrous in their political potentials. As Sarah Brouillette and Joshua Clover argue in their essay "On Artistic Autonomy as a Bourgeois Fetish," it is more important to understand, from a totalizing standpoint, how capitalist value flows through art and culture in a dynamic way, stressing the historical trajectory of capitalism's development, de-development, eclipse, and the shifting forms of cultural expression that emerge and decline alongside. Is it not even less wise now, they ask, to celebrate the aesthetic for its enlightening and non-commodified potentials? It is the feeling of being beleaguered, of being ensconced in threatened institutions, protected by weakening fortifications, that produces much of the energy behind the current return to the aesthetic, which comes to appear, in this light, more and more like a defense of the relative wealth accorded one pocket of encultured whiteness.

Saying that capitalist value flows through everything is different from saying that our lives, experiences, and cultural activities have been slowly, and are by now entirely, "subsumed" by capitalism. Culture cannot be "really subsumed": it is made and experienced in ways that aren't maximally profitable and that cannot readily be made more so, in ways that are non-accumulative, ungovernable, non-productive, non-developmentalist, dwelling in affects and pleasures that aren't directly value producing (but that of course can be, like anything, transformed and repurposed to serve the dominant regime of labor). Culture in general retains this potential for counterproductive expression, making, and being, but it is not alone in this—the same could be said of friendship, or care, or simply living. Elite culture that makes claims to its own exceptionality effectively denigrates this regular activity, this "ordinary" culture, to use Raymond Williams's famous terms. Cultural activity performs many roles, of course, in relation to the requirements of waged capitalist life, and half-employment, and wagelessness—from pacification, to amelioration of unease, to temporary respite, to training in particular attitudes and styles of comportment. The sphere of so-called autonomous art is one site of such activity. Though not unique, it prizes its own insights, trumpets its own ostensible exceptionalism, values its own affordances and status vis-à-vis other culture practices. We need not help it constitute itself as such.

Indeed, we have a more urgent task at hand: the social reproduction of capitalism will soon prevent the reproduction of social life as such. The seeming inexorability of climate catastrophe not only all but guarantees the mass extinction of flora and fauna but will also make large parts of the globe uninhabitable for humans, thanks to ocean acidification, fluctuating sea levels, droughts and desertification, and violently turbulent storms. As the elites retreat to bolt-holes in Alaska and New Zealand, the rest of the population will be subject to famines, epidemics, mass relocations, and an increased rate of natural disasters. Our present moment demands a political response commensurate to this crisis, one that includes a clear-headed manner of addressing environmental devastation—and its uneven application across populations—in the capitalist totality. As Brent Ryan Bellamy writes in his essay "Ecology with Totality: The Case of Morton's *Hyperobjects* and Klein's *This Changes Everything*," environmentalism has long aspired toward totality. But, he argues, without a materialist orientation that recognizes "ecological catastrophe and economic crisis . . . [as] two expressions of the same capitalist dynamic," the possibility of overcoming climate change and ensuring the survival of humanity all but disappears.[69]

For many readers, totality may seem old-fashioned and outdated, a dusty relic of a mid-century moment in which historical materialists could theorize capitalism—and its end—without also contending with a bottomed-out rate of profit, ever-growing surplus populations, and inevitable environmental destruction. But as the essays in this collection show, thinking totality—if it is done in a materialist and dialectical manner attendant to the insides, outsides, and "frontiers" of capitalist social relations—is the only approach to our world capable of uncovering and undoing the mechanisms that create, enforce, and endlessly reproduce the varieties of oppression that are essential to the functioning of capitalism. Only when we see the capitalist totality in its fullness can we discern the fault lines through which a new world, one in which all can flourish, might emerge. This is the urgent work of our moment, one we hope to contribute to, both in this collection and on the streets.

Notes

Kevin produced a rough version of this introduction in October of 2018. After he was hospitalized and unable to work, the contributors listed in the byline came together to finish what he started. All insights belong to Kevin; all errors belong to the rest of us.

1. Susan Ferguson, "Intersectionality and Social-Reproduction Feminisms: Toward an Integrative Ontology," *Historical Materialism* 24, no. 2 (June 2016): 38–60.

2. Ibid., 46–47.

3. Ibid., 56.

4. Nancy Fraser and Rahel Jaeggi, *Capitalism: A Conversation* (Hoboken: Wiley, 2018), 52.

5. Richard Westerman underscores this point in his recent work on Lukács. He responds to criticisms against Lukács that charge him for centering a laboring subject outside of history with a special capacity to throw off the social structures that restrain it. Lukács's subject, for Westerman, does not act as a deus ex machina with a special capacity, nor does it correspond to an underlying essence. Rather, Lukács defines the subject by the "structural principle of the subject-object totality"; Westerman, "Spectator and Society: Luckás, Reigl, and the Phenomenology of the Individual Subject," *New German Critique* 45, no. 3 (2018): 135, 177. See also Richard Westerman, *Lukacs's Phenomenology of Capitalism: Reification Revalued* (Cham, Switzerland: Palgrave Macmillan, 2018).

6. György Lukács, *History and Class Consciousness*, trans. Rodney Livingstone (Cambridge, Mass.: MIT Press, 1972), 165–66.

7. Ibid., 166.
8. Ibid.
9. For accounts of how capitalist imperatives have historically shaped the dynamics of settler colonial dispossession and a genocidal logic of indigenous elimination, see Patrick Wolfe, "Settler Colonialism and the Elimination of the Native," *Journal of Genocide Research* 8, no. 4, (2006); Glen Sean Coulthard, *Red Skin, White Masks: Rejecting the Colonial Politics of Recognition* (Minneapolis: University of Minnesota Press, 2014); and Robert Nichols, "Disaggregating Primitive Accumulation," *Radical Philosophy* 194 (November/December 2015), https://www.radicalphilosophy.com/article/disaggregating-primitive-accumulation.
10. Lukács, *History and Class Consciousness*, 83.
11. Ibid., 149.
12. Moishe Postone, *Time, Labor, and Social Domination: A Reinterpretation of Marx's Critical Theory* (Cambridge: Cambridge University Press, 1993).
13. Ibid., 73.
14. See Theodor Adorno, "Dwarf Fruit," in *Minima Moralia: Reflections on a Damaged Life*, trans. E. F. N. Jephcott (New York: Verso, 2005), 49–50.
15. Salar Mohandesi, "Identity Crisis," *Viewpoint Magazine* (March 16, 2017), https://www.viewpointmag.com/2017/03/16/identity-crisis/.
16. Combahee River Collective, "A Black Feminist Statement," 5, https://americanstudies.yale.edu/sites/default/files/files/Keyword%20Coalition_Readings.pdf.
17. Ibid.
18. Ibid., 6.
19. Endnotes, "A History of Separation," *Endnotes* 4 (October 2015), https://endnotes.org.uk/issues/4/en/endnotes-preface.
20. Ibid., 95n16.
21. Ibid., 119, 100.
22. Ibid., 120.
23. Ibid., 128.
24. Ibid.
25. Ibid., 129, 127.
26. Robert Brenner, *The Economics of Global Turbulence* (London: Verso, 1998), 93.
27. Endnotes, "A History of Separation," 75.
28. Ibid., 147.
29. Ferguson, "Intersectionality and Social-Reproduction Feminisms," 45–46.
30. Ibid.
31. Mohandesi, "Identity Crisis."
32. David McNally, "Intersections and Dialectics: Critical Reconstructions in Social Reproduction Theory," in *Social Reproduction Theory: Remapping Class, Recentering Oppression*, ed. Tithi Bhattacharya (London: Pluto, 2017), 97.
33. Nancy Fraser, "Behind Marx's Hidden Abode: For an Expanded Conception of Capitalism," *New Left Review* 86 (March–April 2014): 57, https://newleftreview.org/II/86/nancy-fraser-behind-marx-s-hidden-abode.
34. Susan Ferguson, "Capitalist Childhood, Anti-Capitalist Children: The Social Reproduction of Childhood," unpublished paper, 2015, quoted in Tithi Bhattacharya, "Introduction: Mapping Social Reproduction Theory," in *Social Reproduction Theory: Remapping Class, Recentering Oppression*, ed. Tithi Bhattacharya (London: Pluto, 2017), 2.

35. Bhattacharya, "Mapping Social Reproduction Theory," 2. Though traditionally gendered, this labor is becoming racialized as well in a process Evelyn Nakano Glenn calls a "racial division of reproductive labor"; Glenn, "From Servitude to Service Work: Historical Continuities in the Racial Division of Paid Reproductive Labor," *Signs* 18, no. 1 (Autumn 1992): 3. Roswitha Scholz, in *Marxism and the Critique of Value* (Chicago: MCM, 2014), 136–37, likewise notes in her "Patriarchy and Commodity Society: Gender without the Body" that, as more and more women work outside the home, "well-situated women" turn to "underpaid female immigrant laborers" to complete the tasks of housekeeping and childrearing. Scholz writes that this process redistributes this labor "within the female plane of existence," but we would emphasize that it is being taken up by racialized women, adding more complexity to the challenges of separating labor (of all kinds) from both gender and race (137).

36. Karl Marx, *Capital*, trans. Ben Fowkes (New York: Penguin, 1976), 1:270.

37. Susan Ferguson and David McNally, "Capital, Labour-Power, and Gender Relations: Introduction to the Historical Materialism Edition of Marxism and the Oppression of Women," in *Marxism and the Oppression of Women: Toward a Unitary Theory*, by Lise Vogel (Boston: Brill, 2013), xxvii.

38. These domestic activities, as the authors of "The Logic of Gender" argue, are "structurally made non-labour": in order for labor-power to have a value, the domestic labor that reproduces labor-power has to be dissociated from the circuit of value. The activities of reproductive labor "do not produce value, not because of their concrete characteristics, but rather, because they take place in a sphere of the capitalist mode of production which is not directly mediated by the form of value." Underscoring this crucial point, "The Logic of Gender" suggests that "there must be an exterior to value in order for value to exist. . . . For labour-power to have a value, some of these activities have to be cut off or dissociated from the sphere of value production." Value requires an outside, then, and this different aspiration toward totality accounts for these processes that are necessary for the reproduction of the capital-labor relation but that are not themselves value-producing. "Naturalized into nonexistence," the reproduction of labor power presupposes that the production and circulation of value have a necessary outside. Such activities, as "The Logic of Gender" suggestively puts it, "form an outside within the inside of the totality of the capitalist mode of production." To the extent that waged productive activities receive social recognition as labor precisely via the validation of the wage, unwaged reproductive labor then becomes "the non-social of the social": part of capitalist reproduction, though not socially validated; Endnotes, "The Logic of Gender," *Endnotes* 3 (September 2013): 61–62, https://endnotes.org.uk/issues/3/en/endnotes-the-logic-of-gender.

39. Cinzia Arruzza, "Remarks on Gender," *Viewpoint Magazine*, September 2, 2014, https://www.viewpointmag.com/2014/09/02/remarks-on-gender/.

40. Ibid.

41. In Ferguson and McNally's words, "In order to secure the production and reproduction of current and future supplies of labor power, capitalism requires institutional mechanisms through which it can exercise control over biological reproduction, family-forms, child-rearing, and maintenance of a gender-order"; "Capital, Labour-Power, and Gender Relations," xxvi.

42. Ibid., xxvi.

43. See Christine Delphy, *Close to Home: A Materialist Analysis of Women's Oppression*, trans. Diana Leonard (London: Verso, 2016).

44. See Postone, *Time, Labor, and Social Domination*, and Endnotes, "Logic of Gender," 65–66.

45. Marx, *Capital*, 1:517, quoted in Ferguson and NcNally, "Capital, Labour-Power, and Gender Relations," xxviii.

46. Lise Vogel, *Marxism and the Oppression of Women: Toward a Unitary Theory* (Boston: Brill, 2013).

47. Chris Chen, "The Limit Point of Capitalist Equality: Notes Toward an Abolitionist Antiracism," *Endnotes* 3 (September 2013): 207, https://endnotes.org.uk/issues/3/en/chris-chen-the-limit-point-of-capitalist-equality.

48. Gilles Dauvé, *Eclipse and Re-emergence of the Communist Movement* (Oakland: PM, 2015), 47, quoted in Joshua Clover, *Riot. Strike. Riot* (New York: Verso: 2016), 160.

49. See Jodi Melamed, *Represent and Destroy: Rationalizing Violence in the New Racial Capitalism* (Minneapolis: University of Minnesota Press, 2011).

50. Chen, "Limit Point," 205.

51. Neferti Tadiar, "Decolonization, 'Race,' Remaindered," *Qui Parle* 23, no. 2 (Spring/Summer 2015): 135, and Tadiar, "Life-times of Disposability within Global Neoliberalism," *Social Text 115* 31, no. 2 (Summer 2013): 23.

52. Peter James Hudson, "The Racist Dawn of Capitalism: Unearthing the Economy of Bondage," *Boston Review*, March 21, 2016, bostonreview.net/books-ideas/peter-james-hudson-slavery-capitalism.

53. For example, Robin Blackburn maintains that the important question is not whether capitalism required slavery in some abstract structural sense but the historical fact that slavery contributed directly to the rise of industrialization in England, however we construe that contribution; see Blackburn, *The Making of New World Slavery*, 2nd ed. (New York: Verso, 2010), 515, and John Clegg, "Capitalism and Slavery," *Critical Historical Studies* 2, no. 2 (Fall 2015): 281–304.

54. See Arthur Scarritt, in this volume, Chapter 3.

55. Nancy Fraser, "Expropriation and Exploitation in Racialized Capitalism: A Reply to Michael Dawson," *Critical Historical Studies* 3, no. 1 (Spring 2016): 167.

56. Ruth Wilson Gilmore, *Golden Gulag: Prisons, Surplus, Crisis, and Opposition in Globalizing California* (Berkeley: University of California Press, 2007), 28.

57. Susan Ferguson and David McNally, "Precarious Migrants: Gender, Race, and the Social Reproduction of a Global Working Class," *Socialist Register* 51 (2015): 9.

58. Chen, "Limit Point," 212.

59. Gilmore, *Golden Gulag*, 113.

60. Nikhil Pal Singh, "On Race, Violence, and So-called Primitive Accumulation," *Social Text 128* 34, no. 3 (September 2016): 30, 40.

61. Ibid., 40–41.

62. Ibid., 39.

63. Frank Wilderson, "Gramsci's Black Marx: Whither the Slave in Civil Society," *Social Identities: Journal for the Study of Race, Nation, and Culture* 9, no. 2 (2003): 225.

64. Cheryl Harris, "Whiteness as Property," *Harvard Law Review* 106, no. 8 (June 1993): 1,714.

65. Brenna Bhandar, *Colonial Lives of Property* (Durham, N.C.: Duke University Press, 2018), 8.

66. Orlando Patterson, *Slavery and Social Death: A Comparative Study, with a New Preface* (Cambridge, Mass.: Harvard University Press, 2018).

67. See Martha Woodmansee, *The Author, Art, and the Market: Rereading the History of Aesthetics* (New York: Columbia University Press, 1994).

68. See David Lee, "Creative Networks and Social Capital," in *Cultural Work and Higher Education*, ed. Daniel Ashton and Catriona Noonan (New York: Palgrave, 2013), 195–213.

69. See Brent Ryan Bellamy, in this volume, Chapter 6.

Works Cited

Adorno, Theodor. "Dwarf Fruit." In *Minima Moralia: Reflections on a Damaged Life*, translated by E. F. N. Jephcott, 49–50. New York: Verso, 2005.

Arruzza, Cinzia. "Remarks on Gender." *Viewpoint Magazine*, September 2, 2014. https://www.viewpointmag.com/2014/09/02/remarks-on-gender/.

Bhandar, Brenna. *Colonial Lives of Property*. Durham, N.C.: Duke University Press, 2018.

Bhattacharya, Tithi. "Introduction: Mapping Social Reproduction Theory." In *Social Reproduction Theory: Remapping Class, Recentering Oppression*, ed. Tithi Bhattacharya, 1–20. London: Pluto Press, 2017.

Blackburn, Robin. *The Making of New World Slavery*. 2nd ed. New York: Verso, 2010.

Brenner, Robert. *The Economics of Global Turbulence*. London: Verso, 1998.

Chen, Chris. "The Limit Point of Capitalist Equality: Notes Toward an Abolitionist Antiracism." *Endnotes* 3 (September 2013). https://endnotes.org.uk/issues/3/en/chris-chen-the-limit-point-of-capitalist-equality.

Clegg, John. "Capitalism and Slavery." *Critical Historical Studies* 2, no. 2 (Fall 2015): 281–304.

Clover, Joshua. *Riot. Strike. Riot.* New York: Verso: 2016.

Combahee River Collective. "A Black Feminist Statement." https://americanstudies.yale.edu/sites/default/files/files/Keyword%20Coalition_Readings.pdf.

Coulthard, Glen Sean. *Red Skin, White Masks: Rejecting the Colonial Politics of Recognition*. Minneapolis: University of Minnesota Press, 2014.

Dauvé, Gilles. *Eclipse and Re-emergence of the Communist Movement*. Oakland, Calif.: PM, 2015.

Delphy, Christine. *Close to Home: A Materialist Analysis of Women's Oppression*. Translated by Diana Leonard. London: Verso, 2016.

Endnotes. "A History of Separation." *Endnotes* 4 (October 2015). https://endnotes.org.uk/issues/4/en/endnotes-preface.

———. "The Logic of Gender." *Endnotes* 3 (September 2013). https://endnotes.org.uk/issues/3/en/endnotes-the-logic-of-gender.

Ferguson, Susan. "Intersectionality and Social-Reproduction Feminisms: Toward an Integrative Ontology." *Historical Materialism* 24, no. 2 (June 2016): 38–60.

Ferguson, Susan, and David McNally. "Capital, Labour-Power, and Gender Relations: Introduction to the Historical Materialism Edition of Marxism and the Oppression of Women." In *Marxism and the Oppression of Women: Toward a Unitary Theory*, by Lise Vogel. Boston: Brill, 2013.

———. "Precarious Migrants: Gender, Race, and the Social Reproduction of a Global Working Class." *Socialist Register* 51 (2015): 1–23.

Fraser, Nancy. "Behind Marx's Hidden Abode: For an Expanded Conception of Capitalism." *New Left Review* 86 (March–April 2014). https://newleftreview.org/II/86/nancy-fraser-behind-marx-s-hidden-abode.

———. "Expropriation and Exploitation in Racialized Capitalism: A Reply to Michael Dawson." *Critical Historical Studies* 3, no. 1 (Spring 2016): 163–78.

Fraser, Nancy, and Rahel Jaeggi. *Capitalism: A Conversation*. Hoboken, N.J.: Wiley, 2018.

Gilmore, Ruth Wilson. *Golden Gulag: Prisons, Surplus, Crisis, and Opposition in Globalizing California*. Berkeley: University of California Press, 2007.

Glenn, Evelyn Nakano. "From Servitude to Service Work: Historical Continuities in the Racial Division of Paid Reproductive Labor." *Signs* 18, no. 1 (Autumn, 1992): 1–42.

Harris, Cheryl. "Whiteness as Property." *Harvard Law Review* 106, no. 8 (June 1993): 1,710–91.

Hudson, Peter James. "The Racist Dawn of Capitalism: Unearthing the Economy of Bondage." *Boston Review*, March 21, 2016. bostonreview.net/books-ideas/peter-james-hudson-slavery-capitalism.

Lee, David. "Creative Networks and Social Capital." In *Cultural Work and Higher Education*, ed. Daniel Ashton and Catriona Noonan, 195–213. New York: Palgrave, 2013.

Lukács, György. *History and Class Consciousness*. Translated by Rodney Livingstone. Cambridge, Mass.: MIT Press, 1972.

Marx, Karl. *Capital*. Volume 1. Translated by Ben Fowkes. New York: Penguin, 1976.

McNally, David. "Intersections and Dialectics: Critical Reconstructions in Social Reproduction Theory." In *Social Reproduction Theory: Remapping Class, Recentering Oppression*, edited by Tithi Bhattacharya, 94–111. London: Pluto, 2017.

Melamed, Jodi. *Represent and Destroy: Rationalizing Violence in the New Racial Capitalism*. Minneapolis: University of Minnesota Press, 2011.

Mohandesi, Salar. "Identity Crisis." *Viewpoint Magazine*, March 16, 2017. https://www.viewpointmag.com/2017/03/16/identity-crisis/.

Neferti, Tadiar. "Decolonization, 'Race,' Remaindered." "Decolonization, 'Race,' Remaindered," *Qui Parle* 23, no. 2 (Spring/Summer 2015): 135.

———. "Life-times of Disposability within Global Neoliberalism." *Social Text* 115 31, no. 2 (Summer 2013): 19–48.

Nichols, Robert. "Disaggregating Primitive Accumulation." *Radical Philosophy*, no. 194 (November/December 2015). https://www.radicalphilosophy.com/article/disaggregating-primitive-accumulation.

Patterson, Orlando. *Slavery and Social Death: A Comparative Study, with a New Preface.* Cambridge, Mass.: Harvard University Press, 2018.

Postone, Moishe. *Time, Labor, and Social Domination: A Reinterpretation of Marx's Critical Theory.* Cambridge: Cambridge University Press, 1993.

Scholz, Roswitha. "Patriarchy and Commodity Society: Gender without the Body." In *Marxism and the Critique of Value*, edited by Neil Larsen, Mathias Nilges, Josh Robinson, and Nicholas Brown, 123–42. Chicago: MCM, 2014.

Singh, Nikhil Pal. "On Race, Violence, and So-called Primitive Accumulation." *Social Text 128* 34, no. 3 (September 2016): 27–50.

Vogel, Lise. *Marxism and the Oppression of Women: Toward a Unitary Theory.* Boston: Brill, 2013.

Westerman, Richard. *Lukacs's Phenomenology of Capitalism: Reification Revalued.* Cham, Switzerland: Palgrave Macmillan, 2018.

———. "Spectator and Society: Luckás, Reigl, and the Phenomenology of the Individual Subject." *New German Critique.* 45, no. 3 (2018): 175–203.

Wilderson, Frank. "Gramsci's Black Marx: Whither the Slave in Civil Society?" *Social Identities: Journal for the Study of Race, Nation, and Culture* 9, no. 2 (2003): 225–40.

Wolfe, Patrick. "Settler Colonialism and the Elimination of the Native." *Journal of Genocide Research* 8, no. 4 (2006): 387–409.

Woodmansee, Martha. *The Author, Art, and the Market: Rereading the History of Aesthetics.* New York: Columbia University Press, 1994.

1 / Let the Dead Bury the Dead: Race, Gender, and Class Composition in the U.S. after 1965
TIM KREINER

> The working class is growing, as Marx predicted, but it is not the old working class which the radicals persist in believing will create the revolution and establish control over production. That old working class is the vanishing herd.
> —JAMES BOGGS, *THE AMERICAN REVOLUTION: PAGES FROM A NEGRO WORKER'S NOTEBOOK*

Few specters haunt revolutionary theory more than the rote identification of *proletarians* with industrial workers. That identification has both historical and theoretical sources. The chauvinism of workers' movements bears more than a little of the blame. So, too, do equations of the leading edge of class struggle with manual wage-laborers in traditional Marxism. Particularly in the wake of the Black and Women's Liberation Movements that gained prominence at the height of the New Left in the late 1960s, those orthodox coordinates gave rise to recurring debates about the fate of women and people of color beneath the communist horizon of workers' movements. Today's militants are no strangers to those debates.[1] In spite of the tremendous theoretical affordance on offer, however, the legacy of those debates tends to generate more heat than light, often in the form of crude oppositions between anti-racist, feminist, and anti-capitalist political concerns. Typically, those concerns are indexed by discrete categories of race, gender, and class tied, in turn, to separate social groups. In such schema, class remains the object of a critique of political economy hostile to concerns with race and gender separately annexed to more culturally inclined paradigms. For better or worse—and mostly for worse—those hostilities long ago took on a life of their own.

Those hostilities owe much to coordinates borrowed from workers' movements by bellwether Black Power and radical-feminist organizations in the mid-1960s, however. To note this is not to say that the historical workers' movement determined the course of New Left liberation movements. It is simply to recall that while what made the New Left new was the emergence of new social movements organized outside the workplace, feminist and anti-racist militants were often compelled to organize around figures conceived as analogous to workers. The founding statement of the short-lived Organization for Black Power (OBP) James Boggs helped organize in 1965, for instance, offered a signal articulation of the rising tide of black nationalism. "Negroes," as its authors put it, constitute a "revolutionary social force... play[ing] the role" in America's cities "workers played in the 1930s in bringing about social reform in industry."[2] While Boggs decisively parted ways with both orthodox Marxism and the cultural nationalism that came to hold sway over many black militants in the following years, however, the view that racial identities formed outside the workplace give rise to revolutionary motives in ways analogous to the social-democratic motives born from workers' identities forged inside the workplace cast a long shadow. So, too, did theoretical efforts to define women as a class on the part of early radical feminist organizations. Few were more cogent than the 1969 "Redstockings Manifesto." "Women are an oppressed class," its authors wrote, noting that while the gendered division of labor and sexual violence is typically suffered in isolation, "in reality every such relationship is a *class* relationship, and the conflicts between individual men and women are political conflicts that can only be solved collectively."[3] Much as "Negroes" are analogous to workers in the OBP statement, for Redstockings women form a class oppressed by men that is analogous to but distinct from the class of workers collectively composed against the ruling class. From this theoretical point of view, "worker," "woman," and "black" (or "Negro") name different social subjects similarly organized on the normative basis of a shared collective identity.

In the 1970s, however, oppositional currents *within* anti-racist, feminist, and anti-capitalist movements challenged the core beliefs that gird such normative views today. "The proletariat is not the working-class, it is a social relation," Gilles Dauvé reminded us in 1972.[4] Two years earlier Shulamith Firestone had declared that "just as the end goal of socialist revolution was not only the elimination of the economic class *privilege* but of the economic class *distinction* itself," so, too, "the end goal of feminist revolution must be, unlike that of the first feminist movement, not just the elimination of male *privilege* but of the sex *distinction* itself."[5] Similarly, in the wake of the split between the Black Liberation Army and the Black Panther Party, the Berkeley-based Racism Research Project took stock of "the incongruous position of criticizing race relations while simultaneously embracing racial categories" then providing "a theoretical justification for the present unsavory state of the racially divided organizational workings of the Left."[6] Even *within* movements that are typically composed by the shared interests of uniform social identities in popular memory today, that is to say, opposing currents unevenly confronted by state violence animated recurring organizational dilemmas during the 1970s. In the wake of those dilemmas, however, the tension between militants committed to the emancipation *of* this or that social group and militants committed to emancipation *from* social orders composed by group interests was largely displaced by conceptual oppositions among racial, gender, and workers' identities. Today, therefore, the ghosts of that organizational tension—between the emancipation of particular groups and emancipation from social orders ruled by group interests— cross all divides in revolutionary theory.

The argument that unfolds in the following pages is as simple as those ghosts are formidable: categorical oppositions among race, gender, and class stem from organizational dilemmas. The unfolding of that argument is complicated, however, by the triumph of particular conceptions of gender, racial, and workers' identities over other organizational models within feminist, anti-racist, and workers' movements. Clarifying these organizational dilemmas will not magically resolve our imagination of life without capital, patriarchy, and white supremacy into a common minimum program. Resolving such theoretical debates merely returns us to the practical matter of how we remit the uneasy relationships between anti-systemic struggles today. At the heart of that problem lies the hoary question of what used to be called revolutionary subjects. If we want to grasp that problem in all of its complexity today, therefore, we will need to return, with clear eyes, to the practical questions *who revolts why* and *how it is to be done.*

We will also need to do so without drawing our conclusions in advance from the slogans and costumes of the past. Not all communist projects resemble the chauvinistic sectors of the historical workers' movement. Nor do all feminist or anti-racist politics today resemble their occasionally anti-communist variants. By the same token, class, gender, and race are not incommensurable categories, even as the latter two index differently lived experiences that exceed the grasp of the former. We can ill afford the unhappy luxury of such categorical sparring at this late date. Today, those who dismiss feminist or anti-racist organizing in the name of communism—or vice versa—have corpses in their mouths.

The Making of the Proletariat (1848–Present)

When the League of Communists issued the *Communist Manifesto* Marx and Engels drafted on the eve of revolution in 1848, few people considered *proletariat* synonymous with *industrial workers*. Indeed, the latter-day cognates of *proletarii*, originally coined to designate a class of citizens in the Servian census with nothing to offer Rome but their children, typically referred not only to factory hands and wage-workers but also to farm hands paid in kind, journeymen, peasants, prostitutes, thieves, the poor on relief rolls, and the otherwise unemployed, even in the emerging discourse of political economy.[7] Simonde de Sismondi ushered *prolétaire* into heavy circulation therein with his 1819 *Nouveaux Princips d'Économie Politique* and placed it on firmer conceptual ground in his 1837 *Études sur l'Économie Politique*.[8] The latter occasioned Marx's pithy paraphrase in his 1869 preface to *The Eighteenth Brumaire of Louis Bonaparte*: "People forget *Sismondi*'s significant saying: The Roman proletariat lived at the expense of society, while modern society lives at the expense of the proletariat."[9] Yet for Sismondi, as for many members of the ruling class deposed by the Revolution, *prolétaire* still gathered all those who owned nothing but their ability to labor in a heterogeneous mass opposed to the propertied classes, a mass swollen with semi-proletarianized peasants, wage workers of all types, and the occasionally criminal, idle proletarians rendered redundant by productivity gains in industry or agriculture. The primary threat posed by proletarians was not, therefore, the organization of that mass into an industrial working class. The specter of the proletariat threatened to overwhelm state coffers with demands from paupers and beggars or, worse, follow the lead of the Canut revolts in Lyon as much as it threatened to form trade unions armed with the strike weapon in England.[10] In Sismondi's oeuvre, indigence, unemployment, and criminality were as much attributes of *les prolétaires* as industry and the wage.

Largely derogatory uses of "proletarian" to refer to the dangerously poor and oppressed were widespread during the July Monarchy. By the 1840s, however, *prolétaire* was also a popular *nomme de guerre* in the beer-hall oratory of Parisian workers' societies. Consequently, the term began to refer to an incipient class of wage laborers variously opposed to owners of property by writers such as Prosper Enfantin, Victor Prosper Considérant, Constantin Pecquer, Pierre-Joseph Proudhon, and Louis Blanc. It was Lorenz von Stein's work that cemented the association of *das Proletariat* with the industrious classes in the minds of many Young Hegelians, however. As Stein summarily put it, the growth of capital and concentration of the dispossessed in factories combined to transform "industrial workers into the proletariat of the present."[11] Marx, for his part, first defined the proletariat as "the dissolution of society as a particular estate" in his 1844 "Introduction to a Contribution to the Critique of Hegel's Philosophy of Right" before concluding, famously, "The *head* of this emancipation is *philosophy*, its *heart* the *proletariat*." In between he mentions off-handedly that "the proletariat is beginning to appear in Germany as a result of the rising industrial movement."[12] Only in *The German Ideology*, on which Marx and Engels continued work into 1847, would the *Manifesto's* vision of a proletariat closely associated with manual wage-laborers, who are both the chief product of bourgeois society and its gravediggers, crystalize. In the early writings of Marx and Engels, the identification of *das Proletariat* with industrial workers was a work in progress as well.

Yet in spite of the mixed use of *prolétaire* in the heady context of early workers' movements, the *Manifesto* has repeatedly been read as a programmatic articulation of *the working class* since its rescue from the dustbin of reaction in 1872. In these post-hoc readings, the identity of the proletariat with industrial workers is typically taken as a given. Engels's addendum to the 1888 English translation of the *Manifesto* gave that identity a canonical gloss. "By proletariat," Engels noted, is meant "the class of modern wage labourers who, having no means of production of their own, are reduced to selling their labour power in order to live."[13] But within the *Manifesto*, Marx and Engels presented two views of proletarians. On the one hand, we are told, "the epoch of the bourgeoisie" has "simplified class antagonisms" into "two great hostile camps, into two great classes directly facing each other—Bourgeoisie and Proletariat."[14] On this view, we will recall, the rule of the bourgeoisie has burst asunder the feudal ties that bound peasants to the country and is rapidly concentrating the formerly scattered, rural population in new industrial conurbations. In the process the bourgeoisie "has converted the physician, the lawyer, the priest, the poet, the man of science, into its paid wage-laborers."[15] The perfect aspect of the present tense is not incidental. The simplification of class struggle into a molar antagonism between capitalists and workers gathered in factories, free to need a wage to eat, was a veritable fait accompli. This is the force of many of the *Manifesto's* most celebrated passages. As the cunning of history would have it, however, that force is also the obverse of the *Manifesto*'s best-known formulation. Today the image of workers amassed behind the factory gate, growing more unruly by the hour beneath the historical weight of their immiseration, is a fast-frozen precipitate of the phrase "all that is solid melts into air."[16] Yet from the present-perfect perspective of the *Manifesto* in 1848, a world remade in the image of workers appeared to lie just beyond the grave of the bourgeoisie. All that was left was to smash the gate and seize the levers of production while redistributing the stockpiles of social wealth.

We might call this the *normative view*. It permanently ascribes the *prolétaire* of early workers' movements to the fraction of wage-workers who compose "the typical image of the proletariat—manual workers in factories, foundries, and mines, on the docks, in shipyards, and on the railways."[17] That image became the hallmark of orthodox notions of an industrial proletariat: a working class in-and-for-itself liberated from feudal lords and command over the implements of labor in a cruelly *double freedom*, as Marx put it, defined by the need to work for a wage in order to live. Thus this familiar image also binds proletarians to a certain repertoire of class struggle. Universal (male) suffrage, shop-floor sabotage, and the downing of tools in the workplace are the chief weapons of those who belong to this image of the proletariat. Collective bargaining is its shield, especially in the urban core of the twentieth century. The wage is its watchword, the factory (and, perhaps, the port) its arena, the mass of semi-skilled wage-laborers organized into a party its vanguard if not its final fighting form. The whole of the class-mass party sequence, in short, reposes in this image of the proletariat. So, too, does the normative view of proletarianization. From this vantage, *dispossession of the means of production* and *subsumption beneath the wage* measure class belonging in the last instance.

On the other hand, however, we find the germ of another view of the proletariat in the pages of the *Manifesto*. Here the molar antagonism between capitalists and workers gathered in factories is itself a moment in the ongoing history of class struggles. From this vantage, that antagonism is as likely to precipitate new compositions of the dispossessed and forms of struggle as it is to bring about the abolition of social classes. In the process "the proletariat is recruited from all classes of the population" and, periodically, recomposed by violent outbreaks of "the epidemic of overdevelopment" that leave capital and proletarians idling cheek-by-jowl alongside "too much means of subsistence."[18] In the passages describing that process the present tense typically sheds its perfect aspect. The "small tradespeople, shopkeepers, and retired tradesmen generally, the handicraftsmen and peasants—all these sink gradually," we are told, into the proletarian majority, while "entire sections of the ruling class are, by the advance of industry, precipitated into the proletariat."[19] In decisive moments even "a portion of the bourgeoisie, and in particular, a portion of the bourgeois ideologists, goes over to the proletariat."[20] From the simple-present perspective of the *Manifesto* today, the image of workers amassed behind the factory gate features the partial cast of a particular moment in the long slog toward the communist horizon. That horizon and its imagery are not ours, however.[21] Nor does identifying who counts as a proletarian bring a new horizon into view. Instead, each new crisis opens up new organizational dilemmas for a proletariat riven by differences and conflict. Once they find one another, on this view, proletarians still have it all to do.

We might call this the *critical view*. It ruthlessly insists that "the capitalist process of production, therefore, seen as a total, connected process . . . produces and reproduces the capital-relation itself."[22] That view is brought to fruition in *Capital* where we are told "accumulation of capital is, therefore, multiplication of the proletariat."[23] As we will see in the following pages, however, multiplication of the proletariat is multiplication of the differences between proletarians as well. The critique of political economy simply brings those differences along with the struggles they precipitate into view. From this perspective, movements for reproductive and civil rights as well as riots against gender or racial violence belong to the repertoire of class struggle for proletarians compelled to face enemies beyond the wage. Nor is the wage the only lynchpin therein. Peculiar combinations of direct violence and market dependency unevenly meted out by the gender distinction and color line also enter this theoretical aperture. The resulting image gathers the variously dominated and dispossessed in the same frame as workers within and without the factory gate. *Proletarian*, in short, refers to the combined and uneven forms of waged and wageless life the *Manifesto*—contra Marx's later paraphrase of Sismondi—recalls when Marx and Engels declare the bourgeoisie unfit to rule because it cannot keep proletarians from sinking into a state where "it has to feed [them], instead of being fed by [them]."[24] From this vantage, *differential access to the means of subsistence*, not direct access to the wage *per se*, measures class belonging in the last instance.

These two views sit uneasily side by side in the annals of communist theory, but the normative view of the proletariat exerted enormous influence over the historical workers' movement itself. In Europe the various national workers' movements were the proving ground of those dilemmas and that composition. One crucial development on that soil was the growth of what the Endnotes collective has called, in their important account of the historical workers' movement, an "affirmable workers' identity."[25] In their argument, the construction of some such identity was less a strategic choice than a tactical necessity for early workers' movements to win reforms. "This proletariat was, increasingly, a respectable class. It became respectable in the figure of the male, semi-skilled, heavy industrial worker (which is not to say that all such workers were male, only that they were imagined to be so, ideally)."[26] For better or worse, as they go on to argue, that identity became the face of the historical workers' movement.

But, by the mid–twentieth century, the image of an industrial proletariat associated with classical workers' movements was quickly becoming a thing of the past. With the 1956 eclipse of blue- by white-collar labor, the prospect of industrial workers becoming a numerical majority in the U.S. had come and gone. Clearly if the proletariat were identical with the industrial working class, the *Manifesto*'s projection of communist revolution as a movement of the immense majority no longer held water. Even orthodox expansions of the category to encompass wage-workers *tout court* with industrial workers as the leading edge of class struggle were increasingly difficult to maintain. By the 1970s, therefore, the normative view of the proletariat in traditional Marxism generally and the growing scandal of the "middle class" in particular posed serious problems for Marxist theorists. Indeed, the only thing that these accounts could agree on was that neither the course of class struggle nor its antagonists resembled those typical of the normative view. Heterodox accounts were a dime a dozen in the twilight of the American century.

One of the most consequential new readings of Marx emerged from Italy, however, where a cycle of anti-capitalist struggles spanning more than a decade increasingly gathered women, students, immigrants, and the unemployed outside the factory gate.[27] At the same time, the emergence of new revolutionary subjects also precipitated new readings of *Capital*. Unlike theories preoccupied with the scandal of the middle class, these inquiries were attuned to new forms of struggle on the shop floor in the years prior to the Hot Autumn that inaugurated Italy's "creeping May." In an effort to grasp the contours of those struggles, theorists initially associated with the workerist currents of *operaismo* and, later, the riots, rent strikes, and squats of *autonomia* elaborated a view of class struggle alive to the logical force of Marx's categories but free from the normative view of traditional Marxism.[28] Few did so more incisively than Romano Alquati. In the 1961 essay that introduced the notion of *class composition*, for example, Alquati argued that as Olivetti sought to maximize its return on investments sunk in plant and equipment, transformations in the composition of the workforce occurred in tandem with transformations in the workplace.[29] Those dual transformations, Alquati noted, were driven by the replacement of people by machines Marx described as the domination of living by dead labor, or a rise in the so-called organic composition of capital. At the same time, the reduction in the number of workers necessary for the production of typewriters, in the case of Olivetti, leads to a rise in the technical composition of capital, or the number of typewriters produced per work-hour.[30] Taken together, these dual developments yield a singular result. The greater the increase in Fordist automation and Taylorist efficiencies, the fewer workers are needed to produce more typewriters within a given period of time.

Alquati was equally attentive to the course of class struggle that followed on those developments at the point of production. He offered two pivotal observations on this score. Objectively, displaced workers were redistributed throughout or expelled from the labor force. Subjectively, these technical transformations of the workforce give rise to new political tactics and organizational forms on the factory floor. Thus, as Alquati would go on to argue in his influential studies of FIAT in the years leading up to the Hot Autumn, wildcat strikes and the refusal of work increasingly eclipsed collective bargaining and wage demands. This was the crux of Alquati's insight. For Alquati, as for many communist theorists in Italy at the time, militants no longer simply confronted the growing power of capital. They also confronted the growing dilemma posed by the anachronistic organization of proletarians on the basis of their identity *as workers* by communist parties. At the same time, because the machinations of capital gave rise to new forms of struggle in his theory of class composition, Alquati's early focus on class struggle at the point of production also pointed toward new struggles and revolutionary actors outside the factory gate. Class composition, as Alquati put it, "begins in manufacture, from a revolution in the conditions of production of labor."[31] Yet that revolution places a growing "minority of workers on the path to obsolescence, [namely] the machine workers on the primary fabrication line of a given factory producing consumer goods." Consequently, Alquati presciently observed in 1964, as the concentration of capital in machinery grows, class struggle remains "constrained to unfold within production and capital accumulation, *yet on a social scale or in the piazza.*"[32]

Thus, by the mid-1960s, clear-eyed Marxists had begun to critique both the traditional identification of the proletariat with industrial wage-earners and the equation of class struggle with social contest behind the factory gate. At the same time, as we shall see in the following sections, militants committed to the proliferating demands for *liberation* emanating from the U.S. struggled to articulate collective identities such as *women*, *black*, *Third World woman*, *gay*, *brown*, *American Indian*, and *Asian American*, to mention only some of the nominations current at the time. Just as *worker* had become an inadequate banner beneath which proletarians might march against capital, however, the affirmation of new social identities offered militants only partial responses to the miseries of race, gender, and class in the postwar world. Precisely because those miseries produce a real need to affirm identities born of social antagonism to improve the lot of the variously immiserated within the status quo, the postwar rebellions that peaked around 1968 in the global North confronted feminist and anti-racist militants with the same dilemma plaguing mid-century workers' movements. Can workers, women, or racialized populations eliminate such miseries *as* workers, women, or racialized populations? Or do affirmations of social identities leave in place the antagonisms from which they spring, regardless of whether those identities are composed in the course of struggles for civil rights, freedom from violence, or redistributive claims upon social wealth?

The Nation Thesis and Surplus Population

Few episodes in the postwar U.S. illustrate that dilemma more dramatically than the contest between rival nationalisms among black revolutionaries. For many black militants, the Black Belt thesis promoted by the Comintern during the interwar period was reanimated by theories of *internal colonialism* that routed the relationship between race and class at home through insights gleaned from struggles for national liberation abroad. As much as the retooled nation thesis drew militants together in the mid-1960s, however, divisions over how to organize the black nation and abolish white supremacy also drove them apart. Those divisions were not simply a matter of rival strategies. They were also owed to competing understandings of racial antagonism in the U.S., including the nature of racial-belonging, and whether such belonging was to be affirmed, or "race" itself viewed as an antagonistic relationship to be overcome.

At the height of the Black Power Movement, for instance, there was little consensus concerning either how to define the black nation or who needed to do what in order to free it, even as nearly all currents of black nationalism took cues from Mao and Fanon.[33] For some, the nation thesis referred to the dream of a separate territory.[34] For others, the black nation was an "internal colony" composed of racial ghettos occupied by municipal police forces.[35] Even among those latter militants, however, fierce organizational divisions emerged concerning who, precisely, belongs to the black nation.[36] Many revolutionary nationalists viewed the black bourgeoisie with suspicion. Some, including Huey Newton and Bobby Seale, argued that members of the black middle class were enemies of the black nation in spite of their apparent racial belonging.[37] Cultural nationalists, on the other hand, tended to view national belonging as a function of shared cultural heritage regardless of class.[38] Those divisions were as deadly as they are seemingly permanent.[39] Notoriously figured by the fatal shootout between members of the organization Us and the Black Panthers in 1969, the tragic conflict between revolutionary and cultural nationalists fueled by COINTELPRO has been etched into the tradition of black nationalism ever since.

At the heart of that conflict lie both rival compositions of the black nation and opposing political strategies for the abolition of white supremacy. The less spectacular organizational rifts between Us and the Black Panthers are a case in point. For Maulana Karenga, who cofounded Us, things were black and white. "Race rules out economics and even if it doesn't wipe it out completely it minimizes it. We conceive of the problem today not as a class struggle but a global struggle against racism."[40] That struggle was definitively pitched on the terrain of cultural identity.[41] Thus Karenga's creation of the pan-African holiday Kwanzaa was meant to affirm a uniform Afro-American racial identity contra white supremacist stereotypes.[42] Newton's dissent could hardly have been more emphatic. "Cultural nationalism, or pork chop nationalism," he once bitingly quipped, promotes the view that "returning to the old African culture and thereby regaining their identity . . . will automatically bring political freedom." The Black Panther Party, on the other hand, "realizes that we have to have an identity" but, as he categorically insisted, "we believe that culture itself will not liberate us. We're going to need some stronger stuff."[43]

Such divisions evince more than organizational rivalries. They also offer competing conceptions of racial antagonism that differ in several important respects. For Karenga, because rac*ism* owes to the historical misprision of faulty beliefs and cultural values, political emancipation flows from the construction of an affirmable racial identity rooted in a mythic past. For Newton, the relationship between racial identity and freedom from racial domination is less clear cut. Racial belonging does not guarantee political solidarity any more than racial identity is an obstacle to such solidarity. Thus, for the BPP, the road to emancipation would be paved by "revolutionary solidarity" with organizations such as the Young Lords, Brown Berets, Red Guard, struggles for Women's and Gay Liberation, and the Appalachian militants of the Young Patriots

Organization who formed part of Fred Hampton's short-lived Rainbow Coalition in Chicago, not affirmations of racial identity as such. Imperfectly realized and inevitably plagued by inter-group antagonisms, revolutionary solidarity nonetheless offered many militants a horizon of liberation beyond the affirmation of immutable social divisions and social antagonisms from which they spring.

In such rival conceptions of the black nation and road to freedom, therefore, we also encounter an odd resonance with the project of constructing an affirmable workers' identity. Insofar as black militants placed more or less inclusive notions of racial unity at the heart of their opposition to white supremacy, they too faced problems posed by a normative view of social identity. Like *worker* in the context of workers' movements, that is to say, *black* glossed over divisions between wageless proletarians and wage-earners, men and women, and, for Karenga, workers and bosses, in the name of a political unity grounded in racial belonging. For all its shortcomings, therefore, the Panthers' practice of revolutionary solidarity recognizes the experience of racial belonging as a key determinant in collective struggles not only for black liberation, but for freedom from social domination *tout court*, without making identity the ground of liberation. Revolutionary solidarity thus names what every militant knows. Social identity is an important moment in the organization of collective political projects but does not confer any particular political commitments to members of this or that social group.

The theoretical implications of that view were also worried by critics of the black nation thesis at the time. Few did so more incisively than Harry Chang and his coauthors in their *Critique of the Black Nation Thesis*. Contra the orthodox view of black Americans as a national minority, they offer a critical vantage on "the political economy of racism" in which the pan-ethnic "White-Black opposition" is revealed as a *historical consequence* of racial violence and economic domination, not the *psychological cause* of "a spontaneously developed antipathy between European descendants and African descendants."[44] Thus "racial categories are racist categories" precisely because they name differential vulnerabilities to social death and economic exclusion.[45] To confront racial domination means, therefore, struggling against the forms of violence that give rise to racial categories in the first place, including the indirect violence of market dependency combined with exclusions from the wage. From this vantage, "the essence of racism can be best described as *differential proletarianization*."[46] Peculiar combinations of direct and indirect violence, not cultural identities measured by national belonging (however defined), are what divides proletarians by race on this view.

Black revolutionaries have long confronted that violence even as it has also divided proletarians. Two years before the formation of OBP, for instance, James Boggs described the chauvinism of workers' movements faced with the growing superfluity of black workers to capital in *The American Revolution: Pages from a Negro Worker's Notebook*.[47] Sidney Wilhelm worried about the potential for racial genocide because of automation in his chillingly titled *Who Needs the Negro?*[48] Few will dispute the evident facts of mass incarceration shaping black life in the U.S. today, including the racialized growth of America's prison system that has kept pace with a black unemployment rate twice that of white workers since 1970.[49] Compelled to make ends meet outside the wage, many proletarians have no choice other than to take shelter in the criminalized sphere of the informal economy. Capital cannot accumulate without those exclusions. That non-white proletarians are disproportionately sentenced to the growing ranks of surplus population is, thus, not incidental to capital accumulation. Nor is the seizure of antediluvian racial logics by capital a cultural residue of historical contingency. The accumulation of capital has always been a racial project as much as it is an economic logic. On this view, the ongoing exploitation of wage labor by capital depends as much on racialized exclusions from the wage as those exclusions partly owe to the accumulation of capital. Together, the capital relation and the color line combine to make workers' and racial identities two of the more or less brutal fates awaiting proletarians.

Saying so will not wish away the antagonism between proletarians divided by race, of course. To put things this way is simply to see that to confront white supremacy is to confront the law of value—and vice versa—policing who is denied what they need to live the life they desire. Yet if *differential proletarianization* is too polite a term for the violently racialized logic policing black life in the U.S., Ruth Wilson Gilmore's definition of racism describes what we face in no less certain terms. "Racism," as she puts it, "is the state sanctioned or extralegal production and exploitation of group-differentiated vulnerability to premature death."[50] There is no denying "the difference between those bodies that do not magnetize bullets and those that do" today.[51] Yet there is also no denying, as Fanon once observed, that for those excluded from the wage violence saturates the atmosphere of racial belonging in part because "the economic infrastructure is also a superstructure."[52] From this vantage, to confront the law of value is to encounter the racialized logic of mass incarceration in the U.S. today, just as to struggle against police brutality is to confront the racialized logic of surplus population. For proletarians divided by race, there is no path toward the communist horizon or abolition of white supremacy that does not involve confronting the enemies of both.

The Left Debate and the Logic of Gender

The orthodox coordinates of the Woman Question formed in the context of the workers' movement were also transformed by the emergence of new social movements. A key touchstone in that transformation was the draft of "Sex and Caste" that Mary King and Casey Hayden circulated among women in the Student Non-Violent Coordinating Committee and Students for a Democratic Society during the years 1964–65.[53] With "Sex and Caste," feminists began to insist that male-dominated currents of the New Left take the gender division of labor and patriarchal violence as seriously as imperialism or white supremacy. Within what was quickly christened second-wave feminism, therefore, the *gender distinction* came to hold the key to the persistence of patriarchy in spite of women's suffrage.[54] By the same token, the abolition of patriarchy *tout court* formed the horizon of women's liberation for feminist militants. Figuring out how to get there, however, proved as divisive as the horizon was unifying.

Radical feminists pursued theoretical inquiries into the durable forms of patriarchal domination that made women a revolutionary subject distinct from both workers and racialized populations.[55] Most initially sought to negate the patriarchal norms regulating the gender distinction. After 1970 or so, however, feminists opposed to actions that might be seen as targeting women themselves, such as the 1968 Miss America protest that launched the Women's Liberation Movement onto the national stage, began striving to rehabilitate historically devalued attributes in order to construct an affirmable female identity. Cultural feminists, as the latter became known (often pejoratively), thus found themselves at odds with radical feminists over how to confront misogyny.[56] At the heart of the acrimony lay differing views of what, precisely, the category "women" denoted. For radical feminists, the content of the gender distinction was mutable and in need of transformation. For cultural feminists, however, the trouble lay with the cultural values ascribed to an invariant gender distinction in the present.[57] Those differences quickly hardened into divergent views of gender identity that fractured the WLM into opposed strategies of affirmation and negation.

By 1973, with the last of the bellwether radical-feminist organizations dissolved in the rising tides of cultural feminism, that fracture was compounded by growing divisions among feminists concerning questions of race and sexuality. The uneasy relationship between feminist and anti-racist concerns in the WLM animated recurring organizational dilemmas.[58] The Sex Wars that followed added further fuel to the fires sorting feminists into increasingly hostile camps.[59] Those compound fractures also centered on opposing strategies of affirmation and negation within autonomous feminist organizations. Growing differences *between* feminists made any affirmation of "women" as a collective subject suspect for some, while critiquing the salience of "women" as a shared identity militated against the abolition of patriarchy for others.[60] Where the former debates had divided the New Left along lines of gender, feminists were increasingly divided by proliferating orientations to the gender distinction organized by questions of difference and identity. Gender thus became the watchword of academic debates arranging feminist militants into essentialist and anti-essentialist camps.[61] Those categories have largely been discarded in the decades since. The compound fracture centered on the gender distinction they described, however, continues to haunt feminist theory today. Yet the organizational questions out of which those fractures grew have largely receded into the background of predominantly cultural affairs. Culture, in short, was all the rage for U.S. feminists attuned to the gender distinction in the aftermath of the WLM.

No entry in those debates proved more decisive than Judith Butler's epochal *Gender Trouble: Feminism and the Subversion of Identity*.[62] Lost in the fanfare surrounding Butler's thesis that gender is not who you are but what you do, however, was the fact that the express purpose of *Gender Trouble* was to make collective action possible in the divided train of the Women's Liberation Movement. The crux of Butler's intervention was, in a sense, to make a virtue of a vice. Troubling the norms of compulsory heterosexuality regulating the cultural imperatives of gender, Butler argued, would enable the indeterminacy of the latter category to "serve as a normative ideal relieved of coercive force." By the same token:

> Without the compulsory expectation that feminist actions must be instituted from some stable, unified, and agreed upon identity, those actions might well get a quicker start and seem more congenial to a number of "women" for whom the meaning of the category is permanently moot.[63]

This is why, as she was at pains to insist in her preface to the second edition, the force of her celebrated but vexed discussion of drag as a performance of gender trouble was neither descriptive nor prescriptive but heuristic. It illustrated a feminism the normative force of which was the *refusal of norms* because, as she put it, "the very description of the field of gender is no sense prior to, or separable from, the question of its normative operation."[64]

Here we can't help but note a certain rhyme with the normative view of the proletariat in traditional Marxism. To the extent that feminist militants sought to elaborate "women" as a revolutionary subject analogous to the classical working class, they inherited the problematic of the normative view. Like "working class," that is to say, "women" referred to an invariant revolutionary subject locked in an epochal struggle against class enemies in the early days of WLM. As in Firestone's *Dialectic of Sex*, the analogy was often explicit.[65] It was also frequently compounded by equally explicit analogies to racialized populations as the invariant revolutionary subject of struggles against white supremacy.[66] Radical-cum-cultural feminists no less than black nationalists or orthodox communists, that is to say, faced the problem of how to define class belonging on the basis of social identity. Thus, for feminist militants, the organizational tension between strategies of affirmation and negation played out theoretically as debates over how to map the gender distinction. Butler's *Gender Trouble* essentially ended the debate by placing the gender distinction on the shifting historical terrain of cultural practice. There was nothing to affirm, on this view, but the need to ruthlessly critique everything that exists so that the free development of each sexual identity might enable the free development of all.

Marxist feminists took a different tack, one announced by the pamphlet that gave *Gender Trouble* its subtitle. *Women and the Subversion of the Community* enjoined feminists involved in the soon to be international Wages for Housework campaign to reject both cultural affirmations of the category "women" and cultural critiques of patriarchal norms. Instead, its authors sought to describe the logic of gender within the historical dynamics of capital accumulation. Rather than either troubling or affirming gender identity, that is to say, these feminists sought the origins of the gender distinction itself from the vantage of a critical political economy. They did so, moreover, with an eye toward the hidden abode of reproduction Marx acknowledged was necessary for the production of value but followed capitalists in leaving "to the worker's drive for self-preservation and propagation" in the pages of *Capital*.[67] According to its author, Mariarosa Dalla Costa, capital's need for *unpaid but socially necessary labor* in the daily and generational reproduction of workers has kept women "using in isolation the same broom in the same few square feet of the kitchen for centuries."[68] Yet in spite of the oft-misunderstood slogan "Wages for Housework," the crucial affordance of this view was not the demand for a social wage from Keynesian welfare states. The key insight the pamphlet unlocked was the need for proletarians divided by gender "*to find a place as protagonist in the struggle*" against *both* capital *and* patriarchy.[69] From the critical vantage of *Women and the Subversion of the Community*, a divided proletariat confronts many enemies at once in any given struggle.

"The Logic of Gender" that emerged from post-2008 revisitations of that view places such struggles on firmer ground.[70] It does so, moreover, by rigorously remitting value theoretical arcanae and patriarchal violence within a unitary framework. For Maya Gonzalez and Jeanne Neton, that is to say, what feminists confront today is not gender per se but, crucially, "the form of gender specific to capitalism."[71] That form includes the assignment of certain individuals to the *socially necessary* but, technically speaking, *unproductive labor* of running errands, preparing meals, caring for children, and providing emotional support for wage-earners. It also includes differential vulnerabilities to violence. On this view, the persistence of patriarchy under capital is simply what the gender distinction definitively names "the *anchoring* of a certain group of individuals in a specific sphere of social activities. The result of this anchoring process is at the same time the continuous reproduction of two separate genders."[72] There is ample play in this system as the spheres mutate in accord with the needs of capital. Not all "women" must suffer patriarchal violence or bear offspring for what Gonzalez and Neton call the *gender fetish* to compose the spheres. Nor must all "women" be biologically female or conform to regnant gender norms. Like the increasingly waged performance of formerly unpaid household tasks such as cooking, cleaning, laundry, and childcare, the greater frequency of deviance is built into the postwar motion of value through the spheres of capital. Nonetheless, it is not the shifting terrain of cultural norms to which individuals are anchored in this perspective. It is the reciprocal interdependence between the capital relation and gender distinction in the collective working day that grounds social identity.

By the same token, therefore, it is not the refusal of patriarchal norms that gives this view its political edge. Instead, the logic of gender opens onto the place of *struggles against patriarchy among proletarians divided by gender within class struggle*. From this vantage, that is to say, the communist horizon and the abolition of patriarchy may or may not be identical, but neither can be reached without struggle on both fronts. Nor can either be imagined without struggles against patriarchy *within the proletariat*. To confront the gender distinction is to encounter the law of value—and to encounter the law of value is to confront the gender distinction—which collaborate to police who suffers what to get what they need to live with or without a wage. Gender and workers' identities, on this view, simply describe two of the many fates awaiting proletarians. If the logic of gender and law of value are one fist, however, proletarians are not ipso facto united thereby. As often as not the capital relation and gender distinction combine to divide proletarians. This is true both theoretically and practically. Thus, as Shahrzad Mojab reminds us, feminist theorists have long vacillated between a view that "reduc[es] gender to questions of culture" and one that "reduced gender to class relations."[73]

Militants were not unaware of that dilemma at the time. One of the most important missives to emerge from the new social movements of the 1960s, the *Combahee River Collective Statement*, for instance, articulated the novel idiom of *identity politics* with Marx and Engels's early definition of communism as the *real movement that which abolishes the present state of things*.[74] "We realize that the liberation of all oppressed peoples necessitates the destruction of the political-economic systems of capitalism and imperialism as well as patriarchy," its authors wrote in 1977. "We are not convinced, however," they continued, "that a socialist revolution that is not also a feminist and anti-racist revolution will guarantee our liberation." Hence the Collective, "in essential agreement with Marx's theory" of class struggle in Europe during the age of empire, proposed that his theory of revolt "be extended" to encompass the wretched of the earth as well as relationships of domination and dispossession unique to the postwar world.[75] Less a global theory of revolution than a powerful critique of theories that identify *communism* with male breadwinners, *women's liberation* with suburban housewives, or *black power* with cultural nationalists, the missive draws on the experiences and insights of militants from Algeria to Stonewall to encourage further inquiry into the problem of revolutionary *solidarity* in the wake of the new social movements. Nor, in spite its solicitous modesty, does the missive leave much doubt concerning the nature of the future inquiries that are required. For the Combahee River Collective, as for many militants today, the wave of struggles that peaked around 1968 made it abundantly clear that *an injury to one is an injury to all* never tells the whole story. *Who revolts why* and *how it is to be done* remain matters of contention, even and especially when social movements are afoot.

It is in this sense that, as Linda Martín Alcoff once bravely ventured, "identity politics ... sides with Marxist class analysis."[76] On this view, gender is one of several "differentials across which value can flow."[77] It is not the only one. Nor does it easily intersect with race and class as in theories divorced from a critique of political economy. By the same token, struggles against the dicta of ruling-class patriarchs and sexual violence within radical milieus do not easily align with orthodox views of class struggle. From the view on offer here, however, there is no path to the communist horizon without those struggles today. Among other things, the fate of all proletarians unevenly depends upon their troubled currents.

Conclusion: Proletarians and Social Struggle Today

Today, the self-understanding of postwar militants receives short shrift in theoretical debates over the relationships among race, gender, and class. Caricatures of Marxism and the intersectional tradition as competing if not hostile frameworks for understanding social antagonism tend to stand in for the rich archive of nuanced positions elaborated by militants in the course of social struggle.[78] Beyond assuring that rote accusations of class-reductionism and identitarian particularism remain in heavy rotation, such caricatures continue to gloss over one of the signal dilemmas shared by militants committed to liberation from the miseries of race, gender, and class in the postwar world. Yet for many militants, as we have seen, the need for an affirmable identity around which to organize existed in tension with the desire to eliminate the antagonistic relationships from which those identities spring. While many of today's debates revolve around normative claims concerning the interests of this or that social group, therefore, the efforts of postwar militants to confront the limits of such normative claims offer a compelling set of critical concepts that point toward a way beyond familiar impasses. Even the cursory recollection of a handful of those efforts in the previous pages suggests some preliminary conclusions in this regard.

At a minimum, we might conclude by noting what normative views of rival revolutionary subjects have made especially difficult to see. During the 1960s and '70s, the composition of the *proletariat, women,* and *black nation* alike were hotly contested *within* communist, feminist, and anti-racist organizations in ways that were quickly eclipsed by categorical oppositions among *race, gender,* and *class* in the cultural aftermath of new social movements. Yet those oppositions depend on normative orientations toward *racial, gender,* and *workers' identities* once opposed by feminist and anti-racist militants critical of the forms of wageless life integral to capital accumulation. While that critical vantage had fallen out of fashion by the end of the 1970s, it may nonetheless offer greater purchase on the complexity of social struggles today than the normative views that took its place. Among other things, it admits what organizational conflicts among proletarians divided by race and gender, on the one hand,

and feminist and anti-racist militants divided by racial belonging, sexual orientation, citizenship status, class, and so on, on the other, have long borne out. In spite of the chauvinist construction of an affirmable workers' identity within traditional Marxism and the historical workers' movement, *proletariat* is not synonymous with a uniform working class composed of white, male, industrial wage-workers. Instead, *the proletariat is composed by modes of differential access to the means of subsistence.* On this view, the gendered performance of unpaid but socially necessary reproductive labor and racialized exclusions from the wage subtend the accumulation of capital *no less but differently than* the production of surplus value. By the same token, forms of wageless life composed by the logic of gender and racialized surplus populations are as much the lot of some proletarians as the more or less golden chains of the wage relation are the lot of others. Racial, gender, and workers' identities merely name some of the many differential fates awaiting proletarians.

More maximally, we might be forgiven for noting what many feminist and anti-racist militants have long argued: the accumulation of capital depends on the reproduction of differential fates to keep profits flowing, even if those fates are themselves periodically recomposed. The 1970s offer a telling case in point. Even as Marxist feminists were theorizing the unwaged reproductive labor historically performed by women in the home, women were flooding labor markets with little relief from the gendered division of labor in the home, giving rise to the postwar rhythms of the "double day" for some while exposing many to sexual violence within as well as without the workplace.[79] As black nationalists and critics of the nation thesis alike were theorizing the revolutionary agency of those locked out of the wage relation altogether, meanwhile, unemployed black men were already beginning to populate a massive expansion of America's prison system at nearly thrice the rate of their white counterparts.[80] Moreover, as the rate of profit that has yet to return to its pre-1970 levels slowed to a trickle, a rank-and-file rebellion organized by the shrinking minority of industrial workers was brutally crushed in 1973.[81] In its wake, it left a moribund workers' movement amid an expanding service sector that has only partially absorbed the shares of the workforce relinquished by manufacturers, and continues to do so on ever worsening terms.[82] By the end of the 1970s, in sum, the industrial working class of traditional Marxism was a thing of the past, but neither *women* nor *blacks* were any better able to articulate the variously dominated and dispossessed in its place. Instead, the *composition of the postwar proletariat* was thrown into flux, and militants into disarray along with it, just as many Marxists turned away from the critique of political economy, and feminist and anti-racist theorists increasingly turned toward cultural theories of social identity.

Consequently, the composition of the proletariat underwent considerable transformations behind the backs of many social theorists after 1970. It is hardly surprising, therefore, that debates about the relationship among race, gender, and class have been reignited by the successive emergence of the Movement of Squares, the Movement for Black Lives, the International Women's Strike, and #MeToo since 2008. In response, some observers have doubled down on normative views of traditional working-class agency indifferent to if not openly hostile toward feminist and anti-racist social movements.[83] Others have placed their hopes in the restorative potential of belatedly recognizing that *the working class* encompasses unevenly combined forms of waged and wageless life composed by the gender distinction and color line.[84] Still others lament the bleak outlook of those who adopt a critical view of the composition problem on the grounds that doing so shirks the problem of formal organization.[85] There are, to be sure, no solutions to the problem of organization in the preceding pages. From the vantage on offer here, recognizing that the proletariat is not identical with the classical working class in revolutionary theory does little in and of itself to heal historical wounds. It does less to resolve the organizational dilemmas proletarians divided by race and gender face today. At most, this prospect makes clear that there is no logically necessary opposition between feminist, anti-racist, and anti-capitalist struggles. Proletarians, on this view, still have it all to do.

At the same time, this prospect has the virtue of clarifying just how much proletarians have to do. It does so by taking seriously the many contributions to revolutionary theory by feminist and anti-racist militants, including those most explicitly opposed to capitalist exploitation. Rather than dressing today's social antagonisms in the normative slogans and costumes of the past, this view opens onto the uneven terrain of manifold social struggles that are of a piece but not of a kind. It won't do, for instance, as even the most cogent observers of contemporary social movements sometimes do, to view "identity politics [as] a real expression of class struggle," as though BLM and #MeToo are so many secondary elaborations of some more primary struggle over the means of survival.[86] The question proletarians confront today is not *whether* social struggles against sexual violence, racialized police violence, and economic exploitation are related, but *how to make each struggle a weapon in the real movement to abolish the present state of things tout court.*

That question, in sum, returns the composition problem to the practical matter of how proletarians divided by race and gender can join forces to abolish capital, patriarchy, and white supremacy today. At the same time, it exorcizes the ghosts of categorical oppositions between workers', racial, and gender identities that followed in the wake of "an injury to one is an injury to all" during the last decades of the twentieth century. The question proletarians face today is not how to recognize their shared fate. The question is how to fight on many fronts knowing full well that collective injuries are everywhere unevenly suffered. Above all, proletarians face the difficulty of knowing that those differences mark the beginning, not the end, of social struggle in the twenty-first century.

Notes

1. See, for instance, Cinzia Arruzza, Sara R. Farris, Johanna Oksala, and F. T. C. Manning, "Gender and Capitalism: Debating Cinzia Arruzza's 'Remarks on Gender,'" *Viewpoint Magazine*, May 4, 2105, accessed February 25, 2017, https://viewpointmag.com/2015/05/04/gender-and-capitalism-debating-cinzia-arruzzas-remarks-on-gender/, and "Class, Race, and Marxism," Verso Blog, July 2017, https://www.versobooks.com/blogs?mentioned_book=4218.

2. James Boggs, "The City Is the Black Man's Land," in *Racism and the Class Struggle Today: Further Pages from a Black Worker's Notebook* (New York: Monthly Review Press, 1970), 45.

3. Shulamith Firestone and Anne Koedt, eds., *Notes from the Second Year: Women's Liberation* (New York: Radical Feminism, 1970), 112, 113.

4. Jean Barrot and Francois Martin, *Eclipse and Re-Emergence of the Communist Movement* (Detroit: Black & Red, 1972), 39.

5. Shulamith Firestone, *The Dialectic of Sex: The Case for Feminist Revolution* (New York: Morrow, 1970), 11.

6. Racism Research Project, *Critique of the Black Nation Thesis* (Berkeley: Racism Research Project, 1975), 1.

7. Goetz A. Briefs, *The Proletariat: A Challenge to Western Civilization* (New York: McGraw-Hill, 1937), 52–83. Other notable accounts of cognate drift include Werner Conze, "Vom "Pöbel" zum "Proletariat": Sozialgeschichtliche Voraussetzungen für den Sozialismus in Deutschland," *Vierteljahrschrift für Sozial- und Wirtschaftsgeschichte* 41, no. 4 (1954): 333–64; R. B. Rose, "Prolétaires and Prolétariat: Evolution of a Concept, 1789–1848," *Australian Journal of French Studies* 18, no. 1 (1981): 282–99; and David W. Lovell, *Marx's Proletariat: The Making of a Myth* (London: Routledge, 1988).

8. The evolution of Sismondi's mixed use of *prolétaire* is a sign of the times. In 1819 Sismondi described the Malthusian increase of the poor as proletarians. In his foreword to the second edition of 1826, however, Sismondi also described the dispossessed fortunate enough to be subsumed beneath subsistence wages as proletarians; see J.-C.-L. Simonde de Sismondi, *New Principles of Political Economy: Of Wealth in Its Relation to Population*, trans. Richard Hyse (New Brunswick: Transaction, 1991), 520 and 10.

9. Karl Marx, *The Eighteenth Brumaire of Louis Bonaparte* (New York: International, 1990), 9.

10. While Sismondi was more sympathetic to the plight of proletarians than some deposed aristocrats, in other words, his view of the category as a mixed bag and its

members as more a plague than not upon the social order he held dear was wholly in keeping with the times; see J.-C.-L. Simonde de Sismondi, *Études Sur l'Économie Politique* (Paris: Chez Treuttel et Würz, 1837), 1:196–223, and J.-C.-L. Simonde de Sismondi, "On the Condition of the Work People in Manufactories," in *Political Economy and the Philosophy of Government*, trans. Anonymous (London: Chapman, 1847), 34–47.

11. Lorenz von Stein, *The History of the Social Movement in France, 1789–1850*, trans. Kaethe Mengelberg (Totowa, N.J.: Bedminster, 1964), 268. Apparently sent to France by the Prussian authorities to report back on the Parisian workers' societies, Stein cuts a strange figure in the making of the proletariat. First published as *Der Sozialismus und Communismus des heutigen Frankreich* in 1842, his book was certainly known to Marx and Engels before they wrote the Manifesto, but, whether they knew of his work as an agent of the Prussian state, neither thought much of Stein as a social theorist. Moses Hess, however, reviewed Stein's book in 1843, and Marx and Engels attacked Bruno Bauer in *The Holy Family* for failing to attain even the level of Stein (Karl Marx and Friedrich Engels, *The Holy Family, or, Critique of Critical Critique* [Honolulu: University Press of the Pacific, 2002], 180); and in *The German Ideology* Marx accused Karl Grün of bowdlerizing the "much despised" Stein's monarchical apologetics (Marx and Engels, *The German Ideology: Including Theses on Feuerbach and Introduction to "The Critique of Political Economy"* [Amherst, N.Y.: Prometheus, 1998], 518), while Grün engaged Stein at length in his own *Die Soziale Bewegung in Frankreich und Belgien*. Whatever its direct influence on Marx and Engels, therefore, Stein's book, the 1850 title of which coined the term "social movement," did much to foment the sociological identification of the proletariat with the working class of factory inspectors in the minds of Young Hegelians, as the young Herbert Marcuse argued at length in *Reason and Revolution* (Oxford: Oxford University Press, 1941), 374–88. On Stein's activities as a Prussian agent, see Joist Grolle, "Lorenz Stein als Preußischer Geheimagent," *Archiv für Kulturgeschichte* 50 (1968): 82–96. On Stein's influence on the Young Hegelians and the surrounding controversies, see Kaethe Mengelberg, "Lorenz von Stein, His Life and Work," in *The History of the Social Movement in France, 1789–1850* (Totowa, N.J.: Bedminster, 1964), 26–33; Shlomo Avineri, *The Social and Political Thought of Karl Marx* (Cambridge: Cambridge University Press, 1968), 53–57; and Gareth Stedman Jones, *Karl Marx: Greatness and Illusion* (Cambridge: Belknap Press, 139–41).

12. Karl Marx, *Critique of Hegel's "Philosophy of Right,"* trans. Annette Jolin and Joseph J. O'Malley (Cambridge: Cambridge University Press, 1970), 142. As a number of observers note, this initial tension—between the emancipation of a proletariat often identified with industrial workers and emancipation from a social order identified with the interests of any particular group—runs throughout the Marxian corpus. On the elaboration of *das Proletariat* in the writings of Marx and Engels between the "Introduction" and *Manifesto*, see Gareth Stedman Jones, "Introduction," in Karl Marx and Friedrich Engels, *The Communist Manifesto* (London: Penguin, 2002), 3–184.

13. Marx and Engels, *Communist Manifesto*, ed. Gareth Stedman Jones (London: Penguin, 2002), 219.

14. Ibid., 220.

15. Ibid., 222.

16. Ibid., 223.

17. Geoff Eley, *Forging Democracy: The History of the Left in Europe, 1850–2000* (Oxford: Oxford University Press, 2002), 48.

18. Marx and Engels, *Manifesto*, 228, 226.

19. Ibid., 228, 230.

20. Ibid., 231.

21. On communist horizons, see Endnotes, "Crisis in the Class Relation," *Endnotes* 3 (2010): 3–19.

22. Karl Marx, *Capital: A Critique of Political Economy*, trans Ben Fowkes and David Fernbach (New York: Penguin, 1990), 1:724.

23. Ibid., 764.

24. Marx and Engels, *Communist Manifesto*, 233.

25. Endnotes, "A History of Separation: The Rise and Fall of the Workers' Movement, 1883–1982," *Endnotes* 4 (October 2015): 96–102, https://endnotes.org.uk/issues/4/en/endnotes-preface.

26. Ibid., 108.

27. Robert Lumley, *States of Emergency: Cultures of Revolt in Italy from 1968 to 1978* (London: Verso, 1990).

28. Steve Wright, *Storming Heaven: Class Composition and Struggle in Italian Autonomist Marxism* (London: Pluto, 2002).

29. Romano Alquati, "Organic Composition of Capital and Labor Power at Olivetti," trans. Steve Wright, *Viewpoint* 3 (1961), https://viewpointmag.com/2013/09/27/organic-composition-of-capital-and-labor-power-at-olivetti-1961/.

30. For "technical composition of capital," see Marx, *Capital*, 762.

31. Romano Alquati, "Outline of a Pamphlet on Fiat," *Viewpoint* 3, https://viewpointmag.com/2013/09/26/outline-of-a-pamphlet-on-fiat-1967/.

32. Romano Alquati, "Struggle at Fiat," *Viewpoint* 3 (1967), https://viewpointmag.com/2013/09/26/struggle-at-fiat-1964/.

33. Robin D. G. Kelley and Betsy Esch, "Black like Mao: Red China and Black Revolution," *Souls* 1, no. 4 (1999): 6–41.

34. Imari Abubakari Obadele, *Foundations of the Black Nation: A Textbook of Ideas behind the New Black Nationalism and the Struggle for Land in America* (Detroit: House of Songhay, 1975).

35. Robert Blauner, "Internal Colonialism and Ghetto Revolt," *Social Problems* 16, no. 4 (1969): 393–408, and Robert L. Allen, *Black Awakening in Capitalist America* (New York: Anchor, 1970).

36. For a trenchant theoretical reconstruction of postwar black nationalism, see Michael C. Dawson, *Black Visions: The Roots of Contemporary African-American Political Ideologies* (Chicago: University of Chicago Press, 2007), 85–134. For an overview of the organizational welter therein, see William Van Deburg, ed., *Modern Black Nationalism: From Marcus Garvey to Louis Farrakhan* (New York: New York University Press, 1997).

37. Mikhail Pronilover, "Social Class and the Revolutionary Politics of the Black Liberation Movement: The Black Panther Party and the League of Revolutionary Black Workers," Marxists Internet Archive, https://www.marxists.org/history/erol/1960-1970/lrbw-class.pdf.

38. Maulana Karenga left few doubts on the matter: "The fact that we are Black is our ultimate reality. We were Black before we were born. . . . Nationalism is a belief that Black people in this country make up a cultural nation"; Karenga, *The Quotable*

Karenga, ed. Clyde Halisi and James Mtume [Los Angeles: Us Organization, 1967], 3, 6).

39. By 1970, the postwar division between cultural and revolutionary nationalists had been implicitly projected onto the longue durée of Black Nationalism in America and explicitly theorized by Evan Ofari; see John H. Bracey, August Meier, and Elliott M Rudwick, eds., *Black Nationalism in America* (Indianapolis: Bobbs-Merrill, 1970), and Evan Ofari, *Black Liberation: Cultural and Revolutionary Nationalism* (Detroit: Racial Education Project, 1970).

40. Karenga, *Quotable Karenga*, 16.

41. "If you know you are Black then your purpose is to build Black.... Us is a cultural organization dedicated to the creation, recreation and circulation of Afro-American culture.... You must have a cultural revolution before the violent revolution. The cultural revolution gives identity, purpose and direction"; ibid., 2, 7, 11.

42. Maulana Karenga, *Kwanzaa: Origin, Concepts, Practice* (Los Angeles: Kawaida, 1977), 11–21.

43. Huey Newton, *Huey Newton Talks to the Movement about the Black Panther Party, Cultural Nationalism, SNCC, Liberals and White Revolutionaries* (Chicago: Students for a Democratic Society, 1968), 4.

44. Racism Research Project, *Critique*, 381, 392.

45. Ibid., 393.

46. Ibid., 390.

47. Boggs's book *American Revolution* (1968) was first published in the *Monthly Review* during July 1963.

48. Sidney Willhelm, *Who Needs the Negro?* (Cambridge, Mass.: Schenkman, 1970).

49. Bruce Western, *Punishment and Inequality in America* (New York: Russell Sage, 2006), 17, and U.S. Bureau of Labor Statistics, "Unemployment Rates by Race and Ethnicity, 2010," *Economics Daily*, October 5, 2011, https://www.bls.gov/opub/ted/2011/ted_20111005.htm.

50. Ruth Wilson Gilmore, *Golden Gulag: Prisons, Surplus, Crisis, and Opposition in Globalizing California* (Berkeley: University of California Press, 2007), 28.

51. Frank B. Wilderson, "The Prison Slave as Hegemony's (Silent) Scandal," *Social Justice* 30, no. 2 (2003) (92): 20.

52. Frantz Fanon, *The Wretched of the Earth*, trans. Richard Philcox (New York: Grove, 2004), 5.

53. Mary King and Casey Hayden first issued their clarion call as the (then-anonymous) 1964 "SNCC Position Paper (Women in the Movement)"; see Sara M. Evans, *Personal Politics: The Roots of Women's Liberation in the Civil Rights Movement and the New Left* (New York: Vintage, 1980), 235–38. King and Hayden's 1965 circular "A Kind of Memo" was published the following year as "Sex and Caste" (*Liberation*, no. 10 [1966]: 35–36).

54. The "second wave" coinage is typically credited to Martha Lear: "The Second Feminist Wave," *New York Times Magazine*, March 10, 1968.

55. Alice Echols, *Daring to Be Bad: Radical Feminism in America, 1967–1975* (Minneapolis: University of Minnesota Press, 1989).

56. For signal critiques of cultural feminism, see Brooke Williams, "The Retreat to Cultural Feminism," in *Feminist Revolution*, ed. Kathie Sarachild (New York:

Random House, 1978), 79–83; Alice Echols, "The Taming of the Id," in *Pleasure and Danger: Exploring Female Sexuality*, ed. Carole S. Vance (Boston: Routledge & Kegan Paul, 1984), 50–72; Ellen Willis, "Radical Feminism and Feminist Radicalism," *Social Text*, no. 9/10 (1984): 91–118. For a partisan riposte, see Verta Taylor and Leila J. Rupp, "Women's Culture and Lesbian Feminist Activism: A Reconsideration of Cultural Feminism," *Signs* 19, no. 1 (1993): 32–61.

57. It is not easy to distinguish radical from cultural feminism at this late date, not least because many cultural feminists initially identified as radical feminists. The dynamics of those personal transformations no doubt partly explain the political charge of the theoretical split. What came to be known as cultural feminism had its roots, moreover, in the pro-woman line closely associated with Redstockings, a bellwether radical-feminist organization and the only one still extant today. Today those radical and cultural currents are more often than not confused in a monolithic "second wave" of feminism. Nonetheless, few will dispute the fury surrounding the division at the time.

58. Those dilemmas preceded, of course, the national emergence of WLM in 1968; see Evans, *Personal Politics*; Bettye Collier-Thomas and V. P. Franklin, eds., *Sisters in the Struggle: African American Women in the Civil Rights–Black Power Movement* (New York: New York University Press, 2001); Benita Roth, *Separate Roads to Feminism: Black, Chicana, and White Feminist Movements in America's Second Wave* (Cambridge: Cambridge University Press, 2004); Kimberly Springer, *Living for the Revolution: Black Feminist Organizations, 1968–1980* (Durham, N.C.: Duke University Press, 2005); Dayo F. Gore, Jeanne Theoharis, and Komozi Woodard, eds., *Want to Start a Revolution? Radical Women in the Black Freedom Struggle* (New York: New York University Press, 2009).

59. Ann Barr Snitow, Christine Stansell, and Sharon Thompson, eds., *Powers of Desire: The Politics of Sexuality*, New Feminist Library (New York: Monthly Review Press, 1983); Carole S. Vance, ed., *Pleasure and Danger: Exploring Female Sexuality* (Boston: Routledge & Kegan Paul, 1984); Lisa Duggan and Nan D. Hunter, *Sex Wars: Sexual Dissent and Political Culture* (New York: Routledge, 1995).

60. Linda Alcoff, "Cultural Feminism versus Post-Structuralism: The Identity Crisis in Feminist Theory," *Signs* 13, no. 3 (1988): 405–36.

61. It is important to remember Joan Wallach Scott's observation that "concern with gender as an analytic category has emerged only in the late twentieth century"; Joan W. Scott, "Gender: A Useful Category of Historical Analysis," *American Historical Review* 91, no. 5 (1986): 1,066. Firestone, for instance, spoke of the sex distinction rather than the gender distinction; gender is nowhere to be found in the *Dialectic of Sex*. It is just as important to remember, however, that, as Scott obliquely notes, gender became the category du jour for Anglo-American feminists during the theoretical fallout surrounding organizational divisions within the WLM. In the years after Firestone's groundbreaking work, those divisions pitted militants committed to ahistorical, essentialist views of patriarchy against historicist, anti-essentialist views of gender relations; Scott, "Gender," 1,058–61.

62. Judith Butler, *Gender Trouble: Feminism and the Subversion of Identity*, 2nd ed. (New York: Routledge, 1999).

63. Butler, *Gender Trouble*, 21.

64. Ibid., xxi.

65. Militants who went on to agree on little else agreed, in the initial salvo of radical-feminist manifestos, that the shared experience of oppression by men composed women as a class. See, for example, the manifestos issued by Redstockings, the Feminists, and New York Radical Feminists, in Firestone and Koedt, *Notes from the Second Year*, 111–26.

66. King and Hayden's "Sex and Caste," for example, begins by noting that "there seem to be many parallels that can be drawn between the treatment of Negroes and treatment of women in our society as a whole" (35).

67. Marx, *Capital*, 1:718.

68. Mariarosa Dalla Costa and Selma James, *The Power of Women and the Subversion of the Community* (Bristol: Falling Wall, 1972), 29.

69. Dalla Costa and James, *Power*, 34; emphasis in original.

70. Maya Gonzalez and Jeanne Neton, "The Logic of Gender: On the Separation of Spheres and the Process of Abjection," in *Contemporary Marxist Theory: A Reader*, ed. Andrew Pendakis (New York: Bloomsbury Academic, 2014), 149–74.

71. Gonzalez and Neton, "Logic," 57.

72. Ibid., 78.

73. Shahrzad Mojab, ed., *Marxism and Feminism* (London: Zed, 2015), 5, 6.

74. See Keeanga-Yamahtta Taylor, ed., *How We Get Free: Black Feminism and the Combahee River Collective* (Chicago: Haymarket, 2017), 19; and Karl Marx and Friedrich Engels, *The German Ideology* (Amherst: Prometheus, 1998), 57. It is perhaps worth recalling the sentence that follows Marx and Engels's memorable formula as well: "The conditions of this movement result from the premises now in existence." Spurred by disappointment with the National Black Feminist Organization as well as "disillusionment" (17) with both the women's and black liberation movements, the members of the Collective came together in the course of struggles during the 1960s and '70s. Motivated by a series of organizational dilemmas carefully described in its pages, and originally circulated as a pamphlet under the unassuming title *Combahee River Collective Statement*, their missive famously popularized the idiom of *identity politics*. It bears repeating, however, that the *Statement* helped to launch the career of an idiom that rarely has anything to do—for opponents or proponents—with the "revolutionary concept" (19) unequivocally advanced therein as a means to the end of white supremacy, patriarchy, and capitalism *in toto*. No matter how much a particular polity may need to affirm its rights and dignity within the status quo in order to survive, if not thrive—and such tactics are often an absolute necessity for survival—the latter is not the horizon of *identity politics* that is forwarded in the *Combahee River Collective Statement*. For its authors, no less than for Marx and Engels in 1846, freedom from domination "is not a state of affairs which is to be established, an ideal to which reality will have to adjust itself." Liberation—a term of art synonymous with communism in the opening pages of *The German Ideology*—is "the real movement which abolishes the present state of things."

75. See Taylor, *How We Get Free*, 19–20. On the roots of the Collective in the organizational dilemmas posed by the communist currents its members encountered within the movements for women's and black liberation, see Colleen Lye, "Identity Politics, Criticism, and Self-Criticism," *South Atlantic Quarterly* 119, no. 4 (2020): 701–14.

76. Alcoff, "Cultural Feminism," 433.

77. Joshua Clover and Juliana Spahr, "Gender Abolition and Ecotone War," *South Atlantic Quarterly* 115, no. 2 (2016): 292.

78. Ashley J. Bohrer, *Marxism and Intersectionality: Race, Gender, Class and Sexuality under Contemporary Capitalism* (London: Transcript, 2019).

79. Diane Elson, "Labor Markets as Gendered Institutions: Equality, Efficiency and Empowerment Issues," *World Development* 27, no. 3 (1999): 612–3.

80. Western, *Punishment*, 90.

81. Robert Brenner, "The Political Economy of the Rank-and-File Rebellion," in *Rebel Rank and File: Labor Militancy and Revolt from Below during the Long 1970s*, ed. Aaron Brenner, Robert Brenner, and Calvin Winslow (New York: Verso, 2010), 37–74.

82. Aaron Benanav, *Automation and the Future of Work* (London and New York: Verso, 2020).

83. See, respectively, Mike Davis, "Old Gods, New Enigmas: Notes on 'Historical Agency,'" *Catalyst* 1, no. 2 (2017): 7–40, and Walter Benn Michaels, "Identity Politics: A Zero-Sum Game," nonsite.org, February 11, 2016, http://nonsite.org/editorial/identity-politics-a-zero-sum-game.

84. Tithi Bhattacharya, "How Not to Skip Class: Social Reproduction of Labor and the Global Working Class," in *Social Reproduction Theory: Remapping Class, Recentering Oppression*, ed. Tithi Bhattacharya and Lise Vogel (London: Pluto, 2017), 68–93.

85. Bue Rübner Hansen, "Surplus Population, Social Reproduction, and the Problem of Class Formation," *Viewpoint* 5 (October 31, 2015), https://www.viewpointmag.com/2015/10/31/surplus-population-social-reproduction-and-the-problem-of-class-formation/, and Tim Barker, "The Bleak Left: On Endnotes." *N+1* 28 (Spring 2017).

86. Endnotes, "Onward Barbarians," Endnotes, December 2020, https://endnotes.org.uk/file_hosting/Onward_Barbarians_by_Endnotes.pdf.

Works Cited

Alcoff, Linda. "Cultural Feminism versus Post-Structuralism: The Identity Crisis in Feminist Theory." *Signs* 13, no. 3 (1988.): 405–36.

Allen, James S. *The Negro Question in the United States*. New York: International, 1936.

Allen, Robert C. *Global Economic History: A Very Short Introduction*. Oxford: Oxford University Press, 2011.

Allen, Robert L. *Black Awakening in Capitalist America*. New York: Anchor, 1970.

Alquati, Romano. "Organic Composition of Capital and Labor Power at Olivetti." Translated by Steve Wright. *Viewpoint*, no. 3 (1961). https://viewpointmag.com/2013/09/27/organic-composition-of-capital-and-labor-power-at-olivetti-1961/.

———. "Outline of a Pamphlet on FIAT." *Viewpoint*, no. 3 (1967). https://viewpointmag.com/2013/09/26/outline-of-a-pamphlet-on-fiat-1967/.

———. "Struggle at FIAT." *Viewpoint*, no. 3 (1964). https://viewpointmag.com/2013/09/26/struggle-at-fiat-1964/.

Arruzza, Cinzia. *Dangerous Liaisons: The Marriages and Divorces of Marxism and Feminism*. Pontypool: Merlin, 2013.
Arruzza, Cinzia, Sara R. Farris, Johanna Oksala, and F. T. C. Manning. "Gender and Capitalism: Debating Cinzia Arruzza's 'Remarks on Gender.'" *Viewpoint Magazine* (blog), May 4, 2015. Accessed February 25, 2017. https://viewpointmag.com/2015/05/04/gender-and-capitalism-debating-cinzia-arruzzas-remarks-on-gender/.
Avineri, Shlomo. *The Social and Political Thought of Karl Marx*. Cambridge: Cambridge University Press, 1968.
Barker, Tim. "The Bleak Left: On Endnotes." *N+1*, no. 28 (Spring 2017).
Barrot, Jean, and Francois Martin. *Eclipse and Re-Emergence of the Communist Movement*. Detroit: Black & Red, 1972.
Bebel, August. *Woman and Socialism*. Translated by Meta L. Stern. New York: Co-Operative, 1910.
Benanav, Aaron, and John Clegg. "Misery and Debt: On the Logic and History of Surplus Populations and Surplus Capital." In *Contemporary Marxist Theory: A Reader*, edited by Andrew Pendakis, Jeff Diamanti, Nicholas Brown, Josh Robinson, and Imre Szeman, 585–608. New York: Bloomsbury Academic, 2014.
Berger, Stefan. *Social Democracy and the Working Class in Nineteenth and Twentieth Century Germany*. Themes in Modern German History Series. Harlow: Longman, 2000.
Bestor, Arthur E. "The Evolution of the Socialist Vocabulary." *Journal of the History of Ideas* 9, no. 3 (1948): 259–302.
Bhattacharya, Tithi. "How Not to Skip Class: Social Reproduction of Labor and the Global Working Class." In *Social Reproduction Theory: Remapping Class, Recentering Oppression*, edited by Tithi Bhattacharya and Lise Vogel, 68–93. London: Pluto, 2017.
Big Flame Women's Group, ed. *Fighting for Feminism: The "Women Question" in an Italian Revolutionary Group*. West London: Big Flame Women's Commission, 1976.
Biondi, Martha. *Black Revolution on Campus*. Berkeley: University of California Press, 2012.
Black Panther. "Central Committee, B.P.P. Press Conference," January 4, 1969.
Blauner, Robert. "Internal Colonialism and Ghetto Revolt." *Social Problems* 16, no. 4 (1969): 393–408.
Bloom, Joshua, and Waldo E. Martin. *Black against Empire: The History and Politics of the Black Panther Party*. Berkeley: Univ. of California Press, 2013.
Boggs, James. *The American Revolution: Pages from a Negro Worker's Notebook*. New York: Monthly Review Press, 1968.
———. "The City Is the Black Man's Land." In *Racism and the Class Struggle Today: Further Pages from a Black Worker's Notebook*. New York: Monthly Review Press, 1970.

Boggs, James, and Grace Lee Boggs. *Revolution and Evolution in the Twentieth Century*. New York: Monthly Review Press, 2008.

Bohrer, Ashley J. *Marxism and Intersectionality: Race, Gender, Class and Sexuality under Contemporary Capitalism*. London: Transaction, 2019.

Booker, Chris. "Lumpenization: A Critical Error of the Black Panther Party." In *The Black Panther Party (Reconsidered)*, edited by Charles Earl Jones. Baltimore: Black Classic Press, 1998.

Bovenkerk, Frank. "The Rehabilitation of the Rabble: How and Why Marx and Engels Wrongly Depicted the Lumpenproletariat as a Reactionary Force." *Netherlands Journal of Social Sciences* 20, no. 1 (1984): 13–41.

Bowring, Finn. "From the Mass Worker to the Multitude: A Theoretical Contextualisation of Hardt and Negri's Empire." *Capital & Class* 28, no. 2 (2004): 101–32.

Bracey, John H, August Meier, and Elliott M Rudwick, eds. *Black Nationalism in America*. Indianapolis: Bobbs-Merrill Educational, 1970.

Braunthal, Julius. *History of the International: 1864–1914*. Translated by Henry Collins and Kenneth Mitchell. 3 vols. New York: Praeger, 1967.

Brenner, Robert. "The Political Economy of the Rank-and-File Rebellion." In *Rebel Rank and File: Labor Militancy and Revolt from Below during the Long 1970s*, edited by Aaron Brenner, Robert Brenner, and Calvin Winslow, 37–74. London and New York: Verso, 2010.

Briefs, Goetz A. *The Proletariat: A Challenge to Western Civilization*. McGraw-Hill, 1937.

Briggs, Asa. *The Age of Improvement, 1783–1867: A History of England*. London: Longman, 1959.

———. "The Language of Class in Early Nineteenth Century England." In *Essays in Labour History*, edited by Asa Briggs and John Saville. London: Macmillan 1960.

Brown, Scot. *Fighting for Us: Maulana Karenga, the Us Organization, and Black Cultural Nationalism*. New York: New York University Press, 2003.

Bussard, Robert L. "The 'Dangerous Class' of Marx and Engels: The Rise of the Idea of the Lumpenproletariat." *History of European Ideas* 8, no. 6 (1987): 675–92.

Butler, Judith. *Gender Trouble: Feminism and the Subversion of Identity*. 2nd ed. New York: Routledge, 1999.

Camatte, Jacques, and Gianni Collu. "On Organisation." Libcom.Org. 1969. http://libcom.org/library/on-organisation-jacques-camatte.

Carson, Clayborne. *In Struggle: SNCC and the Black Awakening of the 1960s*. 4th printing. Cambridge, Mass.: Harvard University Press, 2001.

Chen, Chris. "The Limit Point of Capitalist Equality: Notes Toward an Abolitionist Antiracism." *Endnotes*, no. 4 (2013): 202–23.

Chevalier, Louis. *Laboring Classes and Dangerous Classes: In Paris During the First Half of the Nineteenth Century*. Translated by Frank Jellinek. New York: Howard Fertig, 1973.

"Class, Race, and Marxism." *Verso Blog* (blog). July 2017. https://www.versobooks.com/blogs?mentioned_book=4218.

Cleaver, Eldridge. *On the Ideology of the Black Panther Party*. San Francisco: Black Panther Party, 1969.

———. 1972. "On Lumpen Ideology." *Black Scholar* 4, no. 3 (1972): 2–10.

Cleaver, Harry. "The Inversion of Class Perspective in Marxian Theory: From Valorization to Self-Valorization." In *Open Marxism*, vol. 2, *Theory and Practice*, 106–44. London: Pluto, 1992.

Clover, Joshua, and Aaron Benanav. "Can Dialectics Break BRICS?" *South Atlantic Quarterly* 113, no. 4 (2014): 743–59.

Clover, Joshua, and Juliana Spahr. "Gender Abolition and Ecotone War." *South Atlantic Quarterly* 115, no. 2 (2016): 291–311.

Collier-Thomas, Bettye, and V. P. Franklin, eds. *Sisters in the Struggle: African American Women in the Civil Rights-Black Power Movement*. New York: New York University Press, 2001.

Combahee River Collective. "A Black Feminist Statement." In *Capitalist Patriarchy and the Case for Socialist Feminism*, edited by Zillah R. Eisenstein, 362–72. New York: Monthly Review Press, 1979.

Conze, Werner. "Vom "Pöbel" zum "Proletariat": Sozialgeschichtliche Voraussetzungen für den Sozialismus in Deutschland." *Vierteljahrschrift für Sozial- und Wirtschaftsgeschichte* 41, no. 4 (1954): 333–64.

Dalla Costa, Mariarosa, and Selma James. *The Power of Women and the Subversion of the Community*. Bristol: Falling Wall, 1972.

Davis, Mike. 2006. "Old Gods, New Enigmas: Notes on 'Historical Agency.'" *Catalyst* 1, no. 2 (2017): 7–40.

———. *Planet of Slums*. London: Verso, 2006.

Dawson, Michael C. *Black Visions: The Roots of Contemporary African-American Political Ideologies*. Chicago: University of Chicago Press, 2007.

Denning, Michael. "Wageless Life." *New Left Review*, no. 66 (2010): 79–97.

Draper, Hal. "The Concept of the 'Lumpenproletariat' in Marx and Engels." *Économies et Sociétés* 6, no. 12 (1967): 2,285–312.

Du Bois, William E. B. *Black Reconstruction in America: 1860–1880*. New York: Free Press, 1998.

Duggan, Lisa, and Nan D. Hunter. *Sex Wars: Sexual Dissent and Political Culture*. New York: Routledge, 1995.

Echols, Alice. *Daring to Be Bad: Radical Feminism in America, 1967–1975*. Minneapolis: University of Minnesota Press, 1989.

———. "The Taming of the Id." In *Pleasure and Danger: Exploring Female Sexuality*, edited by Carole S. Vance, 50–72. Boston: Routledge & Kegan Paul, 1984.

Elbaum, Max. *Revolution in the Air: Sixties Radicals Turn to Lenin, Mao and Che*. London: Verso, 2002.

Eley, Geoff. *Forging Democracy: The History of the Left in Europe, 1850–2000*. Oxford: Oxford University Press, 2002.

Elson, Diane. "Labor Markets as Gendered Institutions: Equality, Efficiency and Empowerment Issues." *World Development* 27, no. 3 (1999): 611–27.
Enck-Wanzer, Darrel, ed. *The Young Lords: A Reader*. New York: New York University Press, 2010.
Endnotes. "Crisis in the Class Relation." *Endnotes*, no. 3 (2010): 3–19.
———. "A History of Separation: The Rise and Fall of the Workers' Movement, 1883–1982." *Endnotes*, no. 4 (October 2015): 70–192.
———. 2013. "The Holding Pattern." *Endnotes*, no. 3 (2010).
Evans, Sara M. *Personal Politics: The Roots of Women's Liberation in the Civil Rights Movement and the New Left*. New York: Vintage, 1980.
Fanon, Frantz. *The Wretched of the Earth*. Translated by Richard Philcox. New York: Grove, 2004.
Farmer, Ashley D. *Remaking Black Power: How Black Women Transformed an Era*. Chapel Hill: University of North Carolina Press, 2017.
Ferguson, Roderick A. *The Reorder of Things: The University and Its Pedagogies of Minority Difference*. University of Minnesota Press, 2012.
Firestone, Shulamith. *The Dialectic of Sex: The Case for Feminist Revolution*. New York: Morrow, 1970.
Firestone, Shulamith, and Anne Koedt, eds. *Notes from the Second Year: Women's Liberation*. New York: Radical Feminism, 1970.
Foster, John Bellamy, Robert W. McChesney, and R. Jamiml Jonna. "The Global Reserve Army of Labor and the New Imperialism." *Monthly Review* 63, no. 6 (2011): 1–31.
Franklin, Bruce. "Lumpenproletariat and the Revolutionary Youth Movement." *Red Papers*, no. 2 (1969): 28–34.
Freeman, Jo. "The Origins of the Women's Liberation Movement." *American Journal of Sociology* 78, no. 4 (1973): 792–811.
Geary, Dick. "Labour in Western Europe from c. 1800." In *Global Labour History: A State of the Art*, edited by Jan Lucassen, 227–88. Bern: Peter Lang, 2008.
Gilmore, Ruth Wilson. *Golden Gulag: Prisons, Surplus, Crisis, and Opposition in Globalizing California*. Berkeley: University of California Press, 2007.
Goldner, Loren. "The Agrarian Question in the Russian Revolution: From Material Community to Productivism, and Back." *Insurgent Notes*, no. 10 (July 2014).
Gonzalez, Maya, and Jeanne Neton. "The Logic of Gender: On the Separation of Spheres and the Process of Abjection." In *Contemporary Marxist Theory: A Reader*, edited by Andrew Pendakis, 149–74. New York: Bloomsbury Academic, 2014.
Gore, Dayo F., Jeanne Theoharis, and Komozi Woodard, eds. *Want to Start a Revolution? Radical Women in the Black Freedom Struggle*. New York: New York University Press, 2009.
Gorz, Andre. *Farewell to the Working Class: An Essay on Post-Industrial Socialism*. Translated by Michael Sonenscher. London: Pluto, 1982.

Grolle, Joist. "Lorenz Stein als Preußischer Geheimagent." *Archiv für Kulturgeschichte* 50 (1968): 82–96.

Hansen, Bue Rübner. "Surplus Population, Social Reproduction, and the Problem of Class Formation." *Viewpoint*, no. 5 (October 31, 2015). https://www.viewpointmag.com/2015/10/31/surplus-population-social-reproduction-and-the-problem-of-class-formation/.

Hardt, Michael, and Antonio Negri. *Empire*. Cambridge, Mass.: Harvard University Press, 2000.

———. *Multitude: War and Democracy in the Age of Empire*. New York: Penguin, 2004.

Hayes, Floyd W. III, and Francis A. Kiene III. "'All Power to the People': The Political Thought of Huey P. Newton and the Black Panther Party." In *The Black Panther Party (Reconsidered)*, edited by Charles Earl Jones, 157–76. Black Classic Press, 1998.

Haywood, Harry. *Negro Liberation*. New York: International, 1948.

Henderson, Errol A. "The Lumpenproletariat as Vanguard?: The Black Panther Party, Social Transformation, and Pearson's Analysis of Huey Newton." *Journal of Black Studies* 28, no. 2 (1997): 171–99.

Hobsbawm, E. J. "The Making of the Working Class 1870–1914." In *Worlds of Labour: Further Studies in the History of Labour*, 194–213. London: Weidenfeld and Nicolson, 1984.

Hobsbawm, Eric. 1996. *The Age of Revolution 1789–1848*. 1st Vintage Books ed. New York: Vintage.

Hodenberg, Christina von. *Aufstand Der Weber: Die Revolte von 1844 und Ihr Aufstieg zum Mythos*. Bonn: Dietz, 1997.

Hole, Judith, and Ellen Levine. *Rebirth of Feminism*. New York: Quadrangle, 1971.

Jones, Claudia. "An End to the Neglect of the Problems of the Negro Woman!" *Political Affairs*, June 1949.

Jones, Gareth Stedman. "Introduction." In Marx and Engels, *The Communist Manifesto*, 3–184. London: Penguin, 2002.

———. *Karl Marx: Greatness and Illusion*. Cambridge, Mass.: Belknap Press, 2016.

———. *Languages of Class: Studies in English Working Class History, 1832–1982*. Cambridge: Cambridge University Press, 1983.

Joseph, Peniel E., ed. "Black Studies, Student Activism, and the Black Power Movement." In *The Black Power Movement: Rethinking the Civil Rights–Black Power Era*, 251–78. New York: Routledge, 2007.

———. *Waiting 'til the Midnight Hour: A Narrative History of Black Power in America*. New York: Owls, U.S, 2011.

Karenga, Maulana. *Kwanzaa: Origin, Concepts, Practice*. Los Angeles: Kawaida, 1977.

———. *The Quotable Karenga*. Edited by Clyde Halisi and James Mtume. Los Angeles: Us Organization, 1967.

Katz, Henryk. *The Emancipation of Labor: A History of the First International.* New York: Greenwood, 1992.

Kautsky, Karl. *The Class Struggle (Erfurt Program).* Translated by William E. Bohn. New York: Norton, 1971.

Kelley, Robin D. G., and Betsy Esch. "Black like Mao: Red China and Black Revolution." *Souls* 1, no. 4 (1999): 6–41.

King, Mary, and Casey Hayden. "Sex and Caste." *Liberation*, no. 10 (1966): 35–36.

Kocka, Jürgen. "Problems of Working-Class Formation in Germany: The Early Years, 1800–1875." In *Working-Class Formation: Nineteenth-Century Patterns in Western Europe and the United States*, edited by Ira Katznelson and Aristide R. Zolberg, 279–351. Princeton, N.J: Princeton University Press, 1986.

Kollontaï, Alexandra. "Communism and the Family" (1920). In *Selected Writing of Alexandra Kollontai*, edited by Alix Holt, 250–60. New York: Norton, 1980.

———. "Sexual Relations and the Class Struggle" (1911). In *Selected Writing of Alexandra Kollontai*, edited by Alix Holt, 237–49. New York: Norton, 1980.

Lenin, V. I. "Eleventh Congress of the R.C.P.(B)." In *Collected Works*, 33:259–326. Moscow: Progress, 1965.

Lovell, David W. *Marx's Proletariat: The Making of a Myth.* London: Routledge, 1988.

Löwy, Michael. "Marxists and the National Question." *New Left Review* 1, no. 96 (1976): 81–100.

Lukács, Georg. *History and Class Consciousness: Studies in Marxist Dialectics.* Translated by Rodney Livingstone. Cambridge, Mass.: MIT Press, 2013.

Lumley, Robert. *States of Emergency: Cultures of Revolt in Italy from 1968 to 1978.* London: Verso, 1990.

Marcuse, Herbert. *Reason and Revolution.* Oxford: Oxford University Press, 1941.

Marx, Karl. *Capital: A Critique of Political Economy.* Translated by Ben Fowkes and David Fernbach. Vol. 1. New York: Penguin, 1990.

———. *Capital.* Vol. 3. Translated by David Fernbach. New York: Penguin, 1991.

———. "Critical Notes on the Article 'The King of Prussia and Social Reform. By a Prussian.'" In *Early Writings*, translated by Rodney Livingstone and Gregor Benton, Repr, 401–20. London: Penguin, 1992.

———. *Critique of the Gotha Programme.* New York: International, 2009.

———. *Critique of Hegel's "Philosophy of Right."* Translated by Annette Jolin and Joseph J. O'Malley. Cambridge: Cambridge University Press, 1970.

———. *The Eighteenth Brumaire of Louis Bonaparte.* New York: International, 1990.

Marx, Karl, and Friedrich Engels. *The Communist Manifesto.* Edited by Gareth Stedman Jones. London: Penguin, 2002.

———. *The German Ideology: Including Theses on Feuerbach and Introduction to "The Critique of Political Economy."* Amherst, N.Y: Prometheus, 1998.

———. *The Holy Family, or, Critique of Critical Critique.* Honolulu, Hawaii: University Press of the Pacific, 2002.

Matthews, Trayce A. "'No One Ever Asks What a Man's Role in the Revolution Is': Gender Politics and Leadership in the Black Panther Party, 1966–71." In *The Black Panther Party (Reconsidered)*, edited by Charles E. Jones, 267–304. Baltimore: Black Classic Press, 1998.

Mengelberg, Kaethe. "Lorenz von Stein, His Life and Work." In *The History of the Social Movement in France, 1789–1850*, 3–39. Totowa, N.J.: Bedminster, 1964.

Michaels, Walter Benn. "Identity Politics: A Zero-Sum Game." Nonsite.org. February 11, 2016. http://nonsite.org/editorial/identity-politics-a-zero-sum-game.

Mojab, Shahrzad, ed. *Marxism and Feminism.* London: Zed, 2015.

Moses, Wilson Jeremiah, ed. *Classical Black Nationalism: From the American Revolution to Marcus Garvey.* New York: New York University Press, 1996.

———. *The Golden Age of Black Nationalism, 1850–1925.* Hamden, Conn: Archon, 1978.

Newton, Huey. *Huey Newton Talks to the Movement about the Black Panther Party, Cultural Nationalism, SNCC, Liberals and White Revolutionaries.* Chicago: Students for a Democratic Society, 1968.

Obadele, Imari Abubakari. *Foundations of the Black Nation: A Textbook of Ideas behind the New Black Nationalism and the Struggle for Land in America.* Detroit: House of Songhay, 1975.

Ofari, Evan. *Black Liberation: Cultural and Revolutionary Nationalism.* Detroit: Racial Education Project, 1970.

Omi, Michael, and Howard Winant. *Racial Formation in the United States: From the 1960s to the 1980s.* New York: Routledge, 1986.

———. "Racial Formation Rules: Continuity, Instability, Change." In *Racial Formation in the Twenty-First Century*, edited by Daniel HoSang, Oneka LaBennett, and Laura Pulido. Berkeley: University of California Press, 2012.

Palmer, Bryan D. "Fin-de-Siècle Labour History in Canada and the United States: A Case for Tradition." In *Global Labour History: A State of the Art*, edited by Jan Lucassen, 195–226. Bern: Peter Lang, 2006.

Pearson, Hugh. *The Shadow of the Panther: Huey Newton and the Price of Black Power in America.* Reading, Mass.: Addison-Wesley, 1994.

Postone, Moishe. *Time, Labor, and Social Domination: A Reinterpretation of Marx's Critical Theory.* Cambridge: Cambridge University Press, 1993.

Postone, Moishe, and Barbara Brick. "Critical Pessimism and the Limits of Traditional Marxism." *Theory and Society* 11, no. 5 (1982): 617–58.

"Program of the African Blood Brotherhood." *Communist Review* 2, no. 6 (1922): 449–54.

Pronilover, Mikhail. n.d. "Social Class and the Revolutionary Politics of the Black Liberation Movement: The Black Panther Party and the League of Revolutionary Black Workers." Marxists Internet Archive, March 11, 2018. https://www.marxists.org/history/erol/1960-1970/lrbw-class.pdf.

Racism Research Project. *Critique of the Black Nation Thesis.* Berkeley: Racism Research Project, 1975.

Robinson, Cedric J. *Black Marxism: The Making of the Black Radical Tradition.* Chapel Hill: University of North Carolina Press, 2000.

Roediger, David R. *The Wages of Whiteness: Race and the Making of the American Working Class.* London: Verso, 1991.

Rogers, Ibram H. *The Black Campus Movement: Black Students and the Racial Reconstitution of Higher Education, 1965–1972.* New York: Palgrave Macmillan, 2012.

Rojas, Fabio. *From Black Power to Black Studies: How a Radical Social Movement Became an Academic Discipline.* Baltimore: Johns Hopkins University Press, 2007.

Rose, R. B. "Prolétaires and Prolétariat: Evolution of a Concept, 1789–1848." *Australian Journal of French Studies* 18, no. 1 (1981): 282–99.

Rosen, Ruth. *The World Split Open: How the Modern Women's Movement Changed America.* New York: Penguin, 2001.

Roth, Benita. *Separate Roads to Feminism: Black, Chicana, and White Feminist Movements in America's Second Wave.* Cambridge: Cambridge University Press, 2004.

Sagarra, Eda. *A Social History of Germany, 1648–1914.* New York: Holmes & Meier, 1977.

Sassen, Saskia. *Expulsions: Brutality and Complexity in the Global Economy.* Cambridge, Mass.: Belknap Press, 2014.

Scott, Joan W. "Gender: A Useful Category of Historical Analysis." *American Historical Review* 91, no. 5 (1986.): 1,053–75.

Sheehan, James J. *German History: 1770–1866.* Oxford History of Modern Europe. Oxford: Oxford University Press, 1989.

Siegel, Deborah. *Sisterhood Interrupted: From Radical Women to Grrls Gone Wild.* New York: Palgrave Macmillan, 2007.

Sismondi, J.-C.-L. Simonde de. *Études Sur l'Économie Politique.* 3 vols. Paris: Chez Treuttel et Würz, 1837.

———. "On the Condition of the Work People in Manufactories." In *Political Economy and the Philosophy of Government*, translated by Anonymous, 196–223. London: Chapman, 1847.

———. *New Principles of Political Economy: Of Wealth in Its Relation to Population.* Translated by Richard Hyse. New Brunswick: Transaction, 1991.

Smith, Sharon. *Women and Socialism: Class, Race, and Capital.* Chicago: Haymarket, 2015.

Snitow, Ann Barr, Christine Stansell, and Sharon Thompson, eds. *Powers of Desire: The Politics of Sexuality.* New Feminist Library. New York: Monthly Review Press, 1983.

Springer, Kimberly. *Living for the Revolution: Black Feminist Organizations, 1968–1980.* Durham, N.C.: Duke University Press, 2005.

Stein, Lorenz von. *The History of the Social Movement in France, 1789–1850.* Translated by Kaethe Mengelberg. Totowa, N.J.: Bedminster, 1964.

Stirner, Max. *The Ego and His Own: The Case of the Individual against Authority.* Edited by James Joseph Martin. Translated by Steven T. Byington. Paperback ed. Radical Thinkers. London: Verso, 2014.

Stuckey, Sterling, ed. *The Ideological Origins of Black Nationalism.* Boston: Beacon Press, 1972.

———. *Slave Culture: Nationalist Theory and the Foundations of Black America.* New York: Oxford University Press, 1987.

Taylor, Verta, and Leila J. Rupp. "Women's Culture and Lesbian Feminist Activism: A Reconsideration of Cultural Feminism." *Signs* 19, no. 1 (1993): 32–61.

Théorie Communiste. "Much Ado about Nothing." Libcom.org. n.d. Accessed January 24, 2018. http://libcom.org/library/much-ado-about-nothing-théorie-communiste.

Thoburn, Nicholas. "Difference in Marx: The Lumpenproletariat and the Proletarian Unnamable." *Economy and Society* 31, no. 3 (2002): 434–60.

Thompson, Edward P. *The Making of the English Working Class.* New York: Vintage, 1966.

Turchetto, Maria. "From 'Mass Worker' to 'Empire': The Disconcerting Trajectory of Italian Operaismo." In *Critical Companion to Contemporary Marxism*, edited by Jacques Bidet, 285–308. Leiden: Brill, 2008.

U.S. Bureau of Labor Statistics. "Unemployment Rates by Race and Ethnicity, 2010." *Economics Daily*, October 5, 2011. https://www.bls.gov/opub/ted/2011/ted_20111005.htm.

Van Deburg, William L., ed. *Modern Black Nationalism: From Marcus Garvey to Louis Farrakhan.* New York: New York University Press, 1997.

———. *New Day in Babylon: The Black Power Movement and American Culture, 1965–1975.* Chicago: University of Chicago Press, 1993.

Vance, Carole S., ed. *Pleasure and Danger: Exploring Female Sexuality.* Boston: Routledge & Kegan Paul, 1984.

Vogel, Lise. *Marxism and the Oppression of Women: Toward a Unitary Theory.* Chicago: Haymarket, 2013.

Wacquant, Loïc. "From Slavery to Mass Incarceration." *New Left Review* 2, no. 13 (2002): 41–60.

Western, Bruce. *Punishment and Inequality in America.* New York: Russell Sage, 2006.

Wilderson, Frank B. "The Prison Slave as Hegemony's (Silent) Scandal." *Social Justice* 30, no. 2 (2003) (92): 18–27.

Willhelm, Sidney. *Who Needs the Negro?* Cambridge, Mass.: Schenkman, 1970.

Williams, Brooke. "The Retreat to Cultural Feminism." In *Feminist Revolution*, edited by Kathie Sarachild, 79–83. New York: Random House, 1978.

Williams, Rhonda Y. "Black Women, Urban Politics, and Engendering Black Power." In *The Black Power Movement: Rethinking the Civil Rights–Black Power Era*, edited by Peniel E. Joseph, 79–104. New York: Routledge, 2006.

Williams, Robert F. *Negroes with Guns*. Detroit: Wayne State University Press, 1998.

Willis, Ellen. "Radical Feminism and Feminist Radicalism." *Social Text*, no. 9/10 (1984): 91–118.

Worsley, Peter. "Frantz Fanon and the 'Lumpenproletariat.'" *Socialist Register* 9, no. 9 (1972): 193–230.

Wright, Erik Olin. *Classes*. London: Verso, 1985.

———, ed. *The Debate on Classes*. London: Verso, 1989.

Wright, Steve. "The Limits of Negri's Class Analysis: Italian Autonomist Theory in the Seventies." *Reconstruction*, no. 8 (1996). https://libcom.org/library/limits-negri-class-analysis-steve-wright.

———. *Storming Heaven: Class Composition and Struggle in Italian Autonomist Marxism*. London: Pluto, 2002.

Young, Lowell, ed. *The 1928 and 1930 Comintern Resolutions on the Black Question in the United States*. Washington, D.C.: Revolutionary Review Press, 1975. http://www.marx2mao.com/Other/CR75.html.

2 / (Un)making Value: Reading Social Reproduction through the Question of Totality

MARINA VISHMIDT AND ZOE SUTHERLAND

Introduction

The history of feminism, like that of other broad-based social movements, is marked by a dynamic of unity and separation, in which political organization around an identity—such as "woman"—invariably gives way to contestations of that identity.[1] Within emancipatory forms of political struggle, such wagers of unity are often formulated negatively, projecting a shared narrative of subjugation for specific social groups. But if the ultimate horizon of struggle is the nonreproduction of those identities that confine us, a future in which their politicization is unnecessary, the problem emerges of how feminists might organize collectively without valorizing and further consolidating those same identities.

The problem of collective identities and their potentially fragmenting effects can be articulated in relation to the issue of "universality," understood both in terms of the unifying horizon of political desire and the political and ethical norms that are held to be unifying for groups in resistance. These articulations are always fragile ones, prone to generating antagonisms within groups as well as producing tensions in reaction to external demands and projections. Feminist movements have often been criticized for operating around a "false universality," either for promising a unity or inclusivity they cannot deliver or for the attempt to universalize per se. Appeals to universals are considered inherently oppressive by some because of their tendency to subsume actual particularity and difference in an ideal unity that can cloak domination of already socially powerful actors.

Yet the distinct way in which these antagonisms play out in part depends upon the horizons of the political forms. The critique of universalism departs from philosophical universalism/s, especially those emanating from eighteenth-century Enlightenment philosophy and its Kantian legacies, which continue to be interrogated over their links to the history of colonialism, racism, and the constitution of gender and sexual normativity in modernity. "Political universality" is often considered the keystone of a liberal feminist "rights-based" approach, concerned primarily with social inclusion, recognition, and equal admission to participation in economic circuits and representative politics. The bourgeois public sphere is the model for this conception of the social whole, and the political universal is accessed through a formal—as the premise for a substantive—equality of rights. One of the main keystones for critiques of this rights-based framework is Hannah Arendt's description of displaced or "stateless" persons after World War II as those who lacked "the right to have rights." For Arendt, the "stateless" were denied access to the means of recognition that were issued by the nation state or international agencies, leaving them to exercise the only legal instrument in their possession as refugees, their "human rights."[2] Yet these rights remained abstract, specifically because they lacked any means of enforcement. Such a tenuous status continues to define the legislative, contractual framework—the basic architecture of liberal universalism that serves to underpin formal political demands.

Like Marxist standpoints on the whole, Marxist and materialist feminisms have been consistently skeptical of the liberal universal of formal equality before the law and of a feminist politics that demarcates its horizon as the fight for recognition and inclusion. Instead, it has framed its problematic at the scale of capitalist value relations as a whole and the reproduction of gender within a "social totality." As Kevin Floyd explains, Marxist "totality thinking" aims to critique capital's fragmentation of social life and to understand the multiple mediations that articulate different horizons of social reality. He writes, "The Marxian critique of capital then endeavors to comprehend what this ontological and epistemological atomization makes it impossible to apprehend: capital as the systemic, global source of this enforced social dispersal."[3] As an ongoing process of the articulation of mediations, the Marxian critique understands the social totality not as an undifferentiated system, but as internally fractured and contradictory in determinate ways. So, while universality and its attendant moral precepts are held to operate in the realm of "pure politics," disregarding the forces and processes of a social organization overdetermined by capital and emphasizing the contingent articulations of social conflict (as in the post-Marxist work of Laclau and Mouffe), the concept of social totality aims to be more systematic, yet not beholden to a mechanical style of analysis.

Despite this, it is precisely this emphasis within Marxism upon thinking a totality of social relations that has produced skepticism toward Marxist feminism, especially in its more orthodox formulations. The word "totality" has a dual connotation: an additive, numerical whole on the one hand and finality and completion on the other. This image of "totalizing" systems has accrued negative political connotations, associated as it is with twentieth-century modernist tendencies toward management of a society conceptualized as a unified and coherent body of subject-citizens, and is seen to have culminated in the mass movements of the twentieth century, in mass industry, and in "total" war. And it has also accrued negative theoretical connotations, wherein Marxist thinking itself is often presented as though responsible for such totalization. As Amy De'Ath has written, "A familiar feminist criticism of Marxist feminism's 'totalizing' tendencies [is] a complaint which tends to rhetorically position a historical materialist Marxist-feminism as if it were the cause, rather than the critique, of capitalism's totalizing movement."[4] This is the context in which left politics saw a large-scale rejection of totality-thinking within social movements oriented more explicitly to gender, race, and sexuality. The term acquired a distinct meaning in the consolidation of the neoliberal order in the 1970s and 1980s, strengthened through the conflation of "totality" and "totalitarianism" in some postmodernist work—and the subsequent retreat and relegation of unifying frameworks, which influenced the shape of politics to come.

Because of its methodological and political preference for more totalizing frameworks, deep skepticism toward the capacity of Marxist feminism to meaningfully articulate issues of race and sexuality became a constant in the field. Emerging as one of the challenges to the unmarked masculinism of left politics—a challenge both to the New Left, and a mark of its further diversification—much feminism of the 1960s and 1970s was itself criticized for peddling a bad universalism in its impoverished relation to issues of race, class, ability, sexuality, and nonbinary gender.[5] This became an issue for many movements fighting racism, sexism, ableism, and heteronormativity, which were often considered "bourgeois deviations" that were "splitting" the class for the sake of "identity" issues. While some Marxist and socialist feminists toed the line, effectively subsuming gender under the more pressing and "unifying" concern of class, in other cases a particularistic notion of woman—white, middle-class, heterosexual, and cisgendered—was itself universalized. Both tendencies culminated in the "dual-systems debate." The proposition at the core of this debate—that patriarchy and capitalism are two distinct social systems—not only aggravated existing antagonisms within the feminist movement; it helped to consolidate the theoretical tendency to position race and sexuality as discrete and supplementary issues of "identity politics." And this idea lingers in many variants of left politics, especially in those keen to avoid universalizing or totalizing parameters in their critical analyses and organizing strategies.

Kevin Floyd has suggested that it was precisely this historical Marxian tendency to subordinate questions of sexuality to supposedly more "total" concerns, representing sexuality and its politics as inherently localized and particularized, which largely framed and conditioned queer thought as it emerged in the 1990s.[6] And a similar story could perhaps be told of the emergence of specific forms of radical, black, and materialist feminism in the 1970s, some of which coalesced into more explicit theoretical positions in the 1990s. An example would be the Combahee River Collective, which emerged in response to the subsumption of the concerns of women of color under a class-focused socialist-feminist movement. Turning away from an exclusive focus on class toward a materialist analysis of the specifically gendered and racialized body, the Combahee River Collective revealed the universalism of the socialist-feminist movement to have been a de facto white agenda. For Floyd, the *appearance* of sexuality as localized and particularized within a capitalist world is precisely the issue that needs challenging. While there has been a tendency in Marxist thought to deprioritize questions of sexuality, Floyd argues that this does not require queer theory to abandon attempts to articulate sexuality within a mediated social whole, but instead requires a "convergence," which will enrich both queer theory and Marxism. This is important not merely for understanding the role of sexuality in capitalism, but in understanding the character of capital itself. The marginalization of "identity politics" not only renders the dynamic of the ongoing reproduction of identities difficult to grasp; it also turns capital into an abstract, thus fetishized, totality, echoing what Marx calls an "imagined concrete" or a "chaotic conception of the whole." Rather than seeing these interconnected particulars as constitutive of and systematically reproduced by capital, such theorizations produce both "capital" and "identity" as fetishized forms whose interrelation becomes difficult to articulate. For Floyd, it is in part this insufficient form of totality thinking that gave way to the need for a more encompassing perspective on the interaction of a whole range of different forms of oppression.

Despite historical problems with the ways in which the concept of totality has been used, for Floyd, critical "totality thinking" can help us to define a set of structural logics that render social relationships both unifying and contradictory. In light of this, our essay considers how the articulation of a structural logic remains necessary for a feminist theory and praxis that aims to understand and to navigate the inherent tensions of identity-based political struggle and explores what formulation of the notion of totality is adequate to this aim. In relation to this, might an insistence upon mediation through the totality offer a different picture of the tension between universalism and difference, one that prevents them lapsing into fetishizations? Could it be a useful approach to the realities of both unity and fracturing within movements? We will begin by looking at some recent attempts to reintroduce a framework of totality in such a way that avoids the fetishized trappings outlined earlier. One such attempt can be seen in the desire to formulate a more materialist version of intersectional thinking.

The Challenge of Intersectionality

Intersectional and Marxist frameworks are often taken to be irreconcilable opposites. However, this may be due more to the programmatic rejection within intersectional thinking of totalizing modes of thought as opposed to its rejection of materialism per se, as some critiques suggest. For this reason we can envision a potential dialogue between the two modes of theorizing.[7] Intersectional responses to second-wave feminism criticized its tendency to universalize the conditions of the white, middle-class, heterosexual woman, arguing that experience is in fact composed of several intersecting systems of oppression. In doing so, intersectional theory destabilized what it took to be reductive formulations of identity in a way that revealed the conflict-ridden terrain of experience rather than resolving those conflicts too easily into a universal "we." Forms of intersectional thinking existed long before its formalization into an explicit theoretical framework by the legal scholar and civil rights activist Kimberlé Crenshaw in 1989. Early reference points for intersectional thinking could include the writings of Sojourner Truth in the nineteenth century, as well as those of black women activists on the peripheries of communist party organizations in the first part of the twentieth century.[8] Examples would include Louise Thompson Patterson, whose organizing with African American domestic workers generated the concept of "triple exploitation" to refer to gender, racial, and class status in Depression-era

United States, or Claudia Jones in the United Kingdom.[9] It is also possible to point to the contributions of earlier revolutionary theorists and activists such as Angela Davis, for whom "women, race, and class" were neither politically nor analytically separate as positions or politics.[10] However, while the work of these activists acknowledged several vectors of oppression and exploitation, presenting the social relations of capitalism as racial and patriarchal in practice, we might distinguish them from those who adhere more specifically to an intersectional analysis. It is Crenshaw's formulation of intersectionality that has come to define it as a discrete framework and that has subsequently become the subject of much theoretical debate.

To illustrate her understanding of intersectionality, Crenshaw refers to the 1976 legal case of *DeGraffenreid v. General Motors*, in which black women were denied access to jobs that were open to both white women and black men. As the legal system was only equipped to consider discrimination along lines of either race or gender, it was unable to recognize the specificity of the discrimination faced by black women. For Crenshaw, this case revealed the inherent reductivism of the legal framework, which could only consider discrimination along a single axis. Crenshaw's analysis shows that the bourgeois legal subject is constituted through a set of socially and institutionally ascribed "structural intersections"—composed of abstractions such as "race" and "gender"—which bind us together into social groups, but which manifest differently in lived experience. The legal framework was unable to capture the fact that gender often takes a racialized form and race a gendered form. As a result, Crenshaw's analysis warns us that seemingly progressive antidiscrimination laws should be treated with suspicion: they tend to obscure more complex forms of discrimination, exacerbating and legitimizing them. While Crenshaw's development of intersectionality is shaped, and also limited, by the legal framework from which it emerges, it remains a powerful critical tool. Her analysis captures the "false universality" of the figure of the liberal subject who is equal before the law and of the discrete categories of identity it reifies in practice. And as Crenshaw saw the legislative as productive for the horizon of more radical struggle, she was also warning against uncritical forms of organizing around those reified identity categories. Ultimately, Crenshaw is not only interested in legal representation and recognition, but in the way that intersecting oppressions are consolidated in everyday social life—in the workplace, in political groups, and in personal relations. Her metaphor for the articulation of intersecting oppressions pointed beyond the legal to account for multiple grounds of identity in considering how the social world is constructed. So, while Crenshaw's work points toward greater visibility for the experiential complexities produced by multiple oppressions, it also implicitly calls for the reinvigoration of radical social struggles in and against the reproduction of those oppressions, at least in the sense of political acts of disidentification from the reductive categories that represent us.

Rematerializing Intersectionality

Despite the potential of the critical legal element of intersectional theory, a number of Marxist feminists, while insisting that feminism should be intersectional, have criticized the lack of "systemic" or "totality" thinking in the dominant approaches. While "intersectionality" for Crenshaw was never meant to be "some new, totalizing theory of identity,"[11] but rather a critical tool for revealing the blind spots produced by a one-dimensional politics of recognition, a more materialist intersectional approach seems possible. The critical practice of describing how identity categories *appear* as discrete through our encounters with institutionalized processes of identity formation is a meaningful starting point for the development of a more materialist critique. However, as Johanna Brenner has argued, some intersectional analyses fail to go any further than a description of experience, leaving capitalist power relations, and thus potential resistance to them, un- or under-theorized.[12] The radical potential of the intersectional model might thus lie in revealing how the production and reproduction of those identity formations are analytically situated within a broader terrain of capitalist social relations.

Recently there have been several attempts to articulate this problem more substantially. David McNally notes that subsequent intersectional theory has struggled to escape the shadow of its inherent "ontological atomism" and its attendant spatial metaphor of the "intersection."[13] For McNally, Patricia Hill Collins's appeal to "interlocking" systems of oppressions, which comprise a "matrix of domination that constitutes a 'single, historically created system,'" or Sherene Razack's characterization of these interlocking systems as codependent, fall into this spatial and atomistic metaphor. Many other Marxist and materialist feminists have argued that the concept of "intersections" first presupposes the existence of coherent and autonomous—yet, somehow comparable—locations of identity and, second, implies the external, and thus contingent, nature of their coincidence. For example, Sue Ferguson claims that while intersectionality describes how specified social locations give shape to individual experience and identity, it cannot show how such locations interact as part of a dynamic set of social relations in which processes, ideas, and institutions reproduce and challenge these intersecting identities.[14] When conceptualized as what Tithi Bhattacharya describes as an "aggregative reality," intersectional theory is, for McNally, premised upon a "static metaphysics" in which ontologically separate axes of difference are mapped onto a neutral social space.[15] But, as he points out, such an atomistic picture cannot explain why these axes would interact in the first place: what is the force that brings them together? Or, as Bhattacharya puts it, what is the *logic* of their intersection?[16] For McNally and Bhattacharya, as for others, it is the "dynamic" aspect of capitalism that needs articulating to overcome ontological atomism—an atomism that could be seen to be strengthened by attempts to complexify the discrete abstractions of identity established in legal systems.[17]

This is not simply a theoretical issue. Since the 1990s, intersectional thinking has become common sense for much political organizing that prioritizes the mutual determinations of gender, race, sexuality, ability, age, and migration status, among other forms of ascribed identity. And this common sense is reflected within the academy's approach to emancipatory politics, where intersectional theory is often presented as a fully comprehensive description of social relations, one whose virtue lies in its appearance of inclusivity and its rejection of "totalizing" tendencies. However, this disavowal of the need for a more totalizing horizon for thinking about how systems of oppression work can tend toward the deflation of political struggle into individualized, "rights-based" issues, admittedly of a now more variegated nature. However, since the 2008 global financial crisis, there has been a resurgence of Marxist feminism—both in and beyond the academy—that aims to revise the assumed division between socioeconomic analysis and identity critique.

Social Reproduction Theory and/as Totality

Recent developments in what has become known as "social reproduction theory" are premised on the construction of something like a "more materialist" intersectional theory, one that anchors gendering and racializing processes within a thinking of "totality," or, at the very least, their reproduction. While there exists variation between thinkers, social reproduction theory takes labor—and its stratification, division, and "multiplication"—to be the basis of this totality. As Bhattacharya explains, "The fundamental insight of social reproduction theory is, simply put, that human labor is at the heart of creating or reproducing society as a whole."[18] In light of this, Ferguson has been developing the concept of an "integrative ontology of labor" as the kind of non-idealistic, yet systematic, notion of totality that feminism should be working with.[19] She describes this integrative ontology in the following terms: "At the heart of social reproduction feminism is the conception of labor as broadly productive—creative not just of economic values, but of society (and thus of life) itself."[20] Here labor means any human activity that creates "all the things, practices, people, relations, and ideas constituting the wider social totality."[21] For Ferguson, the social reproduction framework can also begin to link this totality to lived experience through analyses of embodied subjects in "socio-historically, geographically specific locations," thus addressing Himani Bannerji's call for the structuralist bias in Marxist feminism to be overcome by the incorporation of the experiential.[22] This expansive framework promises a more global and integrative picture of the diverse concrete positions and experiences of—especially, but not only—women to be theorized, one that avoids the pitfalls of an "additive" intersectional model as well as the functionalist tendencies imputed to Marxist feminism.

A central insight of social reproduction theory is, as Meg Luxton describes, that the "production of goods and services and the production of life are part of one integrated process."[23] However, it is primarily the complex and messy form this integration takes—that is, how it is produced and reproduced—that needs articulation. Because of the sheer expansiveness of the concepts involved—such as "life"—this is not at all a straightforward process. As the concept of "the social" is already, perhaps inherently, prone to radical indeterminacy, the same applies to what counts as its reproduction. At the same time, linking social reproduction to an account of "totality" also faces pitfalls. While the everyday understanding of totality simply designates the "all" or "whole" of something, this can often lead to overly vague formulations, which can stretch the definition of the term beyond analytic utility. The category of "capitalism" is perhaps one of the most susceptible to this conceptual slippage, often taken to designate not merely a mode of production, but the entire social world.[24] This capacity for slippage and extension is further encouraged by theories that assume at some level a tendential "total subsumption" of life under capital. If the global triumph of capital over its previous antagonists in the last few decades has generalized capital's domination to all spheres of social life, it confronts us as the sole basis of our very reproduction, making the link of social reproduction to the totality somewhat tautological. For the framework to be meaningful, what is included within this "all" needs specifying, not simply as a list of connected or overlapping aspects, but as the unity of *distinct, but interdependent* moments.

The totality is not a pregiven object. The analysis of the various determinations at play needs to be undertaken with the aim of breaking down an abstract and vague conception of a whole, reproducing it in the process as internally differentiated—that is, as "concrete."[25] It is this equating of concretion with internal differentiation that renders Marx's critical method amenable to thinking totality as the "unity of the diverse," and it is specifically the attempt to register such concreteness that gives social reproduction theory so much potential.

Despite this, it is worth considering the critical and political consequences of the tendency of some versions of social reproduction theory to bracket questions around global value chains, finance, and politics to centralize this "integrative ontology of labor." Although intended as synthetic, such an expansive notion of labor can itself be left significantly underdetermined. The "integrative ontology" seems to include all labor that reproduces the conditions for that labor—that is, as labor-power that is brought to market—and not just labor that is value producing. And it extends even further than this, to all activities that maintain and reproduce life in any social formation. Social relations, in all their heterogeneity, can be critically encompassed through the category of labor, rather than through an articulated, mediated social whole. So, while the expansive notion of labor appears to answer the need for a more unitary theory—originally articulated by Lise Vogel and recently reformulated by Cinzia Arruzza, among others—avoiding the dualisms of previous Marxist-feminist programs, it risks erasing important distinctions and lines of causality, subsuming a wide range of activities, forces, and gendered and racialized dynamics to the category of "labor."

The consequences of blurring the activities that reproduce life with the activities that reproduce "capitalist life" can render the terrain of feminist struggle ambiguous. This ambiguity is in fact familiar for feminist politics, and indeed any emancipatory politics that departs from membership in a stigmatized or marginalized group. For further clarity it is important to draw analytic distinctions between activities that might merely appear reproductive (of life) in their concrete characteristics—domestic chores, care work—and those that are socially validated by the wage and thus reproductive of capital. Without such distinctions, the use of socially reproductive labor as a key analytic-cum-political category could court the same danger that Marxist feminist critique once spotted in the "workerist" politics of the factory—the moralized affirmation of labor. In the context of feminist theory and politics, this affirmation has been lent credence by the fact that the labor of reproduction is universally devalued: the devaluation of labor becomes subject to a call for recognition, be this of an ethical, economic, or political nature. Reproductive labor can be defined as a specific set of gendered activities, whose devaluation can be redressed in terms of their "social value" in the reproduction of (social) life. Yet at the same time these activities are located in circuits of abstract value, whether or not they receive a monetary wage, and hence need to be considered from the standpoint of the reproduction of capital. Once the recognition of the social value of socially reproductive work becomes a political goal, this can be extended to the gendering of the labor as well as the labor itself, thus risking the affirmation of feminized people in the traditionally gendered terms of caregivers.[26] In this way, the negativity of the reproduction of life in capitalist society is occluded, along with the transformative potential of this negativity, and reproduction takes on an independent and positive value. Rather than social reproduction and the reproduction of capital being collapsed into an ontology of labor, an analysis of value relations, of "value in motion," might be key to avoid producing an affirmative account of gendered labor and therefore an affirmative account of the society it helps to reproduce. By "value relations," we mean that the abstract value that is characteristic of capital as a social relationship does not only manifest itself in the direct exchange of values (such as labor power for a wage or a commodity for a set amount of money) but that these relations are mediated by the value-form in a number of indirect ways as well, often naturalized in asymmetries other than the "economic." Such a theorization of the socialization of the form of capitalist value is key to arguments that gender and race are as operative within capitalist value relations as commodified labor power. This is so insofar as they contribute to the differential pricing of labor power, but also to the production of subjectivity in social antagonism and to the intricacies of situated and historical class formation.

Theories of social reproduction grounded in an integrative ontology of labor may not offer the resources necessary for situating the relationship between social reproduction and the reproduction of capital as "value in motion." While such an ontology has the advantage of elasticity, it ultimately falls short as an analysis of gender, race, or capital in a landscape of social reproduction determined by a number of value relations, not all of which are collapsible into labor. This ontology risks blurring the distinctions between labor "as such" and labor within the (gendered, racialized, normative, violent) capitalist mode of (re)production itself—thus between life and labor, the social and the financial, and ultimately, between capital and life. All social forms get integrated in an ontology of labor that, as Kevin Floyd has noted when writing about self-valorization in autonomist Marxism, cannot ultimately be distinguished from an ontology of capital.[27] Social reproduction feminism conceptualizes a more complex and "concrete" totality through a materialist intersectional thinking that accounts for the *logic* of the intersection, articulated through different historical dynamics of the logic of capital rather than as separate, distinct systems, such as class, gender, and race, which collide haphazardly. Yet it is in the proposition that this logic is the "worldmaking" ontology of labor, rather than the spectrum of value relations, that some versions of the theory meet the limit of their explanatory power and political salience.

As an additional question, we might ask whether an analysis dedicated to figuring the capitalist mode of production as a world produced by "labor" might be a normative fantasy in an era of mass un- and underemployment and highly monitored and often abandoned surplus populations, with the lived negativity of value relations (lived in many ways through race and gender) coming to the fore. To insist upon this point is to underline how social reproduction opens up into "nonreproduction" and the *totality* of capitalist accumulation and the forms of structural hyper-violence and extraction it dictates. An integrative ontology of labor does not capture well a historical moment in which the necessity of abolition is posed by the proliferation of "wageless" and "surplus" life rather than a maldistribution of surplus value. Under these conditions it becomes clear that neither race nor gender can be adequately explained as a rank in the labor market, which would be the implication of an ontology premised on labor to explain all varieties of structural oppression.[28] We need to look at how gender and race pose an "outside" to the capitalist value relation that enables it to function. By "outside" we mean the kind of historical and phenomenological aspects of capitalist social life that seem to be left out of an "orthodox" Marxist picture of the reproduction of that life, those aspects that seem not to be directly mediated by the wage relation and yet shape it at every level. Without taking into account how such "outsides" and "insides" are produced at this level of analysis, there is a risk of reproducing a class-reductivist politics that defaults to a white identity politics. An interrogation into the violent apparatus of value in capitalist social relations and the violence of their reproduction might require looking beyond the category of labor to financial, state, and libidinal economies. Here is where the perspective of an internally differentiated and contradictory "totality" can be helpful.

Negative Totality and Insurgent Universality

It is precisely this "outside" to which we turn now in the process of developing a concept of totality that takes into account value relations as stratified social relations. This could be conceived as a "negative totality" that would situate the logics of gender, race, and normativity within the form of value. That may involve situating social reproduction within capitalist social relations as an antagonistic form of social unity from the perspective of its overcoming and not of its maintenance or "reproduction." We will go on to articulate this concept with some recently proposed revisions to the political concept of universality as ways to reframe what we have identified as a point of weaknesses in the rich and influential work being done under the headings of intersectionality as well as some forms of social reproduction theory.

In "The Logic of Gender," Maya Gonzalez and Jeanne Neton argue that "there must be an exterior to value (and labor), in order for value (and labor) to exist," while rejecting the dualistic thinking of autonomist and commons-based theories, which too simplistically affirm this "exterior."[29] The perspective of totality allows us to approach gender and race as constitutive internal outsides to value relations. In a similar move, Marxist system ecologist Jason W. Moore describes how an uncommodified "outside" is crucial for capitalist growth as it keeps its costs down: if everything were wholly commodified, capital would "eat itself."[30] Moore highlights the importance of free appropriation as a core dynamic of accumulation, of the indispensability of free or cheap inputs to capitalist valorization, of keeping some things off the value map, both financially and socially. Such an analysis takes into account the crucial insights of Marxist social reproduction theory on the structural significance of the "unpaid" and the "unvalued," extending this work not just to devalued human labor but to nonhuman and geophysical forces appropriated by capital in its production of "nature." Feminist geography, such as that of Maria Mies, is a key influence here as well, and it is shaped by historiography and ecology in its approach to critical political economy, offering a formulation of totality that avoids one of the foremost criticisms that have been levied against the concept—that it is too "deterministic," expunging all sense of agency and contingency. This criticism, following that of Althusser, initially targeted the Lukácsian notion of "expressive totality" before his own work became the target of similar charges of formalism and foreclosure. Such notions of totality posit an overall systematic horizon in which reality is an effect of structures that can be comprehensively mapped and are autonomous of personal or collective agency. A negative totality, however, is the attempt to see how different structures are contingently articulated in a moving historical process (itself fractured by disjunctive and contradictory temporalities).

As Chris O'Kane puts it, "Not only would such a notion of negative social totality point to the negativity of the capitalist social form, and the internal reciprocal domains of the economy and the state; but also the realms of nature, subjectivity, and civil society integral to the perpetuation of capitalist social totality."[31] Such a formulation departs from Marx's methodological note in the 1857 "Introduction" to the *Grundrisse* about arriving at a rich and concretely determined totality composed of multiple realities and relations only as the result, and not as the presupposition, of a dialectical method of inquiry.[32] This is of course not a straightforward matter, since it is precisely an immediate relation to a multiple and complex whole that must first be boiled down into "simple abstractions" (such as "population") before the process of reconstructing it through observation, research, and political analysis can commence. This emphasis on totality as a result, an articulation rather than an assumption, renders it a speculative concept, which both allows for contingency and lends a determinate framework to what would otherwise be a simple "conjunction" or "intersection" of more or less decontextualized particulars. Here the "negativity" in O'Kane's notion of the social totality can be related to Hegel's idea of negativity, which is to say, the lack of finality of any state of affairs in thought or praxis, because they are mediated and transformed from one state to another and because of the "negativity" of contradictory social relations that naturalize themselves as static and unchanging. Yet this question of negativity needs to be taken up again, not simply as a characteristic of the capitalist totality but as an aspect of the relation between totality and universality, as we will see.

Likewise, for Floyd "totality" has to be speculative and critical, rather than a positive concept.[33] Because for Floyd the greatest producers of difference, atomization, and reification are the social relations of capital, no radical materialist politics can afford to dispense with a "rigorously negative practice" of totality thinking, one opposed to the kind of positive imposition of totality of which Marxism has long been accused.[34] For Floyd, totality is a regulative category that operates at the level of epistemological transformation. Starting from our discrete positions, such critical practice would have a theoretical and political commitment to unify all those moments of social life that have been atomized by capitalist relations. He emphasizes that this process is necessarily ongoing and never final, but it is nevertheless through such a commitment that we can hope to avoid epistemically and politically stultified conceptions of social life.

So far, we have pointed to the need to revisit the category of "totality" as well as providing an outline of what form this might take. It remains to do the same for "universality," the other synthetic concept at issue in this essay. As we saw at the beginning, "totality" and "universality" have traditionally been opposed as respectively constituting a materialist and an idealist conception of a social whole. There are various ways of outlining the reductive implications of such an opposition, but here we will confine ourselves to citing some recent discussions of the problem of universality in emancipatory politics as developed by political philosophers Massimiliano Tomba and Cinzia Arruzza. In Tomba's recent analysis of "insurgent universality," he refers to the French 1793 Declaration of Rights as the outcome of revolutionary struggles of women, *sans-culottes*, and enslaved people in the French colonies, notably in Saint-Domingue.[35] Whereas the 1789 Declaration of the Rights of Man presumes an "abstract citizen," granted rights from above, the 1793 one is redrafted "from below," with its radicalization of the freedoms of speech, assembly, and right of insurrection against oppression.[36] Within but against the formal or "political" freedom of the bourgeois revolution, those excluded or occluded from the Rights of Man claimed their social and economic rights from a system that ratified the principles of popular sovereignty while dispensing with their participation from the beginning. In this way, the universality of the figure of "Man" is eroded and negated by a more encompassing universality, one committed to dismantling the naturalized hierarchies of sex and race, public and private, that the legal nation state upheld in continuity with the absolute monarchy.

Arruzza picks up on this framework, proposing a "political insurgent universality" as a ground for contemporary feminist politics.[37] This is a dynamic ground that jettisons even strategic presumptions of a unity of shared interests for the human species or for feminized genders, but rather posits the "universality of reality" of capital as the historically actual ground for social reproduction, whose tendency is to expand and displace all other forms of providing for this reproduction.[38] Arruzza counterposes "political insurgent universality" to "political universalism," which is seen to create a false binary between universalism and difference as vague and reified categories, useless for theory and the practical work of organizing.[39] Arruzza additionally refers to the basis of real universality as not just the actuality and pervasiveness of capitalist social relations but as capital's "totalization effect."[40] Here she is careful to distinguish her argument from sociological analyses of the homogeneity attendant on "globalization" or a notion of the objectivity of common interests among a global population increasingly rendered "surplus" by a capitalism driven by speculation and extraction, rather than production. Setting out the dangers of ontological and functionalist arguments, she concludes that it is the "constraints" on social reproduction and subjectivation brought about by capitalist rule that is the key element of the totalizing logic she identifies. This is intended to clarify the stakes of feminist universalism and its ability to go beyond the additive structure of intersectionality.

Returning to totality in light of this, one way to avoid impasses in the conceptualization of capitalist totality is to understand capitalism's totalizing effect in terms of constraints and not in terms of functions. In other words, capitalist accumulation produces or contributes to the production of varying forms of social hierarchy and oppression. While various forms of oppression interact or even grow together, capitalist accumulation poses constraints that determine to a large extent all other forms of social relations. The reality that no form of oppression cannot be alleviated by ready access to money seems to underline this overdetermination. Thus, that the constraints posed by capitalist accumulation are pervasive and have the capacity of coloring all other social relations provides the grounds for speaking of the capitalist world as a contradictory and articulated moving totality.[41]

This brings us once again to the earlier-cited formulation of "negative totality." Here the "capitalist world" is figured as a "contradictory" and "moving" totality, which is increasingly experienced by its subjects as a series of constraints rather than possibilities. This experience can potentially be translated into an "political insurgent universality" as the political articulation of the various forms and scales of constraint that the reproduction of the capitalist social whole entails.[42] Here we could return briefly to the Hegelian inflection of the relationship between totality and universality as a mediation between the "objective" and the "subjective" that develops through forms of dialectical negativity. Jamila Mascat, in her recent reconstruction of the category of "abstraction" in Hegel's work, notes that "the intimate connection between formalism, universality, and abstraction can be deduced, *via negativa*, from Hegel's understanding of the concrete as opposed to the formal universal."[43] In other words, universality can be composed of concrete rather than abstract (or formal, "ideal") mediations of speculative thought that hypothesize something other than the status quo, fostering the actual (political) praxis capable of enacting transformation. It is realized as the *product* of emancipatory struggles, as well as being a premise that animates those struggles. The universal is, again, a result and not a presupposition. This formulation is reflected in a number of other current analyses of the political utility of universality emerging on the Marxian left, such as that enunciated by Asad Haider, for whom universality emerges through the principle of solidarity with alterity. This is founded on the alterity of any political subject to themselves, rather than the policed unity of "identity" or the relationship between Self and Other that subtends liberal, rights-based conceptions, capable of reproducing colonial relations of victimhood and humanitarian intervention.[44]

Conclusion

Both intersectionality and social reproduction feminism arose in response to a lack of accounting for social locations of "extra-economic" oppression and domination in capitalist modernity by Marxism. While the two perspectives often run together in contemporary theoretical and activist practice, the difference is that intersectional views have a tendency to dispense with an account of a "totality" of capital as determining of social life, while social reproduction feminism understands itself as a "unitary theory" that can articulate the contradictions of capitalist social life, through an ontology of labor, wherever and however they may be encountered. Some thinkers from within this paradigm, such as Arruzza, make a stronger claim: that there can be a dimension of universality that pervades those struggles that unfold on the terrain of social reproduction, a universality "from below" that is presupposed by the emancipatory orientation of struggles against differentiated forms of violence and exploitation. Concomitantly, the prioritization of specific identities immanent to the intersectionality paradigm can be shown to prematurely dismiss the reference to a logic of totality as performing the epistemically oppressive act of "totalizing." Acknowledging that the capital relation is the social horizon of the production and maintenance of these identities doesn't mean that it is not a contradictory or constitutively incomplete one. What it does mean is that the negativity of that totality is perceived through its systematic shaping of everyday existence. Here we can note Floyd's observation that totality is only thinkable from situated perspectives: "The totality of capital, Marx suggests, can be accounted for only through this movement through a range of particular, immanent points of view.... Any pretension to a bird's-eye view is revealed here to be the effect of a failure to account, within the very effort to think totality, for the specific social location of that same effort."[45]

Feminist movements, including revolutionary, anti-capitalist ones, cannot eradicate internal antagonism. Regardless of the insights of its members, antagonism will always develop, both out of the specific material conditions and the dynamics of the movement itself. The nature of struggle is that it is inherently self-limiting and internally unstable in a way that no amount of organizational magic or good intentions can remedy. In the context of such antagonisms, movements may well still make important gains, so long as a certain momentum can be maintained, but they will ultimately come apart or dissipate in foreseeable and unforeseeable ways. And what is more, that moment of dissipation can often itself be generative of radical potential. Despite this, the projection of emancipatory horizons and of the nature of the unity those horizons allow can be understood in ways that can bring such potential antagonisms into focus to greater or lesser extents, allow them space to breathe, and sharpen awareness and understanding of them. As Arruzza puts it, echoing Audre Lorde, diversity "must become our weapon, rather than an obstacle or something that divides us."[46] In those situations where the working through of internal antagonisms—or at least their holding in productive tension—may be possible, the various *internal* relations between distinct forms of oppression, as well as the constant drive for oppressed identities toward reification, requires ongoing articulation and critique. Such attempts can be seen by the group Sisters Uncut in the UK, whose fight against violence—domestic, sexual, gendered, and state—in the context of austerity has brought them into solidarity with a vast range of movements in ways that have enriched an understanding of capitalist social relations. In addition to this, the International Women's Strike is a contemporary movement that has placed at its center a conscious aim to avoid the structural limitations of liberal feminism and to aim at "political universality"—exemplified by the annual Women's Marches since 2016—through its organizational approach. Having emerged in response to a host of other gender struggles—the Polish strike against a more violent abortion law, the Argentinian *Ni Una Menos* strike against male violence, and the International Day for the Elimination of Violence against Women—its strategy has been to develop in and through dialogue with a wide range of already existing networks of grassroots organizations, in an attempt to mediate the production of a dynamically evolving class-based, anti-racist feminism, inclusive of trans women and queer and nonbinary people, without subsuming the issues and demands of these organizations under a universal "we." More recently, the resurgence of the Black Lives Matter movement indicated how an abolitionist vision contesting the systemic devaluation of racialized communities could include demands around trans rights and labor issues during the pandemic (with anti-blackness a labor issue for the greatly disproportionate casualties among key workers), firmly situating social reproduction on its agenda as a matter of both survival and transformative political power.

Concepts such as Arruzza's "totality of constraints" and Haider's solidaristic universality by means of and across alterity can help us understand how neither an integrative ontology of labor nor a subsumptive conflation of capital and life are necessary to develop the grounds for analytic concreteness and political articulation. This is the articulation between social locations that fosters organized struggle, a mode of struggle capable of dealing with the specificity and systematicity of the "outside" to value represented by gendering, racialization, and other "devaluations" in the reproduction of the capitalist whole, rather than dismissing these as secondary to a reified "class." This is not to suggest that the vicissitudes of practical politics diminish the usefulness of any "totalizing" paradigm. Instead, we would propose that taking a dialectically negative approach allows for social locations to be politically and theoretically read as structural without thereby being made functional or integral and for difference to be a nonreified social experience that has political significance open to determination and inflection in situated emancipatory struggles. Without some form of practical universality, the whole notion of emancipation is rendered tenuous, and it is the jettisoning of this notion that is responsible for the increasing salience of a "politics of survival" that often finds itself operating on a mainly representational plane within unchanged structures. Social reproduction feminism, seen through the lens of materialism, can be seen as an intersectional theory, with an added appeal to a "unifying" analysis of capitalist dynamics, such as the way the form of value is determined by patterns of hierarchical social value experienced as gender, race, sexuality, and ability. But this theoretical appeal to unity is not obligated to only take the form of a labor analysis that has only partial or limited purchase as an explanation of the real abstractions of global capital in people's lives. Any analysis that aspires to a unitary exegesis on political grounds has to acknowledge its constitutive incompleteness and the need to be supplemented by unforeseen conjunctions that are both socially determinate and historically contingent.

Notes

1. Jules Joanne Gleeson points out that the current transfeminist movement also exhibits all these tendencies, spanning a spectrum from liberal inclusion to gender abolition; see Gleeson, "Transition and Abolition: Notes on Marxism and Trans Politics," *Viewpoint*, July 19, 2017, https://www.viewpointmag.com/2017/07/19/transition-and-abolition-notes-on-marxism-and-trans-politics/.

2. Hannah Arendt, *The Origins of Totalitarianism* (New York: Harcourt Brace Jovanovich, 1973).

3. Kevin Floyd, *The Reification of Desire: Toward a Queer Marxism* (Minneapolis: University of Minnesota Press, 2009), 6.

4. Amy De'Ath, "Gender and Social Reproduction," in *Sage Handbook of Critical Theory* (Thousand Oaks, Calif.: Sage, 2018), 1540.

5. Most recently, this criticism has echoed in the association of "radical feminism" with an essentialist and trans-exclusionary politics that has a generational, albeit not exclusive, bent.

6. Floyd, *Reification*, 5.

7. For a sustained argument about the compatibility of Marxism and intersectionality, see Ashley J. Bohrer's *Marxism and Intersectionality: Race, Gender, Class and Sexuality under Contemporary Capitalism* (Bielefeld, Germany: Bielefeld University Press, 2020).

8. The inseparability of "women, race, and class" is reflected in the title of Angela Davis's essay collection from 1981. Her decades-long activism in the prison abolition movement also testifies to an intersectional understanding of incarceration as it affects communities both on the inside and outside of prison walls; Davis, *Women, Race, and Class* (New York: Vintage, 2011).

9. Louise Thompson Patterson, "Toward a Brighter Dawn (1936)," *Viewpoint Magazine*, October 31, 2015, https://www.viewpointmag.com/2015/10/31/toward-a-brighter-dawn-1936/. See also, in the same issue, Esther Cooper Jackson, "The Negro Woman Domestic Worker in Relation to Trade Unionism" (1940), https://www.viewpointmag.com/2015/10/31/the-negro-woman-domestic-worker-in-relation-to-trade-unionism-1940/, and 1950 texts by Mary Inman and Marvel Cooke. For Claudia Jones, see Carole Boyce-Davies, *Left of Karl Marx: The Political Life of Black Communist Claudia Jones* (Durham, N.C.: Duke University Press, 2008), and a second book by Boyce-Davies on Jones in 2011: *Claudia Jones: Beyond Containment* (Oxfordshire: Ayebia Clarke, 2011).

10. See note 8.

11. Kimberlé Crenshaw, "Mapping the Margins: Intersectionality, Identity Politics, and Violence against Women of Color," *Stanford Law Review* 43, no. 6 (July 1991): 1,241–99.

12. Johanna Brenner, "Intersections, Locations, and Capitalist Class Relations: Intersectionality from a Marxist Perspective," in *Women and the Politics of Class* (New York: Monthly Review Press, 2000): 293–324.

13. David McNally, "Intersections and Dialectics: Critical Reconstructions," in *Social Reproduction Theory: Remapping Class, Recentering Oppression*, ed. Tithi Bhattacharya (London: Pluto, 2018), 96.

14. Sue Ferguson, "Canadian Contributions to Social Reproduction Feminism, Race, and Embodied Labour," *Race, Gender & Class* 15, nos. 1/2 (2008): 42–57.

15. Tithi Bhattacharya, "Introduction: Mapping Social Reproduction Theory," in *Social Reproduction Theory* (London: Pluto, 2018), 17, and McNally, "Intersections," 98.

16. Bhattacharya, "Introduction," 17.

17. McNally, "Intersections," 97.

18. Bhattacharya, "Introduction," 2.

19. Sue Ferguson, "Intersectionality and Social-Reproduction Feminisms: Toward an Integrative Ontology," *Historical Materialism* 24, no. 2 (2016): 38–60.

20. Ibid., 48.

21. Ibid.

22. Ibid., 53, and Himani Bannerji, "But Who Speaks for Us? Experience and Agency in Conventional Feminist Paradigms," in *Unsettling Relations: The University as a Site of Feminist Struggles*, ed. Himani Bannerji, Linda Carty, Kari Delhi, Susan Heald, and Kate McKenna (Toronto: Canadian Scholars Press, 1991).

23. Meg Luxton, "Feminist Political Economy in Canada and the Politics of Social Reproduction," in *Social Reproduction: Feminist Political Economy Challenges Neoliberalism* (Montreal: McGill-Queen's University Press, 2006), 36.

24. For a deeper analysis of the inherent indeterminacy in categories such as "the social" and "capitalism," see Endnotes, "Error," *Endnotes 5: The Passions and the Interests* (Autumn 2019). See also Rob Lucas, "Feeding the Infant," in *What Is to Be Done under Real Subsumption* (Berlin: Archive, forthcoming in 2021).

25. Ibid.

26. The extent to which this is an issue for social reproduction theory per se has been a point of debate; see Melinda Cooper, *Family Values: Between Neoliberalism and the New Social Conservatism* (Cambridge, Mass.: Zone and MIT Press, 2017). See also Kate Doyle Griffiths, "Labor Valorization and Social Reproduction: What Is Valuable about the Labor Theory of Value?" *Comparative Literature and Culture* 22 (2020).

27. Kevin Floyd, "Automatic Subjects: Gendered Labour and Abstract Life," *Historical Materialism* 24, no. 2 (June 2016): 61–86.

28. In Chris Chen's analysis, for example, race is posited as an "ascriptive process," a form of structural coercion; Chen, "The Limit Point of Capitalist Equality: Notes Toward an Abolitionist Anti-Racism," *Endnotes* 3 (September 2013), https://endnotes.org.uk/issues/3/en/chris-chen-the-limit-point-of-capitalist-equality.

29. Maya Gonzalez and Jeanne Neton, "The Logic of Gender: On the Separation of Spheres and the Process of Abjection," in *Contemporary Marxist Theory: A Reader*, edited by Andrew Pendakis, Jeff Diamanti, Nicholas Brown, Josh Robinson, and Imre Szeman (London and New York: Bloomsbury), 149–74.

30. As Rosa Luxemburg already indicated more than one hundred years ago in *The Accumulation of Capital*, Moore also argues that capital is swiftly running out of these outsides as the planet descends into a geophysical crisis of "cheap nature"; see Jason W. Moore, *Capitalism in the Web of Life: Ecology and the Accumulation of Capital* (New York: Verso, 2015).

31. Chris O'Kane, "The Path of Negative Totality: From the Critique of Political Economy to a New Reading of the Critical Theory of The Negative Totality of Capitalist Society," https://jjay.cuny.edu/sites/default/files/contentgroups/economics/chrisokaneTotality.pdf, 33.

32. Karl Marx, *Grundrisse: Foundations of the Critique of Political Economy*, trans. Martin Nicolaus (New York: Penguin, 2005), 100.

33. Floyd, *Reification*.

34. Ibid., 6.

35. Massimiliano Tomba, "1793: The Neglected Legacy of Insurgent Universality," *History of the Present* 5, no. 2 (Fall 2015): 109–36.

36. Tomba, "1793," 125.

37. Cinzia Arruzza, "Capitalism and the Conflict over Universality: A Feminist Perspective," *Philosophy Today* 61, no. 4 (Fall 2017): 847–61.

38. Ibid., 849. Here Arruzza draws upon Étienne Balibar's distinction among three forms of universality—"universality as reality," "fictive universality," and "ideal

universality." See Étienne Balibar, "Ambiguous Universality," in *Politics and the Other Scene* (London: Verso: 2011), 146–76.

39. Arruzza, "Capitalism," 851.

40. Ibid., 853.

41. Ibid., 854–55

42. One example of a constraint that resonates across different scales of a capitalist totality and takes oppressive forms that are striated by social norms would be a gendered or racialized disadvantage in relation to land rights, which is exacerbated during an enclosure or dispossession process (the constraint being how private property is exacerbated by gender and race) or the gendered and racialized disparities in the experience of illegalized migration.

43. Jamila M. H. Mascat, "Hegel and the Advent of Modernity: A Social Ontology of Abstraction," *Radical Philosophy* 2, no. 1 (February 2018): 33.

44. "Universality does not exist in the abstract, as a prescriptive principle which is mechanically applied to indifferent circumstances. It is created and recreated in the act of insurgency, which does not demand emancipation solely for those who share my identity but for everyone; it says that no one will be enslaved. It equally refuses to freeze the oppressed in a status of victimhood that requires protection from above; it insists that emancipation is self-emancipation"; Asad Haider, *Mistaken Identity: Race and Class in the Age of Trump* (New York: Verso, 2018), 113.

45. Floyd, *Reification*, 13.

46. Cinzia Arruzza, "From Social Reproduction Feminism to the Women's Strike," in *Social Reproduction Theory: Remapping Class, Recentering Oppression*, ed. Tithi Bhattacharya (London: Pluto, 2018), 196.

Works Cited

Arendt, Hannah. *The Origins of Totalitarianism*. New York: Harcourt Brace Jovanovich, 1973.

Arruzza, Cinzia. "Capitalism and the Conflict over Universality: A Feminist Perspective." *Philosophy Today* 61, no. 4 (Fall 2017): 847–61.

———. "From Social Reproduction Feminism to the Women's Strike." In *Social Reproduction Theory: Remapping Class, Recentering Oppression*, ed. Tithi Bhattacharya. London: Pluto, 2018.

Balibar, Étienne. "Ambiguous Universality." In *Politics and the Other Scene*, 146–76. London: Verso, 2011.

Bannerji, Himani. "But Who Speaks for Us? Experience and Agency in Conventional Feminist Paradigms." In *Unsettling Relations: The University as a Site of Feminist Struggles*, edited by Himani Bannerji, Linda Carty, Kari Delhi, Susan Heald, and Kate McKenna. Toronto: Canadian Scholars Press, 1991.

Bhattacharya, Tithi. "Introduction: Mapping Social Reproduction Theory." In *Social Reproduction Theory: Remapping Class, Recentering Oppression*, edited by Tithi Bhattacharya. London: Pluto, 2018.

Bohrer, Ashley J. *Marxism and Intersectionality: Race, Gender, Class and Sexuality under Contemporary Capitalism*. Bielefeld, Germany: Bielefeld University Press, 2020.

Boyce-Davies, Carole. *Claudia Jones: Beyond Containment*. Oxfordshire: Ayebia Clarke, 2011.
———. *Left of Karl Marx: The Political Life of Black Communist Claudia Jones*. Durham, N.C.: Duke University Press, 2008.
Brenner, Johanna. "Intersections, Locations, and Capitalist Class Relations: Intersectionality from a Marxist perspective." In *Women and the Politics of Class*. New York: Monthly Review Press, 2000.
Chen, Chris. "The Limit Point of Capitalist Equality: Notes Toward an Abolitionist Anti-Racism." *Endnotes* 3 (September 2013). https://endnotes.org.uk/issues/3/en/chris-chen-the-limit-point-of-capitalist-equality.
Cooper, Melinda, *Family Values: Between Neoliberalism and the New Social Conservatism*. Cambridge, Mass.: Zone and MIT Press, 2017.
Crenshaw, Kimberle. "Mapping the Margins: Intersectionality, Identity Politics, and Violence against Women of Color." *Stanford Law Review* 43, no. 6 (July 1991): 1241–99.
Davis, Angela. *Women, Race, and Class*. New York: Vintage, 2011.
De'Ath, Amy. "Gender and Social Reproduction." In *Sage Handbook of Critical Theory*. Thousand Oaks, Calif.: Sage, 2018.
Endnotes. "Error." *Endnotes 5: The Passions and the Interests* (Autumn 2020).
Ferguson, Sue. "Canadian Contributions to Social Reproduction Feminism, Race and Embodied Labour." *Race, Gender & Class* 15, nos. 1/2 (2008): 42–57.
———. "Intersectionality and Social-Reproduction Feminisms: Toward an Integrative Ontology." *Historical Materialism* 24, no. 2 (2016): 38–60.
Floyd, Kevin. "Automatic Subjects: Gendered Labour and Abstract Life." *Historical Materialism* 24, no. 2 (June 2016): 61–86.
———. *The Reification of Desire: Toward a Queer Marxism*. Minneapolis: University of Minnesota Press, 2009.
Gleeson, Jules Joanne. "Transition and Abolition: Notes on Marxism and Trans Politics." *Viewpoint*, July 19, 2017, https://www.viewpointmag.com/2017/07/19/transition-and-abolition-notes-on-marxism-and-trans-politics/.
Gonzalez, Maya, and Jeanne Neton. "The Logic of Gender: On the Separation of Spheres and the Process of Abjection." In *Contemporary Marxist Theory: A Reader*, edited by Andrew Pendakis, Jeff Diamanti, Nicholas Brown, Josh Robinson, and Imre Szeman, 149–74. London and New York: Bloomsbury, 2014.
Griffiths, Kate Doyle. "Labor Valorization and Social Reproduction: What Is Valuable about the Labor Theory of Value." *Comparative Literature and Culture* 22 (2020).
Haider, Asad. *Mistaken Identity: Race and Class in the Age of Trump*. New York: Verso, 2018.
Jackson, Esther Cooper. "The Negro Woman Domestic Worker in Relation to Trade Unionism (1940)." *Viewpoint Magazine*, October 31, 2015, https://www.viewpointmag.com/2015/10/31/the-negro-woman-domestic-worker-in-relation-to-trade-unionism-1940/.

Lucas, Rob. "Feeding the Infant." In *What Is to Be Done under Real Subsumption*. Berlin: Archive, forthcoming in 2021.

Luxton, Meg. "Feminist Political Economy in Canada and the Politics of Social Reproduction." In *Social Reproduction: Feminist Political Economy Challenges Neoliberalism*, edited by Kate Bezanson and Meg Luxton. Montreal: McGill-Queen's University Press, 2006.

Marx, Karl. *Grundrisse: Foundations of the Critique of Political Economy*. Translated by Martin Nicolaus. New York: Penguin, 2005.

Mascat, Jamila M. H. "Hegel and the Advent of Modernity: A Social Ontology of Abstraction." *Radical Philosophy* 2, no. 1 (February 2018): 29–46.

McNally, David. "Intersections and Dialectics: Critical Reconstructions." In *Social Reproduction Theory Remapping Class, Recentering Oppression*, edited by Tithi Bhattacharya. London: Pluto, 2018.

Mezzadra, Sandro, and Breet Neilson. *Border as Method, or, the Multiplication of Labor*. Durham, N.C.: Duke University Press, 2013.

Moore, Jason. *Capitalism in the Web of Life: Ecology and the Accumulation of Capital*. New Verso, 2015.

O'Kane, Chris. "The Path of Negative Totality: From the Critique of Political Economy to a New Reading of the Critical Theory of The Negative Totality of Capitalist Society." https://jjay.cuny.edu/sites/default/files/contentgroups/economics/chrisokaneTotality.pdf.

Patterson, Louise Thompson. "Toward a Brighter Dawn (1936)." *Viewpoint Magazine*, October 31, 2015, https://www.viewpointmag.com/2015/10/31/toward-a-brighter-dawn-1936/.

Tomba, Massimiliano. "1793: The Neglected Legacy of Insurgent Universality." *History of the Present* 5, no. 2 (Fall 2015): 109–36.

3 / Tripartheid: How Global White Supremacy Triumphs through Neoliberalism

ARTHUR SCARRITT

> The means of the extravagant rentier diminish daily in inverse proportion to the growing possibilities and temptations of pleasure. He must, therefore, either consume his capital himself, and in so doing bring about his own ruin, or become an industrial capitalist.
> —KARL MARX, *ECONOMIC & PHILOSOPHIC MANUSCRIPTS*

> The seeds of the fiasco of an election in November 2016 in the United States, where the less affluent of European descent, including more than half of the women of this group, found their tribune in a vulgar billionaire, has roots in the cross-class coalition that spearheaded colonial settlement in the seventeenth century at the expense of the indigenous and enslaved Africans.
> —GERALD HORNE, *THE APOCALYPSE OF SETTLER COLONIALISM: THE ROOTS OF SLAVERY, WHITE SUPREMACY, AND CAPITALISM IN SEVENTEENTH-CENTURY NORTH AMERICA AND THE CARIBBEAN*

For the past fifty years, the neoliberal reassertion of elite power has triumphed around the world. A new aristocracy concentrates "masters of the universe" wealth and power, even amidst weak economic growth. Upwards of half of the world's population, meanwhile, has "dropped out of history . . . written off as hopeless or terminal cases."[1] And the once stable middle class faces fearsome insecurity and downward mobility.

Students of these globe-changing processes emphasize structural factors, a point corroborated by neoliberalism's own prescriptions and structural adjustment programs (SAPs). David Harvey, for instance, describes neoliberalism as a "*political* project... to restore the power of economic elites."[2] Neoliberalism restructures social institutions to funnel wealth from the poor to the rich, justified as supply-side economics.

At the same time, however, overt racism has powered political projects across the globe, such as white rage fueling Trump's triumph in the U.S., the growth of white supremacy and xenophobia in Europe, and anti-indigenous, fear-fueled politics in Latin America. The largely class-based structural analyses of global change therefore need to better incorporate the explicitly racial nature of neoliberal transformations. For their part, the great strides in racial studies have largely understood race as a country-specific issue, as so many parallel but unrelated cases. Indeed, some of the greatest disputes have hung on how race works differently in different countries.[3] Such a perspective, however, undercuts racial analysis from understanding race as global, or what Charles Mills has termed "global white supremacy."[4]

I argue that linking national racial analyses and global class analyses requires recognizing that key defining characteristics of the neoliberal order stretch back to colonialism and have persevered across history—despite facing major challenges—to now enjoy a vigorous reinvention through neoliberal reforms. Foremost, a new financial elite rules neoliberalism, a rentier class who wrested control from the industrial bourgeoisie and whose fortune and thus command center on windfalls from speculation rather than profit from investing in the means of production. I argue that this group traces its roots back to the rentier class that dominated Europe for centuries prior to industrialization and who made colonialism in their own image.

This essay therefore traces the strange persistence of the rentier class, a group predicted to disappear by most observers, including Marx, Weber, Adam Smith, John Maynard Keynes, and many others. Put simply, "the basis of rent is the monopolisation of particular portions of the globe by a certain class demanding a payment for its use."[5] Rentiers largely rule, then, through setting up a political system that enables them to demand these payments, a system that politically creates shortages that can be captured by this class. Industrial capitalism, in contrast, requires the political conditions for exploiting labor to expand productivity and generate profit, and therein create wealth. Rent captures value from shortages, whereas profit depends on increasing output. Michael Hardt explains the difference between rent and profit:

In the collection of rent, the capitalist is deemed to be relatively external to the process of the production of value, merely extracting value produced by other means. The generation of profit, in contrast, requires the engagement of the capitalist in the production process, imposing forms of cooperation, disciplinary regimes, etc.[6]

Mining and other extractive enterprises are classic examples of rent, whereas industrial production epitomizes profit generation. Importantly, where industrialism relies on wage relations so that worker well-being is linked to productivity, rentiers distribute resources paternalistically, with proletarian well-being dependent upon fealty to the powerful. The dynamism of industrialism compared to the self-defeating parasitism of the rentier inspired Keynes to predict the "euthanasia of the rentier."[7]

Yet over the past forty years, neoliberalism and its host of finance-favoring laws have created new forms of rent collecting that hegemonically define the economy: patents, copyrights, and intellectual property; new financial instruments, such as collateralized debt obligations, that transfer money from the poor to the rich without generating new wealth; and myriad inventive ways of transforming common rights to such things as education, health care, housing, and roads into lucrative windfalls for financial interests while generating unprecedented debt for the majority. Guy Standing condemns this rise of the rentier as the corruption of capitalism, as the rich simply profiting from their wealth and therein undermining the productivity that actually generates new wealth.[8]

This chapter places new focus on the rentier as the protagonist behind the global system of white supremacy and its revitalization through neoliberalism. I argue that rentiers survived through setting up a tripartite racialized system during colonial crises. Across fraught historical circumstances, this tripartheid system provides a modicum of racial privilege to a middle stratum group such that they fracture non-elite groups and therein preserve the aristocratic order.

In this analysis, the relative racial privilege of non-elite actors centers on the privilege to benefit from the immiseration of their more deeply racialized counterparts. As Theodore Allen's work on *The Invention of the White Race* argues, colonial elites in North America gave poor whites a limited amount of resources more than blacks for the express purpose of dividing these groups' mutual class interests.[9] Poor whites therein did the elites' dirty work lest they lose their relative privileges. I take this one step further. Much of these limited resources, I argue, involved the privilege of directly benefitting from the degradation of the fully racialized. Not only did the middle get relatively better access to resources like land, but most of the main aspects of their daily lives—work, family, home, and community—were institutionally set up to depend on the abasement of the racial Other. The relatively privileged garnered their well-being from maintaining the system that made the Other vulnerable and the gentry untouchable, so their racism was highly rational.

To argue my point, I compare two seemingly disparate countries across three major eras: the U.S. and Peru during early colonialism, the golden age of controlled capitalism, and neoliberalism. I choose these locations precisely because of their large differences. The similarities not only reveal the core nature of this racialized system across disparate territory but also the inherent systemic interconnectivity. Understanding race in one area requires seeing it as part of a global system.

The comparison argues against the academic consensus that race is fundamentally about economic exploitation. Instead, it reveals the defining core of racial hierarchy as the *political* maintenance of an aristocratic social order commanded by a global rentier elite. That is, rather than colonial elites racializing society to command cheap labor, the comparison shows the establishment of a highly costly system whose investments were not driven by maximizing economic returns but by keeping an elite class in power no matter the cost—a traditionally feudal system of rentier rule enabled by racialization.

Labor exploitation clearly occurs under racialization. But we need to distinguish between systems that use oppression as one among many tools to prioritize exploitation and those systems centered on oppression wherein any exploitation occurs secondarily, as a byproduct. This is of great historical importance—and made poignantly so, as under neoliberalism "the chance to be exploited in a long-term job is now experienced as a privilege."[10] That is, elites' pressing concern has shifted from how to exploit labor to how to control surplus populations.[11]

To be more specific, capitalists seek a system that maximizes labor exploitation. Colonial rentiers, in contrast, sought to maintain a system of indelible inequality. Exploitation in the capitalist drive for profit entails some form of capitalist dependence on both the maintenance and renewal of labor—paying wages and filling vacancies.[12] Colonials, in contrast, set themselves apart as inherently superior, with underlings naturally and fully dependent on the benevolence of their supposed betters. For rentiers, any profit or exploitation occurred incidentally, enslaved to the oppressive purpose of maintaining the aristocratic order.

Unlike capitalists, rentiers could not invest in the maintenance of labor. Instead, colonials valued labor for its expendability, for demonstrating the complete control elites exercised and thus reaffirming their supposedly innate superiority. Admitting any rentier dependence on labor would undermine the unassailability of the elite. And thus the wage relation, a core defining feature of capitalism, could only exist haphazardly. Rentiers therefore addressed the issue of the renewal of labor by treating labor as a limitless and highly disposable resource. They treated human life with utter contempt and witnessed genocides upon non-elite populations.

The contradiction of ultimately depending on labor continuously threatened the aristocratic order and made it inherently unstable. Colonials bitterly acknowledged this dependence. But they rabidly fought against any structural recognition—any kind of inclusive reforms—thus deepening their commitment to undermining the labor source they depended upon and further destabilizing their system of rule. Indeed, there are many indications that the god-like rentiers running neoliberalism have realized colonialists' greatest fantasies: how to free themselves of dependence on labor. The staggering inventiveness currently poured into primitive accumulation, into rent collecting, has generated mechanisms that make labor increasingly superfluous. And therein neoliberalism addresses the central conundrum of colonialism and sets up a more perfect feudal order.

My comparative study demonstrates this: looking at early colonialism shows the creation of modern race and the establishment of tripartheid. The similarities show that the colonial project fundamentally centered on saving and extending European feudalism. Racialization only occurred well into the colonial project as a response to colonial crises, with the gentry employing it specifically to preserve their feudal order rather than to innovate exploitation. Racialization therein indelibly marked feudal relations, and reciprocally, feudalism characterized racialization.

Skipping ahead to look at the golden age of controlled capitalism reveals the greatest threat to the tripartheid system. Industrialization created capitalists with sufficient funding and motivation to challenge rentier rule. The economic successes of this era disrupted racial rule as, for the first time since early colonialism, the corporatist class compromise between workers and owners made these groups see their racial interests as undermining their much more lucrative class interests. But, as this historical account shows, the rentiers and their racialized system persevered through making themselves useful to industrial capitalism. With the uncertainty of the crumbling of the Keynesian compromise in the 1970s, labor fought to keep the bourgeoisie fighting for its class interests, while the rentiers worked to draw the capitalists over to their racialized system.

Coming forward to our current era therein reveals the neoliberal triumph as best understood in racial rather than class terms, pace David

Harvey and so many others. With the corporatist crisis, industrialists chose to abandon their cross-class alliance against racialization and side with the rentiers and their white supremacy. Rather than face a leap in the socialization of the means of production, industrialists chose to subject themselves to a new extreme financial regime seeking quick windfalls rather than steady growth. Inverting Marx's prediction of the rentier's ruin, capitalists elected to consume their own capital in bids to amass speculative fortunes, abandoning innovations in the means of production to instead help revolutionize the means of appropriation. The multi-race class alliances fell apart. Instead, the new elite disciplined the middle racial groups, generating uncertainty for middle-class whites in the U.S. and *mestizos* in Peru, prompting the deeper racialization of the Other who struggles for relations of feudal-like dependence over lawless oblivion.

Colonialism: Writing Feudalism across the World

Most analyses agree that Europe brought feudal relations to their colonies, if simply for the mundane reason that feudal relations defined Europe and it would have been hard if not impossible to bring any other relation.[13] My point is much stronger: any other achievements measured in terms of plunder, land, or labor only occurred and had any success through the transposing of highly unequal feudal class relations to the New World. In other words, colonialism was primarily about preserving and extending the vaunted positions of the gentry, with all else bent toward that end. Indeed, as George Fredrickson comments, the gentry treated commoners with subhuman contempt, seeing themselves as naturally and inherently superior, presaging the essentialist construction of race.[14]

Setting up and maintaining an elitist society drove colonialism, with economics harnessed to rather than working independently of the reproduction of social hierarchy. As Polanyni famously observed, only under industrialization did economics stop being "merely a function of the social" and exhibit their independent processes.[15] Thus, under colonialism, maximizing exploitation was not the goal but rather maximizing subordination and social polarization. That is, the establishment of colonialism did not center on setting up an extractive system, imperial bureaucracy, or a racial hierarchy. Extraction, empire, and racism indeed occurred, but only well after and dependent upon the establishment of a feudal society based on polarized social disparity. Thus, at its core, coloniality means the perseverance of an aristocratic rentier elite, with later changes such as racialization serving this end and being defined by it.

The contrasting cases of early British and Spanish colonialism illustrate this well. Financed through private charter companies, the shoestring early North American colonization effort relied on imported indentured and other impoverished European labor to establish feudal relations. Looking toward Spain and Portugal, sixteenth-century Britain may have longed for empire, but certainly lacked one. Colonizing North America may have established some form of beachhead to compete against these empires, but the process lacked funding on the Iberian scale. Instead, British colonialism largely served to address the crises of British feudalism.

Sixteenth-century Tudor rule faced major shortages of food and employment. Elite-driven enclosures accelerated rapidly despite the crown and Parliament repeatedly passing anti-enclosure acts.[16] Feudal relations therein created ever larger superfluous populations that the elites regarded as irredeemable "indolent rogues" who needed controlling through workhouses, prisons, and even slavery.[17] The almost ten-year Civil War only exacerbated instability and uncertainty. The problem of shiftless masses did not arise from land shortages—Britain was much less densely populated than other European areas such as the Papal States. Rather, this crisis reflected the unwillingness of the landed aristocracy to alter social relations to include a greater part of the population. Indeed, the elite enclosed ever more lands to serve their opulent lifestyles, generated more starving vagabonds, and triggered more revolts. Feudal methods therein deepened feudal crises.

Feudalism in conjunction with colonialism, however, saved feudalism, largely by exporting its problems. Kidnapping adults, snatching children and selling them as slaves, and transporting convicts and prisoners of the Civil War, without their consent, all sought to relieve England's problems by addressing the labor needs of the colonies.[18] In these "barbarous years" in North America, low life expectancy, heavy workloads, and hazardous living conditions meant a large portion of indentured servants failed to live out their servitude in order to realize their freedom.[19] Early colonialism established an elite who dominated land ownership and had fewer labor requirements, though they largely lacked sufficient leisure to engage in the socializing that undergirds true elite class formation.[20] While the British elite in particular may have held negative views of the indigenous population, colonial survival depended on the native society. That is, despite the early presence of racist attitudes, racial hierarchy did not structure society.

In the seventeenth century, a new, more class-creating aristocracy arose, using improved conditions largely to impose a deeper feudal order dependent upon non-racialized labor.[21] In 1629 New York, the Dutch granted massive estates, with one, Rensselaerswyck, making up one million acres, or over a fifth of the available land. Tenant farmers worked the fields, much like in the home country. Elites in Virginia and Maryland emulated England and thus "wanted to join in the creation of an inequality that could never be breached," crafting a system of large landed estates and government by a small clique of gentry.[22] To enable this, the headright system provided gentry with fifty acres for each indentured servant brought from England. Land became concentrated among the few, while servants made up the great majority of people, such as three-fourths of the mid-seventeenth-century Virginia population.[23]

Both the legal structure and the brutality led Edmund Morgan to argue that indenture prefigured the formal enslavement of Africans.[24] Many contemporaries denounced indenture as nothing more than slavery.[25] Indeed, "most [North] American historians have agreed that the prevalence of servitude, in tandem with the growth of slavery, made unfreedom of varying degrees the common denominator of colonial work until the American Revolution."[26] Whites made up the majority of plantation workers in Chesapeake until 1690, a full ten years after the institutionalization of slavery.[27] In all, the first hundred years of North American colonization, even under the most brutal conditions, centered on cementing a feudal system of a landed rentier aristocracy dominating the highly degraded but nonracialized working masses.

Feudal Disorder and Native Stability in Peru

The Spanish crown, in contrast, underwrote much of its colonization efforts. Since King Phillip II was unwilling or unable to make the rapacious aristocracy pay any taxes, he created the largest empire in many centuries through becoming the "debtor from hell": obligations reached half of the GDP, with the debt to British banks eventually helping launch the Anglo empire.[28] Colonial expansion helped the Spanish confront the crises of continuous bankruptcies, a mercenary gentry, and an immiserated and ever restive peasantry. But how much of an empire did the early Spanish presence in Peru actually constitute? Francisco Pizarro's band of 130 ruthless soldiers achieved the seemingly impossible by conquering the Inca in 1532. But bloody Spanish infighting meant Pizarro and three of his four brothers on this mission were killed within ten years, only Hernando surviving because he was incarcerated in Spain for treason.[29]

Francisco arrived in Peru already rich from his position as *encomendero* in Panama. The *encomienda* system gave lordly oversight to conquerors, granted leave to squeeze labor and tribute from native populations as they could and begrudgingly give 20 percent, the Royal Fifth, to the Throne. Regarded as inhumane even by the standards of the day, the crown eventually passed the New Laws in 1542 to try to end the system. This sparked a bloody rebellion in Peru and the killing of the viceroy, the king's representative. But this was not the first Peruvian battle between Spaniards. Almost immediately after conquest, the Spanish began infighting. After several battles in the 1530s, disagreements over the size of their newly rising *encomiendas* brought the forces of Diego "El Mozo" de Almagro II to kill Francisco in a 1541 coup, with Pizarro supporters returning the favor the very next year at the battle of Chupas.[30]

While fighting civil wars rather than forming civil society characterized much of early Spanish rule, the Andean *encomiendas* proved much more indigenous than European.[31] Rather than creating a new system of domination, the Spanish adapted the Incan system of ruling through a privileged local aristocracy (*curacas*), while deepening ethnic rivalries and exacerbating incipient class differentiation inherent in Andean social relations.[32] When the Spanish removed the Inca, most natives gladly refocused their organization around their local group, particularly as their complex networks of kinship ties were the primary means of accessing resources, and the *curaca* could present themselves as liberators from Incan rule.[33]

Such near total reliance on the native socioeconomic system severely limited the depredations the Spanish could unleash. Spanish America abounded with racialized horrors, such as hunting natives for sport.[34] But, as Stern describes it, "The colonials remained foreign, extraneous elements superimposed on an autonomous economy in which they served little purpose."[35] This *encomienda* system granted lordly oversight to Spanish settlers over tremendous areas and large native populations. While natives reviled *encomenderos* for their impunity and random violence, the colonials depended upon reciprocal relations with the local *curacas* who controlled native labor and resources. The most successful *encomenderos* lavished gifts upon their *curacas* to assure both the continual flow of tribute and the safeguarding of their own positions.[36]

Under these conditions, strategic alliances with the Spaniards helped preserve the integrity of local society and gained protection from rivals, while providing some new routes to social mobility.[37] The *ecomenderos* competed much more than they cooperated, only weakly launching class-formation activities and therein failing to develop a resilient civil society.[38] The imperial presence in Peru therein constituted a battling group of rival lords. At this point, Peru lacked an organized colonial infrastructure.

Instead, it retrofitted feudal relations such that the *encomendero* class could realize feudal status and wealth through preserving Andean society, the crown largely unable to impose its laws and only begrudgingly given its fifth.

Thus, in both the impoverished British north and the wealthy Spanish south, empire failed to materialize in any meaningful way. Instead, poorly organized aristocrats straddled and drove society to fulfill their own interests. Feudalism, not empire, defined early colonialism. That is, rather than driven economically, colonialism was principally a political project for imposing an aristocratic feudal system on the world, not simply because Europeans regarded it as normal, but because feudal relations proved themselves as the key tool for realizing the other major goals of elitism, social control, and resource extraction.

And with the dependence on native societies, modern racism had yet to emerge.

Creating Race in Peru

In Peru, after the first forty years of colonialism, serious crises threatened Spanish rule. Colonials eventually addressed these through draconian racialization. As the white population grew and diversified in the later 1500s, the shared desire to exploit native labor exacerbated competition and rivalry among colonials, especially as they lacked the institutional capacity to directly recruit labor. Rather than building the infrastructure for coordinated policy implementation, however, they persisted in their self-splintering strategies of relying on their own patronage networks, increasing their dependence on and exploitation of the *curacas*. At the same time, colonials faced deteriorating economic output at the silver mines in Potosí and across the entire mining sector, heightened rebellions, and the debility of the governing *encomienda* system. Colonials held fast to the idea they could address all these problems by getting more native labor fed into the colonial machinery—by strengthening their control over labor to render it exploitable.[39]

In the countryside, meanwhile, colonial rule through ethnic fracturing increasingly made colonists the final arbiters in local disputes. Concomitant with this rise in political power and legitimacy, the Spanish continually increased their demands for labor and tribute. But such wringing eroded the local system of control. In particular, it dramatically sharpened the contradictory role of the *curaca* middlemen, the direct providers of native labor, threatening to turn them into agents of colonialism. The increased penetration and demands of Spanish authority undermined the motivation for natives to make strategic, autonomy-preserving alliances with the colonists.[40]

With the increased Spanish demand for labor and tribute, colonial desires to consolidate natives into a more fully racialized "Indian" group for the strict end of extraction became increasingly evident. Under these circumstances, appeasing Europeans came to resemble participating in one's own destruction much more than preserving native autonomy. At the same time, the preservation of generally self-sustaining and autonomous indigenous spheres enabled natives to construct, in the midst of colonial rule itself, widespread anti-colonial movements, such as the neo-Inca state in the jungle city of Vitcos, the Taki Onqoy millenarian dancing sickness movement, and various Huanca uprisings in the central Andes.[41]

To address these crises, Spain sent a new viceroy, Toledo, who dramatically remade social relations. Rather than somehow negotiating a more humane social system (natives suggesting several models themselves), the Toledo reforms of the 1570s refashioned colonial society to eventually break the back of the native economy and have its labor directly serve the Spanish. Herein the full racialization of the indigenous population finally occurred. Fully embracing feudal colonialism's utter contempt for life, the reforms reconfigured the diverse ethnic groups that enjoyed various levels of autonomy into a degraded homogeneous Indian population constructed for the purpose of colonial exploitation.[42]

As one of the most brutal parts of the reforms, Toledo forcibly relocated indigenous populations onto concentrated land holdings called "reductions." Native well-being deteriorated precipitously. Aimed at wresting control of the natives from the *curacas*—who had become more demanding and less willing to deliver tribute and labor—relocation truncated traditional dispersed settlements, massively displaced the native populations, and generally uprooted them from the physical terrain through which they reproduced their local cultures. Natives lived in much more squalid conditions, reliant on external labor markets for their reproduction, and were much more susceptible to pathogens, both because of their population concentration and their deteriorated living conditions. Malnutrition and famine spread. While earlier alliances with the Spanish may have staved off the demographic collapse witnessed in other parts of Latin America, Toledo's breaking of native self-sufficiency now brought population collapse to the Andes.[43]

The major contradiction of the Toledo reform era was that it sought to dramatically increase the amount of native labor available for Spanish exploitation at the same time that it drastically eroded the ability of native labor to reproduce itself. As one of the first examples of racially rendering labor exploitable, Toledo's reforms reveal much about labor reserves significantly defining race. In this instance, racialization and the migrant labor system happened at the same time. But the case shows how this is more than correlation. Roughly, such a system entails holding a population in specific geographic locales. Here, the costs of maintaining the labor force—day-to-day subsistence—are lower such that employers can pay them lower wages. At the same time, however, these locales force the population to engage in the larger world as their local resources are structured to be insufficient for reproduction.

The point is that colonials were not setting up a rational system for maximizing economic profit but rather one for entrenching the power of a vaunted elite. The massive contradiction that Toledo expended a giant part of the potential work force to make a larger amount of native labor exploitable than under the previous system demonstrates the non-primacy of economics in their rationale. In more modernist terms, they drew down most of their capital to better access what capital remained. They used race to set up the native population as a truly pauperized mass dependent upon Europeans who set themselves up like gods. The massive waste of life in the transatlantic slave trade parallels this genocide. Further, once established, the Europeans did not even maintain their labor stocks well, but rather kept them in horrible conditions, guaranteeing their demise. They treated labor as totally expendable even though in any longer-term economic rationale they would see themselves as slitting their own throats, as wildly spending the main resource upon which they depended.

British Racialization

By the 1670s, colonials created the same feudal crises they had rescued the motherland from: elites continued to monopolize lands, but people began living out their indenture enough to create "shiftless masses" of freedmen. Morgan finds local estimates of freedmen ranging from 25 percent to 40 percent of the population.[44] Upon gaining freedom, the unwillingness of elites to establish a fairer system of land distribution left these proletarians with only miserable options: dubiously pushing the frontier, renting from landlords, or returning to servitude, with debt peonage rife when tobacco prices fell. Owning no land, freedmen were denied the vote by elites, yet the elites still made freedmen subject to levees and other taxes, such as the quitright owed the king. Rebellion began to flourish alongside frontier wars such as King Philip's War, which almost ended the colonial experiment in New England.[45]

Scholars point to Bacon's Rebellion of 1670 as the beginning of British colonial racialization, largely because these events demonstrated how the alliance of poor Europeans and Africans could threaten colonial society. As Gerald Horne puts it, "When Africans, indigenes, and poorer Europeans began to rebel simultaneously, simple survival meant concessions to one of these groups."[46] Contrary to Horne's otherwise outstanding work, looking more closely at the actual process of racialization through the granting of concessions to poor Europeans shows that the gentry treated the issue as not one of "simple survival" but rather the survival of extremist elite rule.

As the aftermath of Bacon's Rebellion shows, the elite would rather hold the colony in a state of near constant revolt than offer concessions: Virginia governor Berkeley and his cronies doubled down, setting up "legalized plundering by which the loyal party were accumulating property at the expense of everyone they could label a rebel" and "squeezing the people to the point where the king's whole revenue from Virginia might be lost."[47] Rather than suing for peace, the gentry preferred to continue enriching themselves through funneling wealth from the poor and keeping "the colony continually on the brink of rebellion."[48] Racialization, then, was not a process of giving a little to gain a lot in the name of survival. Rather it involved a way for the elite to have their cake and eat it too, for them to offer nonconcessional forms of concessions, ones that cost them almost nothing in terms of status, treasure, or altering their place in the social structure.

Racial hatred proved a perfect resource for meeting this challenge: nurturing it cost the elite very little, but it proved nearly inexhaustible. The Toledo reforms one hundred years previously and thousands of miles south showed a well-funded, highly coordinated, deliberate, crown-run effort to save colonial society from itself, largely through the genocidal institutionalization of racial hierarchy. The later British colonies lacked the Spanish resources and thus the full coherency of Toledo's reforms. Instead, British racialization occurred through a fraught process, accelerating slowly across more than sixty years after Bacon's Rebellion of 1670.

Morgan narrates a host of cumulative policies.[49] First, Virginia reversed its policy on enslaving Indians as a negotiation with Bacon, granting him a virtual "slave-hunting license" in 1676 by allowing him to permanently enslave any captured Indians. This remarkably paralleled the Indian enslavements of New England that helped lay the ground for institutionalizing bondage.[50] In 1670 Bacon and his men had indiscriminately attacked all Indians as unworthy hostiles, even allies to the colonies. This created major problems for the administration—their own people killing their allies. But the 1676 reversal funneled the racial hatred of Bacon's group into an immediately profitable enterprise, providing direct economic, political, and psychological rewards to Europeans for their racist attitudes and behaviors.

The move toward enslaving Indians for life also tied into other racialization processes. Before, policy held that only non-Christian servants imported by sea—Africans—and not by land—Indians from other areas—would be considered slaves for life. This reversal therein homogenized the very radically different populations of Africans and Indians, marking them as degraded people fit only for enslavement and the brutality required to extract work from this form of labor relation. The original colonial intentions to enslave natives was therein spread to the increasing black population. This was a marked shift. From the first slave ship of 1619, Africans had largely been treated like European indentured servants. "Indians and Negroes were henceforth lumped together in Virginia legislation, and white Virginians treated black, red, and intermediate shades of brown as interchangeable."[51]

The gentry worked to deepen the European servants' and freedmen's racial hatred and contempt. Early on, in 1670, it singled out Indians and Africans as prohibited from owning Christian servants. More deeply, legislation prescribed thirty lashes to any—including free and Christian—Indian or African who lifted a hand to *any* Christian. Though the Europeans were of lowlier class status, they gained racial status against free Indians and Africans. And at this time, free people readily treated servants with corporal punishment. It also allowed European servants to bully slaves, "placing them psychologically on a par with masters."[52] Thus, the laws began deliberately disrupting the master-servant dyad, interposing a much more complex master-servant-slave dynamic. And though this was not yet explicitly stated in racial terms, the privileging of European Christians as European Christians rather than as indentured servants began to paint itself along phenotype.

On its way to creating whiteness, the Virginia assembly began increasing the economic rewards of being European. Masters had frequently given property to slaves—a cow or a pig—as a reward for good behavior. But in 1705, Virginia legislated the seizing of slave property by local church parishes, to be used for poor Europeans. The elite took from the poor Africans and gave to the poor Europeans, institutionalizing a practice where any material possessions a slave managed to procure would go to Europeans. This is one of the most blatant examples of poor Europeans participating directly in the exploitation of poor Africans. Poor Europeans thereby came to have a vested interest in the continued immiseration of Africans and Indians. And the gentry incurred no direct costs.

Miscegenation had been highly common, especially with male colonists greatly outnumbering women. But by the early 1700s, new laws punished intermixture, explicitly using the term "white." These laws began explicitly drawing a color line, separating the races. And they did so in such a way that advantaged poor whites as a group. For instance, white women who had mixed children faced a fine that again went to the local parish to benefit poor whites, generally. This also served elite interests, as white servants got time tacked onto their servitude. Free white women necessarily had to have free children, but mixed free children had to serve as parish servants for the first thirty years of their lives.[53] As a rich comment of the gender relations in race, colonists did not punish black women for having children with white fathers. And, of course, the male gentry willingly enslaved any children they sired with their black slaves. The assembly also regularly passed laws declaring mixed offspring to belong to the black race.

In legislation of 1723, the assembly forbade the freeing of slaves. Initially, masters had to pay for the transport of freed slaves out of the colony. But reforms mandated instead that freed slaves could simply be seized and sold. And in 1725, the free blacks and Indians who managed to stay in the colony had their political rights stripped from them—to vote, testify in court, or hold office. Poor whites, on the other hand, began enjoying greater political freedoms. Thus, non-Europeans became "consolidated in a single pariah group," disassociating them with whites, however poor.[54]

As Virginia governor William Gooch himself explained, the retreat from associating free status and political rights such as voting for blacks and Indians aimed "to fix a perpetual Brand upon Free Negros & Mulatos."[55] In other words, the gentry deliberately created a rightless caste based explicitly on skin color. As Allen puts it, the expressed motivations behind these laws revealed it as a system of racial oppression whose "hallmark is the insistence on the social distinction between the *poorest* member of the oppressor group and any member, however propertied, of the oppressed group."[56] As Allen further elaborates, much of the point of this system was not to fend off African slave revolts but to control poor whites. Because of the relative poverty of this British colonial effort—in comparison to Peru but also British Caribbean ventures—these Europeans still represented the biggest threat to the gentry:

> Nothing could have been more apparent than that the small cohort of the ruling elite must have a substantial intermediate buffer social

control stratum to stand between it and "great disturbances," or even another rebellion.[57]

Racialization also provided various forms of privileged employment, such that the immediate well-being of poor whites depended on black and Indian degradation. According to Allen, such mechanisms directly addressed the issue of gaining poor white support for a system of slavery that obviously undermined the viability of free labor. In one of the first North American examples of a color bar, deficiency laws mandated only menial jobs for blacks while reserving skilled jobs for whites, and sometimes even created explicit overseeing positions for whites, such as mandating a quota of white overseers as a ratio of plantation slaves. Whites therein came to demand black exclusion from skilled trades throughout the colonies.[58]

The racialized system also created new income sources for poor whites as the racial police. In 1727, Virginia established militias of white, mostly former indentured servants, to patrol for unseemly meetings among blacks and between blacks and whites. And in 1788, slave patrolling was spread to the entire white population by offering rewards to "any freeman"—except, obviously, those barred from testifying because of their skin color. Together these policies worked to institutionalize racial hatred into a racial hierarchy wherein poor Europeans—now made white—received modest privileges from the immiseration of non-Europeans, therein making poor whites invested in the highly unequal aristocratic society.

The similarities between North and South America reveal much about the initial racialization process. Both emerged out of crises of feudal colonial rule, and, though the respective gentry differed in their capacities, both disregarded costs in terms of funds and human lives in jealously preserving the aristocratic order. Ready contemporary alternatives existed, including moderate reforms suggested by the British crown, but colonists hewed to their extreme regimes. While the Spanish reforms heavily disciplined the intermediary *curacas* and the British newly created an intermediary stratum, this between group proved crucial for racial rule. Both involved an institutional segregation wherein whites had a set of institutions enabling their citizenship while a separate set of institutions served the racialized Others, forcing them to realize their personhood through the intermediary stratum who gained privileges through these arrangements.

In these conditions, the middle group received limited privileges while constantly facing the threat of sliding back into the dehumanized masses. With the system so painfully restructured, ruling now centered on rewards and threats to the middle group such that their conflicted nature resolved itself in favor of the elite—therein avoiding rebellions—without providing so many privileges as to generate competition to elite interests. In each case, racialization involved elites innovating society's structure such that they did not have to compromise with other groups yet preserved their feudal status. Racialization therein did not center on the survival of colonial society, but on the survival of an extremist elite society. Though many important events occurred in the following decades, none proved as great a threat to the aristocratic society as industrialization's post–World War II corporatist compromises.

The Industrial Challenge to White Supremacy

> All fixed, fast-frozen relations, with their train of ancient and venerable prejudices and opinions, are swept away, all new-formed ones become antiquated before they can ossify.
> Karl Marx, "Manifesto of the Communist Party"

Industrialization created the largest challenge ever to the aristocratic order, threatening it both politically and economically. Most importantly, industrialization was a wholly new way to generate capital: productivity instead of plunder, making things instead of taking things, profit instead of rent. When the bourgeoisie finally came to rule and therein shape society to serve its interests, capitalism's great productive capacity made Marx predict the end of the rentier. In this, he and most others saw the industrial reshaping of the world away from personalistic colonial relations, forcing others "to adopt the bourgeois mode of production" under pain of extinction and to reduce relations to nothing more than "naked self-interest, than callous cash payments."[59]

As the history of industrialization shows, in their dark satanic mills, capitalists initially treated workers with the same deadly disregard as under feudalism. The new conditions most immediately created a huge range of novel ways for workers to lose or shorten their lives. But through concentrating so many workers in the small areas of factories and through shifting social relations from paternalism to the wage relation, industrialization also created the conditions for realizing greater successes for popular mobilizations. By the 1930s in North America, popular movements restrained much of the genocidal treatment of labor in the industrial sectors.[60]

The real threat to the rentier order came as the New Deal and Bretton Woods ushered in the golden age of controlled capitalism and the corporatist compromise among capital, labor, and the state. Herein industrial capitalism exhibited its greatest potentials for undoing white supremacy—of structuring society along exclusively class rather than both class and race relations (to say nothing of social democratic, socialist, and communist possibilities). Previously, capitalists had eagerly employed the colonial legacy of paternalistic labor procurement to undermine working-class challenges. As Bonacich explains, "Employer paternalism led black workers to feel they had more to gain by allying with capital than with white labor," therein enabling capitalists to employ race to divide labor as a class.[61] The labor movement proved too small to take race on at a systemic level, instead retreating to organize white workers through the exclusion of blacks. This strategy largely failed by the 1930s, with union membership collapsing, meat cutters in East St. Louis dropping from 1,500 to 30, and the Amalgamated Association of Iron, Steel, and Tin Workers hemorrhaging from 365,000 to just 3,000.

Only in partnership with the state through New Deal legislation could working-class interests challenge the racialized system. In the 1930s, the Wagner Act and the Fair Labor Standards Act established real protections against capitalists' racially divisive strategies. Unions, especially the CIO, successfully recruited blacks to unions and partnered with black organizations such as the NAACP and the Urban League. Black union membership climbed from 50,000 in the 1930s to 1.25 million by the end of World War II.[62] As for the capitalists, in agreeing to the corporatist compromise, they achieved "high levels of trade and capital flows," high levels of investment, and state-enforced limitations on cutthroat competition through the tight regulation of financial markets.[63] Since Marx or before, scholars have emphasized the uniqueness of industrial class relations. But my work shows their singularity in racial terms: for the first time since early colonialism, white proletarians saw their racial interests as actually harmful to their class interests.

Many indicators show the success of the Keynesian compromise. Union membership held steady in the 30 percent range until the 1970s.[64] Unemployment stayed low, generally below 5 percent.[65] Inequality had been mitigated, with the top 10 percent of incomes dropping from taking 45 percent of all income to hold steady at 35 percent until the 1980s.[66] Poverty rates dropped from a high of 22.4 percent to a historic low of 11 percent in 1973.[67] For the capitalist, worker productivity doubled between 1950 and 1976.[68] And an unprecedented twenty years of steady but low levels of inflation between 1950 and 1970 provided for healthy regular capital accumulation.[69] In other words, economic stability, high wages, and robust profits made workers and owners mutually invested in corporatist industrialism, marginalizing the rentiers and their paternalist organization of society.

Racially, this class compromise between workers and capital eclipsed the utility of white proletarians serving as the middle tripartheid group. And the overall growth in manufacturing, wage relations, and the concomitant power of the bourgeoisie undermined racist rentier rule. As such, racial inequality decreased. For instance, migration to the industrializing U.S. North combined with unionization to shrink the racial wage gap between 1940 and 1950: where once black workers made forty-eight cents for every dollar white workers earned, in 1950, they earned sixty-one cents.[70] While the gap remained sizable, this was a huge, 27 percent increase in proportional wages at a time when all wages were rising. But the 1960s U.S. in no way amounted to a paradise of racial equality. Arguably, part of the Civil Rights Movement emerged from limited but regularly stifled black male upward mobility, such as this growth in black incomes getting undercut by reactionary racist legislation.[71]

The class struggle between white workers and owners therein provided the first systemic means for potential deracialization. Seeing the industrial revolution through the lens of its colonial origins means that white class struggles over the control of the means of production also involved a struggle over the terms of racial domination (a similar statement could be made about gender). Through industrial struggles, white owners and white labor negotiated the extent and manner over which white workers would manage the racial hierarchy on behalf of elites. How much patronage would workers receive, and in what forms, for serving as the racial intermediary group? How much would white workers' well-being depend upon their subordination of the racialized Other? Such issues played out in complex and frequently contradictory ways, with outcomes under similar conditions having disparate racial outcomes. But in each, the independent dynamics of race played a constituent part of these class struggles.

To put it another way, the less whites worked in their role as intermediaries in the paternalistic racial stratification system, the better off they were as wage-earning workers in the class stratification system. And since the bourgeoisie shared anti-rentier positions, this was a real possibility. On the other hand, if rentiers could make the continued racial stratification of labor serve industrialists' needs, rentiers could pull the bourgeoisie onto their side, making paternalism useful to industrialization such that the rentiers would persevere, as would the racial hierarchy.

By 1970, rising contradictions and crises presaged the unwinding of the Fordist compromise. Capitalists had to choose between two extremes. Either they continued deracializing through an enhanced partnership with their cross-class labor allies and agreed to dramatic increases in the socialization of the means of production, or they deepened racialization by aligning with rentiers. This would entail capitalists subjecting themselves to a new radical regulatory regime based on windfall profits instead of Fordist steady growth. And it meant unleashing the financial interests that the Keynesian compromise had vowed to never again let run wild. Historical struggle determined the outcome. And, as I hope to make clear in the next sections, industrial capitalism benefited heavily from the rentier-managed imperial flow of capital from the periphery to the center.

Third-World Development

Understanding the scope of the industrial challenge to rentier racism requires understanding the integration of core and peripheral capitalist areas. How much could industrialization in one area challenge the globality of white supremacy? How much could deracialized class relations persist while integrated into world-spanning colonial race relations? How did the persistence of colonial race relations in the Third World affect industrial social relations in the core? Could deracialization happen in one area and not others? Did colonial persistence undermine the industrial challenge, support it in some way, or have no effect at all?

The general answer is that colonialism made itself useful to industrialization and, in so doing, undermined the deracialization project, making industrialization dependent upon racialized rentier rule and thus giving the rentiers a power base from which to continually challenge industrial deracialization. While North American workers experimented with overcoming the racial organization of society and the rentier, the fruits of the Golden Age largely reinforced the colonial order in South America. In Peru, increasingly successful indigenous mobilizations against landlords resulted in a progressive military coup, with the government of General Juan Velasco (1968–75) instituting one of the largest ever land reform programs.[72] But these reforms altered rather than overcame the terms of racialized rentier rule. The powerful simply created new means to dominate locally, such as through staffing the agrarian reform offices; monopolizing key local resources, such as transportation, money lending, and hiring; and openly resorting to violence.[73] The new political entity of peasant communities granted natives political autonomy but strangled these by forcing all resource acquisition through the old clientelist networks. In all, "the revolutionary armed forces reproduced the traditional top-down vertical structures of domination of the oligarchic period."[74]

The military government, however, did refashion the tools of patronage into the productive sphere, qualitatively changing the type of patronage and the ideology rationalizing the rural-urban relations.[75] Under the ideological banner of "the land for those who work it," the new state patron focused on issues of farming infrastructure and markets. The greatest promised patronage was the land itself, but the actual redistribution provided few positive results.[76] From this point forward, however, paternalist control of the countryside achieved a dynamic new ideological cover: economic development. The superior position of the patron was therein reconstructed to promise improved material well-being for the populace.

Racially, developmentalism strengthened the tripartheid middle group of *mestizos* who came to embody the new paradigm. Throughout twentieth-century Latin America, governments and societies variously turned from ideas of inherent racial superiority toward an all-inclusive model of the *mestizo* "Cosmic Race"—a *sui generis* people emerging from the union of natives and Europeans.[77] *Mestizaje* (becoming *mestizo*) newly promised universal citizenship through a celebration of the native heritages of the Americas—though only through assimilationist mixing with European stock.

Rather than overcoming the racialization of society, *mestizaje* helped solve the dilemma faced by the aristocratic *criollo* (white coastal elite) order when confronted by forces pushing for modernist forms of inclusivity.[78] *Mestizaje* effectively splintered subaltern groups, renovating racism through delivering "a double blow, denigrating the unassimilated while inciting the assimilated to wage an endless struggle against the 'Indian within.'"[79] Citizenship became more inclusive, but only through creating a new sector whose rights depended upon continually proving their deservingness by denigrating natives.[80]

Mestizaje therein reconstructs Indians as anti-modern and a serious impediment to the advancement of society. Meanwhile, the fluid, vague, and multifaceted culturally determined racial distinctions within the *mestizo* "race hidden as a culture," and between *mestizos* and Indians, generated continuous intergroup discord.[81] People had to constantly struggle to position themselves within the multiple gradations of the *mestizo* hierarchy while distancing themselves from The Indian—*lo Indio*.[82] Ideologies changed in order to justify continued inequalities, *mestizaje* regularly finding new ways for people to deny real racial differences, thereby intensifying racism.[83] The shift to *mestizaje* thereby provided *criollos* with a motivated force to newly police racial boundaries—and in such a way that largely did not threaten aristocratic *criollo* rule.

In the Velasco reforms, *mestizos* staffed most of the urban development agencies upon which rural villagers depended for resources. And acquiring status and employment in the industrializing urban coastal areas required cultural assimilation to *mestizo* norms. Further, the industrialization policies of subsidizing urban areas with cheap rural food created some of the greatest racial divides. The very well-being of the urban *mestizo* workers depended upon the price controls undercutting rural native incomes. Not only did this new focus on development, then, make people's economic well-being track with their race, but it enhanced the earlier predication of *mestizo* privileges upon native subordination, now spelled out in clear economic terms. Under these conditions, urbanization flourished, with peasants fleeing the stagnant rural economy in favor of the dynamic subsidized cities. The census numbers of indigenous people decreased massively at this time, far outstripping birth, death, and intermixture rates. Nelson Manrique explains this as reflecting (*mestizo*) urban growth on the coast at the expense of the rural, indigenous-associated *sierra*.[84] That is, acquiring urban jobs meant giving up one's indigeneity. Or to put it more broadly, despite developmentalism's promise to improve everyone's well-being, participation came through celebrating the *mestizo* and deprecating the Indian.

The new developmentalism also reinvigorated the atomization of native political engagement while obscuring the racialized content of the policies. Explicitly reformist in character, by legally transforming natives from Indians to peasants the government tossed out natives' patrimonial land rights, replacing them with class rights to work the soil. This successfully defused native struggles away from any indigenous liberatory ideas of transforming the state and toward the exploitative atrocities of local landlords. The state therein became the peasants' champion, removing the rapacious *gamonales*, but severely limiting reforms to the highly local.[85]

As with much of the rest of Latin America, the lofty goals of developmentalist Peru actually resulted in the Lost Decade of heavy indebtedness. Even the largely authoritarian Velasco regime failed to tackle inequality, with subsequent civilian governments choosing to orient their economies toward financing their loans rather than alienating the rentier elite. As many have shown, international development assistance proved a mechanism for propping up authoritarian leaders faithful to the United States.[86] Putting it in explicitly racial terms, though, shows how rather than challenging rentier rule, the international development infrastructure exacerbated internal inequalities to tie rentiers closer together into a worldwide mechanism of extraction from the periphery to the core:

a global white supremacy. And later adept refinancing only increased capital flows and white interconnectedness.

Rentier Racism in the Core

Similar relations of racist colonial dependency existed amid industrialization in the United States, experienced through such policies as affirmative action and welfare that similarly sold themselves as investing in the well-being of racialized peoples. Black agitation in North America gained some of its strongest victories in the form of affirmative action. But as Stokely Carmichael pointed out, these investments worked at least partially to recruit the best prepared among the black population to work at the behest of the dominant white culture.[87] Herein the talented tenth becomes dangerously Janus-faced, owing loyalty to the dominant culture that provided it with unique resources while serving as a unique conduit for their brethren to access the outside world.[88] Thus, they became a new part of the middle-stratum managerial class, structured to at least partially police the subaltern for the benefit of the elite.

Welfare, the other form of investment for most of the rest of the subaltern population, proved highly colonial.

> As the study of Piven and Cloward (1971, chaps. 1, 4) suggests, the distribution of poor relief is designed to meet the conditions for dual dependency upon the state on the one hand and the employer on the other, so that labor may be mobilized and distributed to accommodate the changing demands of the economy. Poor relief, therefore, may be regarded as a functional equivalent of migrant labor, in that both perform the same regulatory function, cushioning the seasonal labor requirements of the agricultural industry.[89]

That is, the elites structured welfare as disempowering of blacks, as a specific means to control labor so that it could be exploited—or not—as needed. Welfare provided resources in such a way that it made recipients dependent and vulnerable to exploitation. The actual functions of the system, of course, enjoyed the ideological cover of empowering through providing resources and therein bringing the downtrodden into the miracles of capitalism.

Meanwhile, the middle racial stratum grew and diversified under corporatism. This provided some openings for challenging the racialized paternalism upon which the system depended. But it also generated new and innovative ways to actively participate, frequently in ways that obscured the racial payoff. As Herbert Gans points out, many diverse sectors thrived off the latent functions of the undeserving poor.[90] Well-meaning social workers, for instance, help perpetuate the system through their palliative efforts at making it less harsh on individuals. Academics receive high salaries for decrying the injustice of the system. Thus, even when they have knowledge about the system and their place in it, they still immediately benefit from the status quo.[91]

Herein the specter of color-blind racism creates powerful ideological tools for indoctrinating the relatively privileged. In their highly segregated milieus, the recently emerged white middle class enjoyed the fruits of privilege, seeing them as normal and totally unrelated to race or hierarchy.[92] Such spaces enable them to think themselves nonracist and fully deserving of the privileges they do not even see as privileges.[93] Every aspect of their lives—home, school, work, and leisure—exist free from the troubles of the global racial political economy. Their everyday existence therein inculcates beliefs that they are innocent and separate from the injustice in the rest of the world. Indeed, their segregation enables them to believe they are doing good through acts of charitable giving that actually reinforce the elitist paternalism that runs the system.[94] While potentially reflective about the bubbles they live in, they spend little of their privileges on confronting the racist system that makes their lifestyles viable. Instead, they can readily blame their non-color-blind counterparts whose short-term well-being is tied much more overtly to the racist system.

In short, industrial capitalism hegemonically characterized corporatism. At the core of this global system, the centrality of profit, the wage relation, and the continued innovation of the means of production created political space that challenged rentier rule. For the first time since early colonialism, proletarians, in limited partnership with the state and capitalists, gained through fighting for their class rights over their racial privileges. As such, racial inequality diminished while overall well-being increased. But rentiers persevered through making themselves useful to industrialists. In much of the Third World as well as in peripheral areas within industrialized countries, rentiers held sway. They provided raw materials, bought market surpluses, and generally managed discontent through maintaining their aristocratic systems. While achieving some cross-race alliances, middle groups' prosperity also developed new forms of racism that perpetuated, justified, and obscured forms of racial privileges that helped maintain rentier status. As corporatism fell into crisis, society faced a divergent decision between greater anti-racist socialization of the means of production and unleashing the gentry and their racist rentier economics.

Neoliberal White Supremacy: Return of the Rentier and Racial Caste

> People getting their fundamental interests wrong is what American political life is all about.
> Thomas Frank, *What's the Matter with Kansas?*

Untold volumes of research have detailed the corporatist crisis and subsequent shift to neoliberalism. But very little articulates this in explicitly racial terms, with the exceptions spelling out neoliberalism as class-related processes with racial consequences. Almost nothing explains neoliberalism as inherently racial, as an explicit form of racial rule with its own independent racial logics. Understanding the core dynamics of racialized society, as generated during colonialism and persevering through corporatism, requires a rereading of today's prevailing relations to see the inherent racialization shaping them. The core neoliberal social relations then involve a polarization between the triumphant lordly rentier and a vast racialized multitude, a population William I. Robinson estimates at over 80 percent in some countries and over half the total global population.[95] From this polarization, neoliberalism created a virulent police force from the middle stratum whose newfound uncertainties and fears motivated its members to unleash much more overt and brutal forms of social control upon the racialized masses lest novel forms of marginalization also sweep them to oblivion.

To get to this point, race played two key and largely untold roles in the corporatist crisis that ushered in neoliberalism. The corporatist compromise ended as business came to believe labor had gained too much control over the means of production.[96] Racially, the successful international anti-colonial mobilizations of the 1950–60s, such as the Civil Rights movements in the U.S. and peasant land seizures in Peru, increasingly disempowered the racial antagonisms between middle and bottom groups. Such racial reconciliation granted class power and threatened capitalist and rentier alike. Second, increasing elite drives toward monopoly and the deregulation of speculative financial markets greatly empowered rentiers—while subjecting industrialists to a radical new set of regulations based on windfall profits rather than, say, workplace safety, wages, or the environment.[97] Thus, a highly polarized situation emerged in which capitalists had to choose between their labor partners in the class system and their rentier partners in the racial system. Though fraught, capitalists ended up siding with the rentiers and engaged in an extremist racial war to undermine working-class cohesion.

The Neoliberal Gentry

The neoliberal unleashing of speculative financial markets as the ultimate overseer of the global economy empowered rentiers to once again become the uncontested world leaders reigning over a rigid social hierarchy. Rather than a return to older forms of colonialism, however, neoliberal reforms creatively invigorated rentier economics, reinventing old colonial relations with a host of new tools. Indeed, neoliberals have successfully repackaged these old relations as the cutting edge of economic innovation, convincing a broad swath of the population of their inherent merit.

Central to this process is the return to prominence of primitive accumulation, what David Harvey terms accumulation by dispossession: concentrating wealth under conditions of weak growth through taking rather than making. Great innovation has occurred in converting all manner of formerly public resources into private gain and the amassing of vast fortunes. But ultimately this is a political process about changing the rules of the game such that money can be attached to things that it had not been previously. And this specifically occurs through new legislation creating artificial shortages: rent, not productivity. New rules allowed for "fiendish, Frankenstein monsters of financial engineering," in the words of apostate Paul Samuelson.[98] These complex tools did the primitive work of accumulation by dispossession, Saskia Sassen explains—for instance, converting ostensible vehicles for black U.S. homeownership, loans, into mechanisms for transferring black wealth to rich whites.[99]

The aggressive assertion of intellectual property rights unleashes fantastic creativity into accumulation by dispossession. This also entices political liberals into the fold by obscuring their dispossessing activities as innovation. As Juliet Schor points out, economic efficiency prices goods at the cost of producing the last batch.[100] Open-source computing therefore creates the greatest efficiency, especially as knowledge begets knowledge, and proprietary access inefficiently restricts its development. Yet the political rules have come to allow people to amass enormous fortunes through making knowledge proprietary, even when their product does not make any money. In classic rentier fashion, legislatively created shortages (proprietary knowledge) rather than productivity amassed fortunes. The inventors of the computer application Snapchat, for instance, made billions from their IPO, though their product had not yet earned any profits. Herein we see the great windfalls available through the privatization of what Marx termed the general intellect.[101] And stock markets fell in line, shifting in focus from delivering funding for production to seeking such rent-driven bonanza payouts.

Now rentiers dominate the global political economy, reinvigorating some age-old practices. The wealthiest people in the world amassed their fantastic fortunes through accumulation by dispossession rather than profit. Carlos Slim acquired his mostly through the privatization of telecommunications, Bill Gates through establishing the laws that made computer code proprietary against the tradition of open source, George Soros on currency speculation, and folks like Charles and David Koch through old-fashioned inheritance and coal extraction.

Not surprisingly, these figures invest their wealth in the traditional rentier fashions that protect their rent-collecting abilities, stunting rather than encouraging the development of innovative alternatives. Transnational oil and coal companies, for instance, while collecting subsidies and proprietary access from governments, have spent billions on stifling the development of solar and alternative energy. On the flip side, they advocate for what they call free trade and open market policies, even as their politically created monopolies openly violate the precepts of these terms. As such, these policies function to funnel money from the poor to the wealthy or, in David Harvey's words, are "draconian policies designed to restore and consolidate capitalist class power."[102] Harkening directly back to feudal paternalism, these elites insist that their charity efforts will redress hardships in the system. They therein once again use others' misery to shore up the highly unequal system and openly advocate for prioritizing relations of dependence rather than merit or humanism.

Neoliberalism therein enables an aristocracy reigning at a distance from their lessers, with many, in Silicon Valley at least, believing they are doing good through their dispossession. Further, though, it innovates colonialism, realizing the great colonial dream of ruling free of their bitter dependence on labor. Herein the emphasis of control shifts. There is always an issue of managing the discontent of the disaffected. But under colonialism, the main focus centered on controlling the population enough to render them exploitable. With the neoliberal turn away from exploitation, the question centers on controlling a population superfluous to the functioning of the system.[103] And a central part of this question focuses on how to extract rents from this population to support the overall aristocratic order.

From Class Solidarity to Racial Privilege

In the neoliberal tripartite racial system, policies have heavily eroded the middle stratum that gained so much during corporatism. In North America, whites predominated in the middle. But in South America, *mestizos* and some whites tended to hold these positions. Capitalism's economic uniqueness enabled successful political mobilization because capitalists needed workers as profit depended upon productivity. The elite consented to collective bargaining and higher wages because it also provided the requisite stable and skilled work force.

The turn to financialization breaks this link and undermines the economic rationale for higher wages, undercutting the wage-relation foundation of middle group stability.

> The bourgeoisie in the classic sense thus tends to disappear: capitalists reappear as a subset of salaried workers, as managers who are qualified to earn more by virtue of their competence (which is why pseudo-scientific "evaluation" is crucial: it legitimizes disparities). Far from being limited to managers, the category of workers earning a surplus wage extends to all sorts of experts, administrators, public servants, doctors, lawyers, journalists, intellectuals and artists.[104]

Neoliberalism alters the terms for deciding wages for even the most privileged workers, generating new forms of uncertainty that force workers to compete across their class where they used to cooperate.

> The evaluative procedure used to decide which workers receive a surplus wage is an arbitrary mechanism of power and ideology, with no serious link to actual competence; the surplus wage exists not for economic but for political reasons: to maintain a "middle class" for the purpose of social stability.[105]

The middle groups must turn from economically leveraging wages to politically garnering paternalistic privileges; from class solidarity for challenging the elite to endearing oneself and one's sector to the wealthy. And they must make their case in terms of maintaining the stability of the new aristocratic order, of helping inure or coerce people into accepting lordly inequalities.

While modern jurisprudence claims it has put an end to them, status-based relationships therein now increasingly predominate across most sectors. As such, these relations determine the distribution of resources. And they do so not based on the economic rationale of maximum return to investment, but on political rationales of maintaining aristocratic rule.

Distribution relies on endearment to the wealthy, convincing them about how they want to hand out their charity. For instance, public higher education, the bedrock of a productive economy, depends for an increasingly large portion of its budget on donations rather than sound economic investments.[106] And career advice from the hegemonic business community says to *Forget a Mentor, Find a Sponsor*.[107] That is, in the new economy, paternalist protections matter more than skills or merit.

Facing such insecurity and the fear that comes with it, the interests of these middle groups no longer center on class solidarity to challenge the elite but on endorsing the forms of austerity that will harm the proletariat, siphoning money to the wealthy while hopefully leaving middle group's privileged surplus wage untouched. That is, through instability rather than inclusion, neoliberalism resolves the middle groups' divided loyalty fully in favor of the aristocracy, a logic that unfurls new deprivations and overt forms of racialized social control upon the bottom group.

Neoliberalism consigns this bottom multitude to misery, in what Mike Davis terms a *Planet of Slums*.[108] But this is an exclusion through the means of incorporation. As a growing body of literature details, these large superfluous populations face expulsions of various sorts.[109] Rather than being a source of potentially exploitable labor, they are, now, finally in the way. Their removal, however, is largely of a specific tripartheid colonial character.

I argue that they are removed *to* conditions of severe paternalist dependence upon groups above them in the racial hierarchy. Instead of being rendered exploitable, they are rendered extractable. For instance, in my own research, I have found that the privatization of indigenous lands in highland Peru converts indigenous land rights to rent-collecting powers for *mestizo*s who predominantly reside in the city but who have strong rural connections.[110] Such a shift undercuts horizontal ties in indigenous spaces and instead makes rural natives beholden almost exclusively to urban *mestizo*s. Without guaranteed access to land for subsistence purposes, rural indigenous life now requires paying rents to the urbanites who control the land. Given poor productivity and markets, people will inevitably fail to pay their rents. This empowers urbanites to take what is due them in any form, including the *prima nocta* rights of feudalism or even neoliberal novelties like organ harvesting. In either case, the indigenous become reduced to the debt slavery of colonialism, fully at the behest of a new set of masters given wide latitude on how to find a use for them.

For their own part, the middle stratum urban *mestizo*s face the precariousness of weak labor and product markets. They, too, face a massive squeeze. But they have proprietary access to rural areas and indigenous populations. Thus, neoliberalism incentivizes them to squeeze their rural connections ever more, extracting whatever they can from the now degraded natives and push these up the racial hierarchy.

In a parallel example, the prison industrial complex in North America exerts miserable forms of total control for paternalist ends. Herein the middle-stratum groups also benefit from collecting rents on these populations. In the case of mass incarceration, though, the paternalist nature of political relations stands out starkly. Politicians farm the patronage of building prisons out to predominantly white areas hit hard by deindustrialization. This becomes a kind of jobs program that teaches a very narrow range of skills but provides income for loyal constituents. With their well-being depending on more incarceration, white areas become highly pro-punishment. Rural whites therein cling to these paternalistic jobs with overtly racist tough-on-crime jealousy, even though these incomes fail to meet the industrial jobs they replaced.[111]

No real productivity comes out of this system. It is merely a costly way to pay for loyalty and one that continues the feudal contempt for life. Further, through the process of prison gerrymandering, patron politicians ensure their positions by counting the racialized victims of this system, the prisoners, as nonvoting constituents. Thus, harkening back to the antebellum two-thirds clause, the white folks in these areas vote on behalf of the black incarcerated, and clearly against their interests.[112]

Processes of exclusion extend beyond the example of mass incarceration. The incarcerial state is hegemonic in this era, though, and therein as the leading edge of the relations of rule defines the larger terms under which the other groups relate. For instance, innovations in this sector have dramatically increased the number of minorities incarcerated in immigration detention centers. Conditions are abysmal. Politically, though, this innovation denies fundamental human rights. One lawsuit, for instance, argues that inmates awaiting the rulings on their immigration status, who are therefore held without being charged—denied habeas corpus—are forced to work for prison wages and therein toil in a slave labor system.[113] Thus, in the larger global racism framework, the expanding prison industrial complex defines much of the overall system: a method for funneling minimal patronage from the European white elite to their loyal retainers, whose maintenance of the system provides daily reminders of how bad things can get for the faithless. Fearing such plights helps drive the system onward, the degradation of the criminalized inspiring ever more tough-on-crime stances.

In sum, neoliberalism reveals itself as an innovative revitalization of racialized colonialism. It enables the imposition of a rigid, race-based social hierarchy. And, outdoing colonialism, it sets up the vast majority of the global population for degrading rent extraction, totally at the mercy of middle groups. These middle groups in turn face unvarnished precariousness. They therefore contemptuously regard lower groups in the hierarchy as worthy only of extraction, so that the middle groups do not share their fate. The elite thereby successfully recruit the middle stratum to do their dirty work while keeping distanced from it themselves.

Herein the elite establish multiple self-reinforcing mechanisms to safeguard and enhance their positions. As under colonialism, the elite feed the middle patronage as the only safety against impoverishment. Loyalty proves the strongest defense against precariousness. As such, the elite recruit the middle to enforce the very policies that created middle group insecurity. Further, the middle group faces the antipathy of the bottom groups. Subaltern groups tend heavily to visit their resentment upon their middle managers. This, however, helps perpetuate the very fracturing and precariousness upon which the system thrives. Thus, echoing one of the great innovations of colonialism, the elite use hostility toward the system to shore up the system itself.

While analysts such as Slavoj Žižek put this in class terms, this tripartite group dynamic makes more sense in the racial terms I have so far outlined. The global rentier class has set itself so far above all others, they behave as though they believe they are inherently better than everyone else, with their aristocratic culture strongly associated with white European sophistication. They have degraded much of the world's population, rendering them irredeemable to the global system. And they rule through promises of relative privileges for the middle group rather than promises of upward mobility. But most importantly, the logic of class relations no longer prevails. Most tellingly, the middle group does not predominantly act according to the economic logic of class, but to the personalistic logic of race. That is, the elite oversee a zero-sum racial game that accrues all wealth to them, rather than a growth-based capitalist game of fighting for control over the means of production, with income accruing accordingly. Neoliberalism ends the class dynamics that wrought racial alliances under corporatism and instead spells out middle-group interests in terms of racial contestation and the marginalization of the Other.

Conclusion

A major piece of the puzzle of grasping racial stratification as a truly global system involves understanding the role and perseverance of the rentier elite. Rentiers did the work of colonialism through setting up and maintaining local fiefdoms. They therein benefited from crown largesse and employed it to do crown business. These petty kingdoms managed local discontent and marshaled local labor through fracturing and creating dependency among the local populations. While initially content to keep the standard European forms of domination, crises in colonial rule inspired them to turn to vicious forms of racism. Rather than undoing the feudal nature of rule, the racial turn embedded it much more deeply into the fabric of society, coloring it anew in racial stratification. The great innovation involved a tripartite system of elites, now deemed white, employing the patronage of limited racial privilege and the fear of racialized degradation to hire a middle stratum to police the racially subjugated bottom. This now racially based autocracy enabled pillage on a much grander scale, windfalls that eventually helped usher in industrialization.

The unprecedented productivity of industrialization brought one of the greatest historical threats to rentier rule. The rising bourgeoisie challenged rentier predominance and eventually, with Bretton Woods, the existence of rentier economics. Crucially, the hegemony of the wage relation uniquely empowered the middle stratum of the tripartite system to fight against their paternalistic racial position through fighting *for* their class rights. Worker reconciliation of traditional middle-stratum racial, ethnic, and national divides helped them align with the capitalists in the fight for the bourgeois mode of production against rentier economics. The rentiers persevered by making patronage politics serve industrial needs, maintaining a vestigial race-based colonialism within the workings of industrialism.

By the 1970s, the corporatist compromise faced a major crisis as increased worker power began threatening capitalist positions. Rather than siding with the increasingly racially reconciled subaltern populations to preserve much of the bourgeois mode of production through making it even more socialist, the bourgeoisie turned to gentry, their minor corporatist partner, such that "the means of the extravagant rentier" did not diminish but came to dominate. Racial hierarchy became hegemonic, the tripartheid structure gaining predominance over the class structure. Misery, poverty, and insecurity spread while rentiers amassed unimaginable fortunes. Racism became more overt as middle group well-being started depending once again on paternalistic controls over subalterns, their class alliances splintered anew by nation, race, and ethnicity.

The centuries-old system of white supremacy therein came to dominate through neoliberalism. Grasping the racial nature of these relations requires understanding racial hierarchy as a truly global system. While nation became an important intersecting factor beginning in the late 1800s, confining racial analysis to such borders limits its utility. Racial domination is both more local and international than this. The rentier sits ensconced in a worldwide network of competing peers, each variously propped up by webs of racialized patronage. And the subaltern groups in their great global variety share similar experiences in the forms of oppression they face. Specifically, rentier elite rule employs the powerful tool of a precariously racially privileged middle group benefitting from the misery of the bottom.

While overall this is a sordid story full of cruelty and suffering, it actually provides some substantive positive openings. Grasping the politically rational but economically irrational nature of racist rentier rule means that considerable funds have always been available for constructing a humanely based society. Profligate waste—of lives and treasure—riddled rentier rule. And these elites cavalierly entered wars of attrition throughout history. Unwilling to alter the structure of society because alternatives threatened their standing, they nevertheless expended untold resources on preserving the system. From the outside perspective of someone without enough money to regard such behavior as normal, sheer cruelty would seem to motivate the hoarding of wealth beyond what a person needs to live in opulent luxury, as revealed by the Mossack Fonseca scandal.[114] Considerable leeway exists, then, for a truly democratic organization of the economy and the experiments and failures it almost inevitably must face. And, even under the worst conditions, subaltern populations have continuously generated creative alternatives directly out of the system's many contradictions.

Notes

1. Slavoj Žižek, "The Revolt of the Salaried Bourgeoisie," *London Review of Books* 34, no. 2 (January 26, 2012): 9–10, citing Fredric Jameson, *Representing Capital* (London: Verso, 2011), 149.

2. David Harvey, *A Brief History of Neoliberalism* (New York: Oxford University Press, 2005), 19.

3. The otherwise informative essays most central to this high-heat, low-light debate are: Eduardo Bonilla-Silva, "Rethinking Racism," *American Sociological Review* 62, no. 3 (1997): 465–80; Eduardo Bonilla-Silva, "More than Prejudice: Restatement, Reflections, and New Directions in Critical Race Theory," *Sociology of*

Race and Ethnicity 1, no. 1 (2015): 73–87; Loïc Wacquant, "Towards an Analytic of Racial Domination," *Political Power and Social Theory* 11 (1997): 221–34; Mara Loveman, "Is 'Race' Essential?," *American Sociological Review* 64, no. 6 (1999): 891; Andreas Wimmer, "The Making and Unmaking of Ethnic Boundaries: A Multilevel Process Theory," *American Journal of Sociology* 113, no. 4 (2008): 970–1,022; and Rogers Brubaker, *Ethnicity without Groups* (Cambridge, Mass: Harvard University Press, 2004). A recent book purporting to elucidate a truly global system disappointingly insists, to the contrary, on the total uniqueness of race in each nation rather than an intersectionality of race and nation; Mustafa Emirbayer and Matthew Desmond, *The Racial Order* (Chicago: University of Chicago Press, 2015).

4. Charles Mills, "Global White Supremacy," in *White Privilege: Essential Readings on the Other Side of Racism*, ed. Paula S. Rothenberg (New York: Worth, 2000).

5. Callum Ward and Manuel B. Aalbers, "Virtual Special Issue Editorial Essay: 'The Shitty Rent Business': What's the Point of Land Rent Theory?," *Urban Studies* 53, no. 9 (2016): 1,780.

6. Michael Hardt, "The Common in Communism," *Rethinking Marxism* 22, no. 3 (2010): 348.

7. Hardt, "Common in Communism," 348, quoting John Maynard Keynes, *The General Theory of Employment, Interest, and Money* (London: Macmillan, 1936), 376.

8. Guy Standing, *The Corruption of Capitalism: Why Rentiers Thrive and Work Does Not Pay* (London: Biteback, 2017).

9. Theodore Allen, *The Invention of the White Race* (London: Verso, 1994).

10. Žižek, "Revolt of the Salaried Bourgeoisie."

11. William I. Robinson, *A Theory of Global Capitalism: Production, Class, and State in a Transnational World* (Baltimore: Johns Hopkins University Press, 2004).

12. Michael Burawoy, "The Functions and Reproduction of Migrant Labor: Comparative Material from Southern Africa and the United States," *American Journal of Sociology* 81, no. 5 (March 1976): 1,050–87; Erik Wright, *Interrogating Inequality* (London: Verso, 1994).

13. See Hugh Thomas, *Rivers of Gold: The Rise of the Spanish Empire, from Columbus to Magellan* (New York: Random House, 2003).

14. George M. Fredrickson, *White Supremacy: A Comparative Study in American and South African History* (Oxford: Oxford University Press, 1982).

15. Karl Polanyi, *The Great Transformation* (Boston: Beacon Press, 1944), 93.

16. M. W. Beresford, *The Lost Villages of England* (Stroud, Gloucestershire: Sutton, 1998).

17. Fredrickson, *White Supremacy*, 60.

18. Bernard Bailyn, *Barbarous Years: The Peopling of British North America; The Conflict of Civilizations, 1600–1675* (New York: Vintage, 2013).

19. Bailyn, *Barbarous Years*, and John Wareing, *Indentured Migration and the Servant Trade from London to America, 1618–1718: "There Is Great Want of Servants"* (New York: Oxford University Press, 2017).

20. Allan Kulikoff, *Tobacco and Slaves: The Development of Southern Cultures in the Chesapeake, 1680–1800* (Chapel Hill: Published for the Institute of Early American History and Culture, Williamsburg, Virginia, by the University of North Carolina Press, 1982).

21. Kulikoff, *Tobacco*.

22. James L. Huston, *The British Gentry, the Southern Planter, and the Northern Family Farmer: Agriculture and Sectional Antagonism in North America* (Baton Rouge: Louisiana State University Press, 2015), 136.

23. Huston, *British Gentry*, 58–62.

24. Edmund S. Morgan, *American Slavery, American Freedom: The Ordeal of Colonial Virginia* (New York: Norton, 1975).

25. Huston, *British Gentry*.

26. John Donoghue, "Indentured Servitude in the 17th Century English Atlantic: A Brief Survey of the Literature," *History Compass* 11, no. 10 (2013): 893.

27. Ibid.

28. Mauricio Drelichman and Hans-Joachim Voth, "Lending to the Borrower from Hell: Debt and Default in the Age of Philip II," *Economic Journal* 121, no. 557 (2011): 1,205–27, and Henry Kamen, *Empire: How Spain Became a World Power, 1492–1763* (New York: HarperCollins, 2003).

29. John Hemming, *The Conquest of the Incas* (New York: Harcourt, Brace, Jovanovich, 1970), and Peter Klarén, *Peru: Society and Nationhood in the Andes* (New York: Oxford University Press, 2000).

30. Hemming, *Conquest*, and Kim MacQuarrie, *The Last Days of the Incas* (New York: Simon & Schuster, 2007).

31. Arthur Scarritt, *Racial Spoils from Native Soils: How Neoliberalism Steals Indigenous Lands in Highland Peru* (Lanham, Md.: Lexington, 2015).

32. S. J. Stern, *Peru's Indian Peoples and the Challenge of Spanish Conquest: Huamanga to 1640* (Madison: University of Wisconsin Press, 1992), and Gonzalo Portocarrero, *Racismo y mestizaje y otros ensayos* (Lima: Fondo Ed. del Congreso del Perú, 2007).

33. Karen Spalding, "Social Climbers: Changing Patterns of Mobility among the Indians of Colonial Peru," *Hispanic American Historical Review* 50, no. 4 (1970): 653, and Stern, *Peru's Indian Peoples*.

34. Portocarrero, *Racismo*.

35. Stern, *Peru's Indian Peoples*, 44.

36. Ibid., and Klarén, *Peru: Society and Nationhood*.

37. Spalding, "Social Climbers," and Stern, *Peru's Indian Peoples*.

38. Scarritt, *Racial Spoils*.

39. Stern, *Peru's Indian Peoples*, and Scarritt, *Racial Spoils*.

40. Stern, *Peru's Indian Peoples*, and Portocarrero, *Racismo*.

41. Karen Spalding, "Hacienda-Village Relations in Andean Society to 1830," *Latin American Perspectives* 2, no. 1 (1974): 107–21; E. P. Grieshaber, "Hacienda-Indian Community Relations and Indian Acculturation: An Historiographical Essay," *Latin American Research Review* 14, no. 3 (1979): 107–28; Florencia Mallon, "Chronicle of a Path Foretold?," in *Shining and Other Paths* (Durham, N.C.: Duke University Press, 1998): 84–117.

42. Stern, *Peru's Indian Peoples*; Karen Spalding, "Kurakas and Commerce: A Chapter in the Evolution of Andean Society," *Hispanic American Historical Review* 53, no. 4 (1973): 581–99, and Klarén, *Peru: Society and Nationhood*.

43. Spalding, "Kurakas," and Scarritt, *Racial Spoils*.

44. Morgan, *American Slavery*, 221.

45. Jill Lepore, *The Name of War: King Philip's War and the Origins of American Identity* (New York: Knopf, 1998).

46. Horne, *Apocalypse*, 148.
47. Morgan, *American Slavery*, 273–75.
48. Ibid., 295.
49. Morgan, *American Slavery*, 328–37.
50. Wendy Warren, *New England Bound: Slavery and Colonization in Early America* (New York: Liveright: 2016).
51. Morgan, *American Slavery*, 329.
52. Ibid., 331.
53. Ibid., 336.
54. Ibid., 337.
55. Allen, *Invention of the White Race*, 242.
56. Ibid., 243.
57. Ibid., 245.
58. Ibid., 252.
59. Marx, "Manifesto."
60. William Greider, *One World, Ready or Not: The Manic Logic of Global Capitalism* (New York: Simon & Schuster, 1997).
61. Edna Bonacich, "Advanced Capitalism and Black/White Race Relations in the United States: A Split Labor Market Interpretation," *American Sociological Review* 41, no. 1 (1976): 43.
62. Ibid.
63. John Gerard Ruggie, "International Regimes, Transactions, and Change: Embedded Liberalism in the Postwar Economic Order," *International Organization* 36, no. 2, *International Regimes* (Spring 1982): 379–415; Bob Jessop, "Post-Fordism and the State," in *Comparative Welfare Systems*, ed Bent Greve (Basingstoke: Macmillan 1996), 165–84; Manfred B. Steger, *Globalization: A Very Short Introduction* (Oxford: Oxford University Press, 2009); Harvey, *Brief History of Neoliberalism*.
64. Bruce Western and Jake Rosenfeld, "Unions, Norms, and the Rise in U.S. Wage Inequality," *American Sociological Review* 76, no. 4 (2011): 513–37.
65. Harvey, *Brief History of Neoliberalism*.
66. Thomas Piketty, *Capital in the Twenty-First Century* (Cambridge, Mass.: The Belknap Press of Harvard University Press, 2014).
67. Jessica L. Semega, Kayla R. Fontenot, and Melissa A. Kollar, "Income and Poverty in the United States: 2016," Washington, D.C.: U.S. Census Bureau (2017), https://www.census.gov/content/dam/Census/library/publications/2017/demo/P60-259.pdf.
68. Mark J. Perry, "Phenomenal Gains in Manufacturing Productivity," American Enterprise Institute (2012), http://www.aei.org/publication/phenomenal-gains-in-manufacturing-productivity/.
69. Harvey, *Brief History of Neoliberalism*.
70. Thomas N. Maloney, "Wage Compression and Wage Inequality between Black and White Males in the United States, 1940–1960," *Journal of Economic History* 54, no. 2 (1994): 358–81.
71. William Sites and Virginia Parks, "What Do We Really Know about Racial Inequality? Labor Markets, Politics, and the Historical Basis of Black Economic Fortunes," *Politics & Society* 39, no. 1 (2011): 40–73.
72. This section relies heavily on Scarritt, *Racial Spoils*.
73. Pierre Van den Berghe and George Primov, *Inequality in the Peruvian Andes* (Columbia: University of Missouri Press, 1977); Jane Collins, *Unseasonal Migrations*

(Princeton, N.J.: Princeton University Press, 1988); Maria Lagos, *Autonomy and Power: The Dynamics of Class and Culture in Rural Bolivia* (Philadelphia: University of Pennsylvania Press, 1986); Deboarah Poole, ed., *Unruly Order: Violence, Power, and Cultural Identity in the High Provinces of Southern Peru* (Boulder, Colo.: Westview, 1994); José Luis Renique, "Political Violence, the State, and the Peasant Struggle for Land (Puno)," in Poole, *Unruly Order*, 223–46; Karl Zimmerer, *Changing Fortunes* (Berkeley: University of California Press, 1996).

74. Paulo Drinot, "Nation-Building, Racism and Inequality: Institutional Development in Peru in Historical Perspective," in *Making Institutions Work in Peru: Democracy, Development and Inequality Since 1980*, ed. John Crabtree (London: Institute for the Study of the Americas, University of London, 2006), 19.

75. Arthur Scarritt, "State of Discord: The Historic Reproduction of Racism in Highland Peru," *Postcolonial Studies* 15, no. 1 (2012): 23–44.

76. Cristobal Kay, "Achievements and Contradictions of the Peruvian Agrarian Reform," *Journal of Development Studies* 18, no 6 (1981): 141–70; Florencia Mallon, "Chronicle of a Path Foretold?," 84–117; Drinot, "Nation-Building."

77. José Vasconcelos, *La Raza Cósmica* (1925) (Los Angeles: California State University, 1979).

78. Nelson Manrique, "Modernity and Alternative Development in the Andes," in *Through the Kaleidoscope: The Experience of Modernity in Latin America*, ed. Vivian Schelling (New York: Verso, 2000), 219–47.

79. Charles R. Hale, "Rethinking Indigenous Politics in the Era of the 'Indio Permitido,'" *NACLA Report on the Americas* 38, no. 2 (2004): 17.

80. Arthur Scarritt, "Broker Fixed: The Racialized Social Structure and the Subjugation of Indigenous Populations in the Andes," *Critical Sociology* 37, no. 2 (2011): 153–77; J. G. Nugent, *El laberinto de la choledad* (Lima: Fundación Friedrich Ebert, 1992); Charles R. Hale, "Does Multiculturalism Menace? Governance, Cultural Rights and the Politics of Identity in Guatemala," *Journal of Latin American Studies* 34 (2002): 485–524.

81. J. C. Callirgos, *El racismo: La cuestión del otro (y de uno)* (Lima: DESCO Centro de Estudios y Promoción del Desarrollo, 1994).

82. Calligros, *El racismo*; Hale, "Rethinking"; Portocarrero, *Racismo*.

83. Calligros, *El racismo*; Marisol de la Cadena, *Indigenous Mestizos* (Durham, N.C.: Duke University Press, 2000); Hale, "Does Multiculturalism Menace?"

84. Nelson Manrique, *La piel y la pluma: Escritos sobre literatura, etnicidad y racismo* (San Isidro, Peru: CIDIAG, 1999).

85. Scarritt, *Racial Spoils*.

86. John Perkins, *The New Confessions of an Economic Hitman: How America Really Took Over the World* (London: Ebury, 2017); Graham Hancock, *Lords of Poverty: The Power, Prestige, and Corruption of the International Aid Business* (New York: Atlantic Monthly Press, 1992).

87. Stokely Carmichael and Charles V. Hamilton, *Black Power: The Politics of Liberation in America* (New York: Vintage, 1967).

88. William J. Wilson, *When Work Disappears: The World of the New Urban Poor* (New York: Knopf, 1996).

89. Burawoy, "Functions and Reproduction of Migrant Labor."

90. Herbert J. Gans, "The Positive Functions of Poverty," *American Journal of Sociology* 78, no. 2 (1972): 275–89.

91. Bonilla-Silva, "Rethinking Racism," 465–80.

92. Douglas S. Massey and Nancy A. Denton, *American Apartheid: Segregation and the Making of the Underclass* (Cambridge, Mass.: Harvard University Press, 1993).

93. Charles A. Gallagher, "Color-Blind Privilege: The Social and Political Functions of Erasing the Color Line in Post-Race America," *Race, Gender & Class* 10, no. 4 (2003): 22–37.

94. Joe R. Feagin, *Systemic Racism: A Theory of Oppression* (New York: Routledge, 2006).

95. Robinson, *Theory of Global Capitalism*.

96. Alan Nasser, "How the Oligarchy Gets Politicized," *CounterPunch* (2011), https://www.counterpunch.org/2011/11/15/how-the-oligarchy-gets-politicized/.

97. Steger, *Globalization*.

98. PBS News Hour, "Nobel Laureates Trace How the Economy Began to Fall Apart," PBS News Hour, Dec 26, 2008, https://www.pbs.org/newshour/show/nobel-laureates-trace-how-the-economy-began-to-fall-apart.

99. Saskia Sassen, "A Savage Sorting of Winners and Losers: Contemporary Versions of Primitive Accumulation," *Globalizations* 7, nos. 1–2 (2010): 23–50, and Saskia Sassen, *Expulsions: Brutality and Complexity in the Global Economy* (Cambridge, Mass.: The Belknap Press of Harvard University Press, 2014).

100. Juliet Schor, *Plenitude: The New Economics of True Wealth* (New York: Penguin, 2010), 19.

101. Žižek, "Revolt of the Salaried Bourgeoisie."

102. David Harvey, *The Enigma of Capital: And the Crises of Capitalism* (Oxford: Oxford University Press, 2010), 10.

103. Robinson, *Theory of Global Capitalism*.

104. Žižek, "Revolt of the Salaried Bourgeoisie."

105. Ibid.

106. Christopher Newfield, *The Great Mistake: How We Wrecked Public Universities and How We Can Fix Them* (Baltimore: Johns Hopkins University Press, 2016).

107. Sylvia Ann Hewlett, *(Forget a Mentor) Find a Sponsor: The New Way to Fast-Track Your Career* (Cambridge, Mass.: Harvard Business Review, 2013).

108. Mike Davis, *Planet of Slums* (London: Verso, 2006).

109. See, for example, Sassen, *Expulsions*.

110. Scarritt, *Racial Spoils*.

111. Heather Ann Thompson, "Why Mass Incarceration Matters: Rethinking Crisis, Decline, and Transformation in Postwar American History," *Journal of American History* 97, no. 3 (2010): 703–34.

112. Heather Ann Thompson, "How Prisons Change the Balance of Power in America," *Atlantic*, October 7, 2013, https://www.theatlantic.com/national/archive/2013/10/how-prisons-change-the-balance-of-power-in-america/280341/.

113. Colleen Slevin, "Former Aurora Immigration Detainees Challenge Private Prison's Labor Practices," *Denver Post*, June 22, 2017, https://www.denverpost.com/2017/06/22/former-aurora-detainees-challenge-labor-practices/.

114. Luke Harding, "Mossack Fonseca: Inside the Firm that Helps the Super-Rich Hide Their Money," *Guardian*, April 8, 2016, https://www.theguardian.com/news/2016/apr/08/mossack-fonseca-law-firm-hide-money-panama-papers.

Works Cited

Allen, Theodore. *The Invention of the White Race.* London: Verso, 1994.

Bailyn, Bernard. *Barbarous Years: The Peopling of British North America; The Conflict of Civilizations, 1600–1675.* New York: Vintage, 2013.

Beresford, M. W. *The Lost Villages of England.* Stroud, Gloucestershire: Sutton, 1998.

Bonacich, Edna. "Advanced Capitalism and Black/White Race Relations in the United States: A Split Labor Market Interpretation." *American Sociological Review* 41, no. 1 (1976): 34.

Bonilla-Silva, E. "More than Prejudice: Restatement, Reflections, and New Directions in Critical Race Theory." *Sociology of Race and Ethnicity* 1, no. 1 (2015): 73–87.

———. "Rethinking Racism." *American Sociological Review* 62, no. 3 (1997): 465–80.

Brubaker, Rogers. *Ethnicity without Groups.* Cambridge, Mass.: Harvard University Press, 2004.

Burawoy, Michael. "The Functions and Reproduction of Migrant Labor: Comparative Material from Southern Africa and the United States." *American Journal of Sociology* 81, no. 5 (March 1976): 1,050–87.

Callirgos, J. C. *El racismo: La cuestión del otro (y de uno).* Lima: DESCO Centro de Estudios y Promoción del Desarrollo, 1994.

Carmichael, Stokely, and Charles V. Hamilton. *Black Power: The Politics of Liberation in America.* New York: Vintage, 1967.

Collins, Jane. *Unseasonal Migrations.* Princeton, N.J.: Princeton University Press, 1988.

Davis, Mike. *Planet of Slums.* London: Verso, 2006.

de la Cadena, Marisol. *Indigenous Mestizos.* Durham, N.C.: Duke University Press, 2000.

Donoghue, John. "Indentured Servitude in the 17th Century English Atlantic: A Brief Survey of the Literature." *History Compass* 11, no. 10 (2006): 893–902.

Drelichman, Mauricio, and Hans-Joachim Voth. "Lending to the Borrower from Hell: Debt and Default in the Age of Philip II." *Economic Journal* 121, no. 557 (2011): 1,205–27.

Drinot, Paulo. "Nation-Building, Racism and Inequality: Institutional Development in Peru in Historical Perspective." In *Making Institutions Work in Peru: Democracy, Development and Inequality Since 1980*, edited by John Crabtree, 4–23. London: Institute for the Study of the Americas, University of London, 2006.

Emirbayer, Mustafa, and Matthew Desmond. *The Racial Order.* Chicago: University of Chicago Press, 2015.

Feagin, Joe R. *Systemic Racism: A Theory of Oppression.* New York: Routledge, 2006.

Frank, Thomas. *What's the Matter with Kansas?: How Conservatives Won the Heart of America.* New York: Metropolitan, 2004.

Fredrickson, George M. *White Supremacy: A Comparative Study in American and South African History.* Oxford: Oxford University Press, 1982.

Gallagher, Charles A. "Color-Blind Privilege: The Social and Political Functions of Erasing the Color Line in Post-Race America." *Race, Gender & Class* 10, no. 4 (2003): 22–37.

Gans, Herbert J. "The Positive Functions of Poverty." *American Journal of Sociology* 78, no. 2 (1972): 275–89.

Greider, William. *One World, Ready or Not: The Manic Logic of Global Capitalism.* New York: Simon & Schuster, 1997.

Grieshaber, E. P. "Hacienda-Indian Community Relations and Indian Acculturation: An Historiographical Essay." *Latin American Research Review* 14, no. 3 (1979): 107–28.

Hale, Charles R. "Does Multiculturalism Menace? Governance, Cultural Rights and the Politics of Identity in Guatemala." *Journal of Latin American Studies* 34 (2002): 485–524.

———. *Más que un Indio.* School of American Research: Santa Fe, 2006.

———. "Rethinking Indigenous Politics in the Era of the 'Indio Permitido.'" *NACLA Report on the Americas* 38, no. 2 (2004): 16–22.

Hancock, Graham. *Lords of Poverty: The Power, Prestige, and Corruption of the International Aid Business.* New York: Atlantic Monthly Press, 1992.

Hardt, Michael. "The Common in Communism." *Rethinking Marxism* 22, no. 3 (2010): 346–56.

Harvey, David. *A Brief History of Neoliberalism.* New York: Oxford University Press, 2005.

———. *The Enigma of Capital: And the Crises of Capitalism.* Oxford: Oxford University Press, 2010.

Hemming, John. *The Conquest of the Incas.* New York: Harcourt, Brace, Jovanovich, 1970.

Hewlett, Sylvia Ann. *(Forget a Mentor) Find a Sponsor: The New Way to Fast-Track Your Career.* Cambridge, Mass.: Harvard Business Review, 2013.

Horne, Gerald. *The Apocalypse of Settler Colonialism: The Roots of Slavery, White Supremacy, and Capitalism in Seventeenth-Century North America and the Caribbean.* New York: Monthly Review Press, 2018.

Huston, James L. *The British Gentry, the Southern Planter, and the Northern Family Farmer: Agriculture and Sectional Antagonism in North America.* Baton Rouge: Louisiana State University Press, 2015.

Jameson, Fredric. *Representing Capital.* London: Verso, 2011.

Jessop, Bob. "Post-Fordism and the State." In *Comparative Welfare Systems*, edited by Bent Greve, 165–84. Basingstoke: Macmillan, 1996.

Kamen, Henry. *Empire: How Spain Became a World Power, 1492–1763.* New York: HarperCollins, 2003.

Kay, Cristobal. "Achievements and Contradictions of the Peruvian Agrarian Reform." *Journal of Development Studies* 18, no. 6 (1981): 141–70.
Keynes, John Maynard. *The General Theory of Employment, Interest, and Money*. London: Macmillan, 1936.
Klarén, Peter. *Peru: Society and Nationhood in the Andes*. New York: Oxford University Press, 2000.
Kulikoff, Allan. *Tobacco and Slaves: The Development of Southern Cultures in the Chesapeake, 1680–1800*. Chapel Hill: Published for the Institute of Early American History and Culture, Williamsburg, Virginia, by the University of North Carolina Press, 1986.
Lagos, Maria. *Autonomy and Power: The Dynamics of Class and Culture in Rural Bolivia*. Philadelphia: University of Pennsylvania Press, 1994.
Lepore, Jill. *The Name of War: King Philip's War and the Origins of American Identity*. New York: Knopf, 1998.
Loveman, Mara. "Is 'Race' Essential?" *American Sociological Review* 64, no. 6 (1999): 891.
MacQuarrie, Kim. *The Last Days of the Incas*. New York: Simon & Schuster, 2007.
Mallon, Florencia. "Chronicle of a Path Foretold?" In *Shining and Other Paths*, edited by Steve J. Stern, 84–117. Durham, N.C.: Duke University Press, 1998.
———. *The Defense of Community in Peru's Central Highlands*. Princeton, N.J.: Princeton University Press, 1983.
Maloney, Thomas N. "Wage Compression and Wage Inequality between Black and White Males in the United States, 1940–1960." *Journal of Economic History* 54, no. 2 (1994): 358–81.
Manrique, Nelson. *La piel y la pluma: Escritos sobre literatura, etnicidad y racismo*. San Isidro, Peru: CIDIAG, 1999.
———. "Modernity and Alternative Development in the Andes." In *Through the Kaleidoscope: The Experience of Modernity in Latin America*, edited by Vivian Schelling, 219–247. New York: Verso, 2000.
Marx, Karl. *Economic & Philosophic Manuscripts*. Marxist Internet Archive (1844). https://www.marxists.org/archive/marx/works/1844/manuscripts/preface.htm.
———. "Manifesto of the Communist Party." Marxist Internet Archive (1848). https://www.marxists.org/archive/marx/works/1848/communist-manifesto/index.htm.
Massey, Douglas S., and Nancy A. Denton. *American Apartheid: Segregation and the Making of the Underclass*. Cambridge, Mass.: Harvard University Press, 1993.
Mills, Charles. "Global White Supremacy." In *White Privilege: Essential Readings on the Other Side of Racism*, edited by Paula S. Rothenberg. New York: Worth, 2000.
Morgan, Edmund S. *American Slavery, American Freedom: The Ordeal of Colonial Virginia*. New York: Norton, 1975.

Nasser, Alan. "How The Oligarchy Gets Politicized." *CounterPunch*, November 11, 2015. https://www.counterpunch.org/2011/11/15/how-the-oligarchy-gets-politicized/.

Newfield, Christopher. *The Great Mistake: How We Wrecked Public Universities and How We Can Fix Them*. Baltimore: Johns Hopkins University Press, 2016.

Nugent, J. G. *El laberinto de la choledad*. Lima: Fundación Friedrich Ebert, 1992.

PBS News Hour. "Nobel Laureates Trace How the Economy Began to Fall Apart." PBS News Hour, Dec 26, 2008. https://www.pbs.org/newshour/show/nobel-laureates-trace-how-the-economy-began-to-fall-apart.

Perkins, John. *The New Confessions of an Economic Hitman: How America Really Took Over the World*. London: Ebury, 2017.

Perry, Mark J. "Phenomenal Gains in Manufacturing Productivity." American Enterprise Institute (2012). http://www.aei.org/publication/phenomenal-gains-in-manufacturing-productivity/.

Piketty, Thomas. *Capital in the Twenty-First Century*. Cambridge, Mass.: The Belknap Press of Harvard University Press, 2013.

Polanyi, Karl. *The Great Transformation*. Boston: Beacon Press, 1944.

Poole, Deborah, ed. *Unruly Order: Violence, Power, and Cultural Identity in the High Provinces of Southern Peru*. Boulder, Colo.: Westview, 1994.

Portocarrero, G. *Racismo y mestizaje y otros ensayos*. Lima: Fondo Ed. del Congreso del Perú, 2007.

Renique, José Luis. "Political Violence, the State, and the Peasant Struggle for Land (Puno)." In *Unruly Order*, edited by Deborah Poole, 223–46. Boulder, Colo.: Westview, 1994.

Robinson, William I. *A Theory of Global Capitalism: Production, Class, and State in a Transnational World*. Baltimore: Johns Hopkins University Press, 2004.

Ruggie, John Gerard. "International Regimes, Transactions, and Change: Embedded Liberalism in the Postwar Economic Order." *International Organization* 36, no. 2, *International Regimes* (Spring 1982): 379–415.

Sassen, Saskia. *Expulsions: Brutality and Complexity in the Global Economy*. Cambridge, Mass.: The Belknap Press of Harvard University Press, 2014.

———. "A Savage Sorting of Winners and Losers: Contemporary Versions of Primitive Accumulation." *Globalizations* 7, nos. 1–2 (2010): 23–50.

Scarritt, Arthur. "Broker Fixed: The Racialized Social Structure and the Subjugation of Indigenous Populations in the Andes." *Critical Sociology* 37, no. 2 (2011): 153–77.

———. *Racial Spoils from Native Soils: How Neoliberalism Steals Indigenous Lands in Highland Peru*. Lanham, Md.: Lexington, 2015.

———. "State of Discord: The Historic Reproduction of Racism in Highland Peru." *Postcolonial Studies* 15, no. 1 (2012): 23–44.

Schor, Juliet. *Plenitude: The New Economics of True Wealth*. New York: Penguin, 2010.

Semega, Jessica L., Kayla R. Fontenot, and Melissa A. Kollar. "Income and Poverty in the United States: 2016." Washington, D.C.: U.S. Census Bureau (2017). https://www.census.gov/content/dam/Census/library/publications/2017/demo/P60-259.pdf.

Sites, William, and Virginia Parks. "What Do We Really Know about Racial Inequality? Labor Markets, Politics, and the Historical Basis of Black Economic Fortunes." *Politics & Society* 39, no. 1 (2011): 40–73.

Slevin, Colleen. "Former Aurora Immigration Detainees Challenge Private Prison's Labor Practices." *Denver Post*, June 22, 2017. https://www.denverpost.com/2017/06/22/former-aurora-detainees-challenge-labor-practices/.

Spalding, Karen. "Hacienda-Village Relations in Andean Society to 1830." *Latin American Perspectives* 2, no. 1 (1975): 107–21.

———. "Kurakas and Commerce: A Chapter in the Evolution of Andean Society." *Hispanic American Historical Review* 53, no. 4 (1973): 581–99.

———. "Social Climbers: Changing Patterns of Mobility among the Indians of Colonial Peru." *Hispanic American Historical Review* 50, no. 4 (1970): 645–64.

Standing, Guy. *The Corruption of Capitalism: Why Rentiers Thrive and Work Does Not Pay*. London: Biteback, 2017.

Steger, Manfred B. *Globalization: A Very Short Introduction*. Oxford: Oxford University Press, 2009.

Stern, S. J. *Peru's Indian Peoples and the Challenge of Spanish Conquest: Huamanga to 1640*. 2nd ed. Madison: University of Wisconsin Press, 1992.

Thomas, Hugh. *Rivers of Gold: The Rise of the Spanish Empire, from Columbus to Magellan*. New York: Random House, 2003.

Thompson, Heather Ann. "How Prisons Change the Balance of Power in America." *Atlantic*, October 7, 2013. https://www.theatlantic.com/national/archive/2013/10/how-prisons-change-the-balance-of-power-in-america/280341/.

———. "Why Mass Incarceration Matters: Rethinking Crisis, Decline, and Transformation in Postwar American History." *Journal of American History* 97, no. 3 (2010).

Van den Berghe, Pierre, and George Primov. *Inequality in the Peruvian Andes*. Columbia: University of Missouri Press, 1977.

Vasconcelos, J. *La Raza Cósmica* (1925). Los Angeles: California State University, 1979.

Wacquant, Loïc. "Towards an Analytic of Racial Domination." *Political Power and Social Theory* 11 (1997): 221–34.

Ward, Callum, and Manuel B Aalbers. "Virtual Special Issue Editorial Essay: 'The Shitty Rent Business': What's the Point of Land Rent Theory?" *Urban Studies* 53, no. 9 (2016): 1,760–83.

Wareing, John. *Indentured Migration and the Servant Trade from London to America, 1618–1718: "There Is Great Want of Servants."* New York: Oxford University Press, 2017.

Warren, Wendy. *New England Bound: Slavery and Colonization in Early America*. New York: Liveright, 2016.

Western, Bruce, and Jake Rosenfeld. "Unions, Norms, and the Rise in U.S. Wage Inequality." *American Sociological Review* 76, no. 4 (2011): 513–37.

Wilson, William J. *When Work Disappears: The World of the New Urban Poor.* New York: Knopf, 1996.

Wimmer, Andreas. "The Making and Unmaking of Ethnic Boundaries: A Multilevel Process Theory." *American Journal of Sociology* 113, no. 4 (2008): 970–1,022.

Wright, Erik. *Interrogating Inequality.* London: Verso, 1994.

Zimmerer, Karl. *Changing Fortunes.* Berkeley: University of California Press, 1996.

Žižek, Slavoj. "The Revolt of the Salaried Bourgeoisie." *London Review of Books*, January 26, 2012, 9–10.

4 / Remapping the Race/Class Problematic
SARIKA CHANDRA AND CHRIS CHEN

Introduction: The Problem of Definition

The present U.S. political conjuncture has reignited ongoing debates over the causal primacy of either race or class or, in the language of pollsters and pundits, racism or economic anxiety, as drivers of contemporary white backlash politics. While such backlash dynamics are not novel features of U.S. politics, the return of these debates to the center of mainstream public discourse presents an opportunity to reassess recent scholarly attempts to theorize what scholars have dubbed the "race/class problematic."[1] Both contemporary scholarship and popular commentary confront persistent theoretical impasses, we argue, generated by the discrepant ways that critics define race and class as basic categories of analysis.

Leaving aside the question of why "economic anxiety" is typically racially coded as white among the multiracial working-class population defined as nonsalaried workers without a four-year college degree, popular analysis of the class character of white revanchist politics depends upon several implicit and interrelated definitional reductions. In much popular and scholarly analysis, race and class are represented primarily as competing group identities or forms of identification that function as synecdoches for broader institutional structures, formative processes, and political objectives. For scholars looking to both contextualize and oppose an emboldened white supremacist right, the semantic ambiguity of the problematic's basic terms is not clarified by recognizing their mutually constitutive character or reiterating a general political commitment to challenging both racial oppression and economic inequality.

Across these discussions, capitalist processes reduced to the concept of inequality and class is narrowed to a socioeconomic status identity described by cultural signifiers or by empirical measures of income, occupation, and educational attainment. While the abbreviation of a capitalist logic of accumulation to class *identity* and economic *inequality* has been the subject of extensive Marxist critique, such elisions continue to hinder attempts to theorize the relationship between capitalism and racial group formation. In our understanding, envisioning simultaneously anti-capitalist and anti-racist political objectives requires a precise definition of capitalism and capitalist processes that is not reducible to references to distributive inequality or the project of assembling affirmative multi-racial working-class identities.

The problem of definition also highlights the urgent need to critically reconstruct the concept of race and its causal linkages to many proximate terms like racial identity, racial difference, racial inequality, racism, and anti-racism. We proceed from the basic assumption that such definitions are politically contested, historically specific, and materially grounded. We thus do not aim to provide a general theory of race but instead focus on theories of U.S. racial group formation and its global implications under capitalist conditions.[2] The writings we examine register how the terms of the race/class problematic have entered into a historical crisis of meaning where existing definitions of each term cannot simply be carried over from theorizations of the problematic in previous eras.[3]

This work is especially urgent in the face of a shifting twenty-first-century "identitarian" white power rhetoric that openly affirms racial difference and hereditarian "race realism" while rehabilitating eugenic reasoning and calling for the protection of "biocultural diversity."[4] The changing ideological terrain, radically reshaped in 2020 by some of the largest political mobilizations in U.S. history against anti-black racism and violence, has dramatically raised the stakes of contemporary scholarly debates over both the race/class problematic and the contested meaning of the very conceptual tools used to represent race as a context of political action for racial groups with radically incommensurable histories.[5]

Such an analysis must break from contemporary attempts to theorize the relationship between race and capitalism within the narrow conceptual parameters of the race/class problematic. Far from an anachronistic and theoretically settled question, the polarized terms of the problematic reemerge not only within electoral commentary on racism and economic anxiety but also across a range of popular and scholarly oppositions between class and "identity politics," culture and political economy, particularity and universality, oppression and exploitation, ontological racial positions and workerist social ontologies of labor, and finally within contemporary Marxist accounts of race that counterpose the logic of capitalist accumulation to the historical formation of contingent racial status hierarchies.[6]

Fundamental problems of definition continue to plague contemporary articulations of the race/class problematic. These pervasive problems of definition call for a methodological strategy of semantically disaggregating the basic terms that have helped construct and reproduce the problematic across this series of oppositions. The semantic ambiguity of race, for example, has generated opposed normative demands to either preserve or abandon the concept. To take one prominent example, the opposition between culture and political economy that dominated earlier Cultural Studies approaches to theorizing the relationship between race and capitalism typically assigns racialization to the terrain of culture, discourse, ideology, and representation. Understood primarily through the idiom of group culture, the concept of race is increasingly detached from an array of changing material practices and policies linking a logic of capitalist accumulation to transnational histories of slavery, settler colonialism, and imperial warfare.

Our attempt to theorize the relationship between race and accumulation moves through four major sections. Beginning with the problem of definition, the first section argues that the ways contemporary critics define race generate three broad normative orientations toward the concept—eliminativist, conservationist, and abolitionist.[7] These orientations are constrained, we argue, by the continued association of race primarily with identity as a basic unit of analysis. After briefly sketching these normative approaches to the concept, we turn toward an emergent body of scholarship, broadly associated with a critical philosophy of race, that has made the question of how to define race, and in particular the concept of racial *identity*, central to its theoretical investigations.[8] Bearing these methodological clarifications in mind, we foreground the definitional premises and normative positions that have come to structure recent recastings of the race/class problematic within contemporary scholarship that has shaped Marxist theories of the imbrication of race and capitalism.[9]

In the second section, our analysis reads the race/class problematic through core definitional arguments advanced in Barbara and Karen Fields's *Racecraft*.[10] We examine how the theorists reconceptualize the problematic by understanding race as a form of ideological mystification that both conceals and justifies underlying class relations and inequality. The Fieldses subsequently coin a term, "racecraft," that analytically detaches racism from economic relations, we argue, and reattaches it to a Durkheimian conception of ritual practice that stands in an alternately arbitrary or purely functional relationship to profit-making and class inequality.

In the third section, we draw upon the work of Michael Dawson, Nancy Fraser, Saskia Sassen, and others to reframe the capitalist organization of class relations through three co-constitutive, recursive, and specifically capitalist mechanisms: *exploitation*, *expropriation*, and *expulsion*. This broadening and analytical clarification of core capitalist imperatives can help reframe the race/class problematic beyond relative measures of income and wealth inequality. Not only have the boundaries between these three core dimensions of accumulation been historically racialized, but their combined action is capable of translating a range of racist practices into capitalist value relations through and beyond the point of production.

In the fourth and final section, we argue that remapping the relation between capitalism and racial formation requires a retheorization of the concept of race itself that registers its dual or split character and its historically specific relational constitution under capitalist conditions. It is a concept that not only describes affirmative or oppressive forms of group belonging but also functions as a dynamic category of struggle oriented toward heterogeneous and historically shifting aims. We argue, through the work of Tommie Shelby and Michael Dawson, that an affirmative conception of race does not describe the innate capacities of biologically distinct populations, but instead a fluctuating sense of "linked fate" that emerges between subjects in response to oppression and exploitation.[11] How experiences of group solidarity are politicized constitutes an evolving repertoire of material strategies of survival, resource sharing, and individual and collective self-defense. Acknowledging the dual character of the concept of race does not foreclose the possibility of either analyzing its strategic limitations as a basis for social movement organizing or exploring how the term encompasses a range of sometimes opposed political objectives.

We argue that current debates about the nexus of race and class frequently conflate three discontinuous though interconnected levels of analysis centered on *identities*, *institutionally mediated social relations*, and *processes of accumulation*. With these broad distinctions in mind, it becomes possible to differentiate between accounts of isolable racial groups, the dynamics of intergroup and intragroup racial conflict, and capitalist processes that systematically reproduce entire social formations over time as internally racially divided. Although these three levels of analysis are not reducible to each other, we argue, how they are articulated or disarticulated within contemporary political demands for racial justice profoundly alter the scope of anti-racist analysis, action, and social transformation.[12]

These three aspects of racial group formation, for us, do not constitute a transhistorical schema for exhaustively representing race as an empirical social phenomenon. Instead, these dimensions of racial ordering function as an heuristic device enabling us to clarify the fluctuating meaning of key terms across existing scholarship and an opportunity to theorize changing relations between component elements of the race/class problematic. By bringing identities, institutionally mediated relational fields, and capitalist imperatives into a single analytical frame, we can theorize the history of race as a concept that synthesizes multiple social determinants without either conflating or isolating specific objects of analysis.

Finally, we conclude by returning to the question of experience. Our preliminary account of the relationship between race and capital does not jettison the concept of lived experience but instead broadly reimagines it within the framework we have elaborated. Such recontextualization, we argue, provides a more robust account of how the experience of racialization is itself subject to different political interpretations that produce the boundaries of the concept not as simply given but as an object of political struggle.[13]

Defining Race

NORMATIVE ORIENTATIONS: RACIAL ELIMINATIVISM, CONSERVATIONISM, AND ABOLITION

Popular commentary on racial and ethnic groups' political preferences routinely collapses heterogeneous political perspectives into a language of racial positionality, or politics into "identity," in ways that render racial groups, or internally differentiated populations within racial groups, ideologically uniform. This representational problem haunts not only nationalist conceptions of racial belonging but later poststructuralist and feminist theories of racial difference formulated in part as a critical response to 1960s-era Black, Chicano, and Asian American nationalist politics. The concept of identity is overstretched, we argue, often eliding significant distinctions between the social forces that position individuals and groups in relation to each other, experiences of racialization, the range of political perspectives racial subjects adopt, and the actions racially positioned subjects take to transform or adapt to their circumstances. Limited to contending visions of a politics of the subject—whether ascribed or asserted, fixed or fluid, homogeneous or heterogeneous, authentic or inauthentic, pure or hybrid—the concept of identity risks trapping the definition of race within an essentialist/anti-essentialist bind and ongoing debates over the properties of individuals and groups.

Acknowledging the conceptual limitations of identity as a unit of analysis, some scholars have reformulated race in terms of regulated relations *between* subjects—from patterns of racial stratification to institutionally mediated forms of group conflict. We engage with this relational turn later in this essay. Building on this scholarship, we reimagine race as a relational form produced by the interplay between a set of material constraints and pressures on the one hand and a range of potential responses to materially constituted worlds on the other.

The contemporary scholarship on identity draws attention to the experiential, epistemic, and psychological impact of racialization on individual and group consciousness and subject formation often missed by eliminativist accounts of race looking to abandon the latter concept. The language of identity also tends to model racial oppression as a process of interpellation designed to produce and regulate normative identities. Resistance to oppression is thus frequently bound to the terrain of a politics of the subject, whether framed as the antinormative subversion of dominant identities and roles or as the working through of pathological attachments to scenes of traumatic injury.

Critics have identified two broad normative orientations toward the concept of race, conservationism (or retentionism) and eliminativism, that call for the preservation or abandonment of the term as a coherent category of analysis. A third approach toward the idea of race has been advanced by many contemporary theorists and activists committed to the abolition of critical institutions, ideologies, and practices that structure the U.S. racial order—ranging from the carceral state to the ongoing reproduction of a cross-class white racial identity that Theodore Allen has called a "ruling-class social control formation."[14] Drawing inspiration from an emancipatory vision of the end of the transatlantic slave trade through the promotion of what W. E. B. Du Bois called "abolition-democracy" in *Black*

Reconstruction,[15] scholarship that might be characterized as abolitionist—from Angela Davis to Ruth Wilson Gilmore, Noel Ignatiev, and David Roediger, for example—offers differing accounts of the meaning of abolition and the role of specific historical agents in realizing social transformation. Fred Moten and Stefano Harney point out, for example, that every call for abolition is at the same time a call for the construction of alternative forms of sociality and social organization based on the augmentation of immanent forms of solidarity in the present. "What is, so to speak, the object of abolition?" they write. "Not so much the abolition of prisons but the abolition of a society that could have prisons, that could have slavery, that could have the wage, and therefore not abolition as the elimination of anything but abolition as the founding of a new society."[16]

While the rhetoric of eliminativism and abolitionism may share similar features, or at moments even converge, they represent different assessments of the strategic significance, meaning, and future of the concept of race. Eliminativist calls to abandon race as a descriptive or explanatory category typically argue that the concept is reducible to a false belief about how biological differences determine the innate human capacities of bounded social groups.[17]

Abolitionist scholarship, on the other hand, understands that race does not merely refer to a kind of cognitive error but also a set of material practices and policies with historical origins in the Atlantic slave trade, in the Spanish and English conquest of the Americas, and, for followers of the work of Cedric Robinson, in a historically durable European collective consciousness that "transmitted a racialism that adapted to the political and material exigencies of the moment."[18] Envisioning the eventual eradication of what they take to be the primary institutional mechanisms of racial domination, abolitionist writers' work raises the question of how the meaning of race itself as a signifier might be altered in a future free of racial oppression.

Social constructionist accounts of race have often asserted a qualified racial conservationism, while eliminativist critiques—most recently advanced by Kwame Anthony Appiah, Robert Miles, Naomi Zack, Paul Gilroy, Antonia Darder and Rodolfo Torres, and Barbara and Karen Fields, among others—remain controversial critical interventions for two broad reasons. First, in popular usage, race is taken to refer directly to social group characteristics rather than to a system of causal explanation, a process of social boundary formation, or an array of structural forces acting upon populations. Thus, calls to discard the concept are frequently interpreted as either a version of conservative "color-blind" rhetoric, effectively hindering attempts to track broader patterns of social inequality, or tantamount to an erasure of the existence, culture, experience, and history of oppressed populations. Second, many theorists argue that eliminativist arguments fail to adequately describe the historical specificity and heterogeneity of race-based political organizing.[19]

Substantive and often unacknowledged differences in how race is defined, we maintain, lie at the root of most basic normative disagreements over whether the concept should be discarded or defended. Some theoretical approaches to the concept borrow elements from both eliminativist and anti-eliminativist positions. However, the quasi-logical structure of the opposition itself registers how race functions as a reference to both a justification for domination and an affirmative signifier of group belonging.

RACE AND IDENTITY AS "SLIDING SIGNIFIERS"

While contemporary scholarship on racism and racial oppression is marked by a broad social constructionist consensus grounded in a rejection of biological-determinist arguments about innate racial capacities or pathologies, the theoretical status of the concept of race itself has remained controversial and contested. The problem of definition implicitly structures a range of contemporary debates over the nature of the U.S. racial order and potential pathways toward its transformation. Pursuing a strategy of semantic disaggregation can reveal how seemingly opposed normative orientations toward the concept may simply be referring to different aspects of a single complex process of group formation. At the same time, pursuing such a strategy helps clarify points of disagreement over how to model the interaction between *different orders of social construction* and how to identify the causal relations and ruptural discontinuities between these orders.

We adopt this approach not to arrive at some definitive meaning of race as a signifier but to disaggregate the discontinuous phenomena that racial categories compress and synthesize.[20] These definitional disputes underscore how race constitutes what Stuart Hall has called a highly elastic "sliding signifier" that not only produces "chains of equivalence ... between genetic, physical, social, and cultural difference" but also how the concept continually shifts between emancipatory and oppressive meanings operating at radically different spatial scales.[21] The concept has been variously understood in terms of biology, ethnic identification, lived experience, shared history, ressentiment, libidinal economy, legal rights or rightlessness, subjects and objects of aesthetic representation, or some combination of all of these. The work of semantic disaggregation can help us clarify the role of capitalist imperatives in transforming the meaning and material context of comparative racial differences between groups over time.

CLASS/IDENTITY

By pursuing a strategy of semantic disaggregation, we attempt to navigate long-standing deadlocked debates over the causal primacy of either race or class as principles of social organization and competing forms of political identification. We argue for a rethinking of the basic terms that structure the opposition and adopt alternative processual categories of analysis. We proceed from the theoretical assumption that race and class are internally related categories that cannot be synthesized through an additive account of race *and* class as isomorphic "identities." These categories do not merely refer to subjects but to a single complex and changing relational structure reproduced by an array of formative processes mediated through capitalist value relations.

Marxist critiques of racial "identity politics" as symptomatic of a broad postwar social movement turn away from explicit class-wide political demands often reduce the historical relationship between race and capitalism to the psycho-political idiom of identity itself framed in terms of competing forms of politicized racial or class identification. Critiques and defenses of racial "identity politics" often assume that identity categories imply fixed political aims and strategies and that "identity" is an adequate basic unit of analysis for theorizing class formation, racialization processes, and a range of differentiated political objectives.

The contemporary meaning of identity invoked by "identity politics" is an arguably recent invention. Popularized during the U.S. postwar period, the term emerges from several different sources: mid-century ego psychology, the language of advertising and mass consumer culture, and early statements of political activists in the latter half of the 1970s. As many scholars have noted, one of the earliest explicit uses of the term "identity politics" is contained in the Combahee River Collective's foundational 1977 "A Black Feminist Statement."[22] Despite early black feminist attempts to claim the term, "identity politics" was not widely adopted by anti-racist movements to frame their political activity. Despite later scholarly attempts to offer more nuanced readings and defenses of the term, it has instead become a derogatory label applied by critics across the political spectrum to such movements in order to criticize their perceived failures in contrast to a nominally universalist class politics and dream of race-blind social democratic redistributive policies.[23] Entering widespread use in a post–New Left "culture war" context beginning in the 1980s, the designation has remained an amorphous placeholder for emergent anti-racist, feminist, and queer liberation movements thought to have contributed to the fragmentation of a broader New Left coalitional movement.[24]

The manner in which the term "identity politics," like race, functions discursively as what Stuart Hall calls a "sliding signifier" raises the question of how identity as a modifier in this formulation compresses a subject, history, and horizon of "politics." Refusing to abandon the term as irredeemably homogenizing and essentialist, philosopher Linda Alcoff has made a persuasive case for understanding identity as a marker of social location that produces distinctive epistemic as well as phenomenological effects:

> Identities are not lived as a discrete and stable set of interests, but as a site from which one must engage in the process of meaning-making and thus from which one is open to the world. The hermeneutic insight is that the self operates in a situated plane, always culturally located with great specificity even as it is open onto an indeterminate future and a reinterpretable past not of its own creation. The self carries with it always this horizon as a specific location, with substantive content—as, for example, a specifiable relation to the Holocaust, to slavery, to the *encuentro*, and so on—but whose content only exists in interpretation and in constant motion.[25]

Responding to the perceived limitations of cultural and poststructuralist feminist conceptions of the category of "women" as a political subject in need of redefinition or deconstruction, Alcoff proposes a complex multidimensional referent for the concept of identity that highlights its dynamic processual character. Resisting both essentialist reduction and a fetishization of indeterminacy characteristic of poststructuralist critiques of the subject as a mystified social form, Alcoff extends the concept of identity to reimagine race as a social location that informs but does not absolutely determine specific political commitments. This more nuanced understanding of the term raises several broad questions about anti-racist political objectives, the highly mediated relationship between individuals and groups, and the social forces that construct social location for individuals and groups. How might we theorize the impact of different institutions that mediate intragroup political conflicts, for example, between individuals who might share the same social location but not the same political commitments, or that work to transform individuals with shared identities into organized groups with specific and sometimes conflicting political aims?

The open-ended, "indeterminate future" of racially positioned subjects brackets specific political visions that seek to ultimately transform not only the meaning of identity but the practices and relations that consistently reproduce it experientially as an oppressive social location. Educational theorist Zeus Leonardo, for example, has posed the question of how the possibility of social transformation might alter "the future of the race concept" in which "race without racism simply would not be race as we know it."[26]

RACE AND GROUP FORMATION

Philosopher Paul C. Taylor has pointed out how the semantic ambiguity of race as a concept is not only produced by significant historical shifts in meaning but continuing debates over the nature of the social groups that racial categories delimit. "White supremacist societies created the Races they thought they were discovering," Taylor notes. He argues that "the ongoing political developments in these societies continued to recreate them":

> Anti-racist activists turned them into political interest groups, cultural nationalists treated them as incubators for ethnic groups, shifts in immigration patterns problematized and expanded their boundaries, and economic changes redefined their relations to the productive forces of society.
>
> All of this is to say: our Western races are social constructs. They are things we humans create in the transactions that define social life. Specifically they are the probabilistically defined populations that result from the white supremacist determination to link appearance and ancestry to social location and life chances.
>
> To talk thematically about race, then . . . is to talk about the field of forces and dynamics that produce and follow from the linkage between body and social location. To speak categorically, or taxonomically, of races . . . is to speak of the specific populations that racial dynamics, or racial formation processes, create. And to speak of a racial identity is to speak of an individual's perspective on and location in the field of racializing social forces.[27]

This compact definition identifies what the philosopher takes to be core features of the term over time—in this case the association of intrinsic capacities and relative worth with differences in physical appearance and ancestry. Taylor's definition then connects these ideas with a history of political projects aiming to distribute material resources, civic status, and relative vulnerability to state and civilian violence along racial lines.[28] Race is thus a concept that establishes a kind of feedback loop or "link" between two orders of social construction: a system of beliefs and a set of practices.[29] The resulting changes in the material circumstances of racialized populations, in turn, transform beliefs about racial difference.

The causal relations established by "linking" are not unidirectional. Racial categories are rendered materially consequential, while the social consequences of racist practices come to materially redefine the meaning of racial belonging. Populations are positioned not only in thought but in practice. Whether ascribed or asserted, the concept of racial identity synthesizes an array of contested formative processes.[30] Though race is regularly invoked as an explanation for historical forces acting upon individuals and groups, the premise that identity *causes* unequal life chances is for Taylor itself a form of mystification.

Taylor's definition implies that racist thinking renders life chances an innate or intrinsic feature of racial groups, believing that the latter *causes* the former and thus naturalizing the link. If according to Taylor's definition, the societal forces that construct race as a social location cannot be derived from the concept of race itself, then we must ask about both the specific ends of racialization processes and about the mechanisms through which race is produced as a materially consequential social location. The institutional processes that structure the material distribution and enforcement of "life chances" for one racial group also comparatively structure them for others. As a model for theorizing the relationship between race and capitalism in particular, Taylor's definition allows us to conceive how political economy has historically shaped race as ideology and material linkages between an array of racist practices. Taylor's definition raises the question of what historically specific practices and policies the concept of race synthesizes and how those mechanisms have changed over time.

The philosopher's attempt to redefine and clarify basic terms reminds us that the meaning of race, racial categories, and racial identity is neither historically unchanging nor reducible to biology or culture. His effort to disaggregate the various meanings of race serves as a methodological reminder of the importance of reading historical conditions, contexts, and conflicts back into categories whose meaning has drastically altered over time. Such categories are not merely neutral demographic descriptors of isolable populations in the U.S. but signify compressed histories of materially interlinked worlds created through a global process of European colonial expansion.

Taylor's definition of race also illuminates a key definitional distinction whose elision arguably generates the eliminativist/anti-eliminativist opposition. The philosopher makes what may appear as a counterintuitive claim when read against popular discourses that often conflate race, group culture, and beliefs about innate racial (in)capacity. "Races, as I have defined them, are not cultural groups strictly speaking," Taylor asserts, "but they are features of the social landscape around which social groups can form."[31] If race is understood as a project of naturalizing the linkage between racial location and "life chances," it indexes a set of practices and beliefs that most theorists contend must be eliminated in the interest of justice. If the concept is taken to describe an affirmative sense of shared group history or culture, then for many theorists it describes a social phenomenon in need of preservation, augmentation, and continual reinvention.

These distinct ways of imagining the semantic referent of race, of course, do not indicate an absolute division between what are historically interconnected social processes. Instead, the definitional divide highlights a theoretical problem of deploying the same concept to describe both the oppressive and affirmative nature of group belonging—a move that within contemporary scholarship often conflates race and group culture. While affirmative conceptions of race need not be understood in precisely cultural terms, analytically disaggregating race and culture avoids reducing racial domination to the misrecognition or nonrecognition of cultural difference. It is a distinction that would offer both conceptions a more differentiated sense of race as a context for a range of meaning-making activities subsumed under the category of culture—especially in cases where references to racial and cultural groups do not describe the same bounded populations.

Identity, Inequality, and the Problem of Definition in "Racecraft"

Offering perhaps one of the most influential defenses of racial eliminativism, *Racecraft*, by Barbara and Karen Fields, offers a sweeping denaturalizing critique of how race—whether understood in biological, cultural, or ancestral terms—is seen as the cause of racism as well as its retroactive justification.[32] The book builds its account around the central problem of defining race and ultimately argues that the concept is simply the ideological byproduct of racism. As an influential analysis that has informed a range of contemporary Marxist accounts of race as a concept, *Racecraft* foregrounds the political stakes of the problem of definition that equates anti-racism with a political strategy of asserting a unified racial identity. At the same time, the definitional reduction of race to a cognitive error in *Racecraft* compels the authors to argue for the abandonment of race as a coherent category of analysis. The book then goes on to theorize the practice of racism as a bundle of simultaneously arbitrary and functional rituals that they call "racecraft." The question at the heart of the study—why a widespread belief in race persists—is left mostly unresolved.

Three theoretical problems are raised by how the Fieldses frame the problematic and define its basic terms. First, a theoretically unstable understanding of racism emerges across these writings as either absolutely functional to the reproduction of capitalist inequality, and as such an unmediated expression of class interests, or as a set of arbitrary and false beliefs. Second, the potential structural linkages between capitalism and racial formation are narrowed to the conceptual bottleneck of class location or patterns of class inequality. The framework of inequality itself instead tends to foreground maldistributive or disproportional effects within an already naturalized economic structure and posit relative incorporation within this structure as the horizon of racial justice. Third, the problematic relies upon a truncated theory of race as an entirely ascriptive status identity and form of ideological mystification without a corresponding account of how the concept has also historically functioned as a politically contested signifier of group solidarity and shared histories of oppression and exploitation. Racial distinctions come to be defined not only by deterministic assumptions about the meaning of appearance and ancestry, we maintain, but through a range of historical strategies of social reproduction and self-defense undertaken by groups in response to their changing racial positioning across long histories of colonial conquest and subsequent capitalist development.[33]

Racecraft offers a warning that perhaps one of the most pernicious effects of racism is how its targets are made to appear responsible for their domination and subordination. Race is thus not merely a biological fiction in their account, but a specious form of causal explanation that conceals an array of routinized racist practices and permeates social constructionist attempts to reformulate race in alternative political or cultural terms. "No operation performed on the fiction," the Fieldses assert, "can ever make headway against the crime."[34] However, we maintain that it is possible to separate the critique of race as a marker of biological kinds from race offered as a causal explanation. *Racecraft* traces the origins of U.S. racial hierarchies back to the institution of black chattel slavery. The book contends that the ongoing reproduction of racial categories is grounded in a self-perpetuating illusion that alternately obscures economic inequality and thwarts the formation of interracial class solidarity.

While we do not arrive at their eliminativist conclusions, the Fieldses' intervention into contemporary debates about race emphasizes the need to examine how even within social constructionist theories the concept is often discursively mobilized as a self-evident explanatory category. Racial difference does not explain racial oppression but is itself in need of explanation. We concur with the Fieldses' powerful critique of the explanatory power of race as a concept and with their understanding of the inseparability of racism and economic inequality.

However, we believe that *Racecraft* reformulates the race/class problematic by assessing the functional or nonfunctional character of race-making to profit-making. It is an argumentative move that limits the explanatory reach of the book's arguments in two broad ways. First, the book provides only a partial mapping of processes of racial formation. Race doesn't merely translate racist beliefs and practices into the seemingly objective characteristics of racial groups but also describes a range of potential responses to materially consequential forms of racial positioning. The deliberately limited definition of race as biological fiction or cognitive error forwarded here presumes that any alternative understanding of the "sliding signifier" of race would involve rehabilitating the biological premises of scientific racism. Accounting for how populations subject to racism have reimagined the meaning of racial belonging would help to explain the concept's durability as a site of ongoing definitional struggle.

Second, for us, the book raises the question of the adequacy of the concept of racism itself and whether the concept that the Fieldses call "racecraft" offers an adequate map of how race-making is inscribed into the path-dependent historical trajectory of capital accumulation and state formation.[35] Despite broadly noting that class relations mediate what they call the collective conjuring rituals of race, racecraft itself stands in an at times purely functional and at others nonfunctional relationship to accumulation processes. The book explains the persistence of "racecraft" through a Durkheimian account of collectively internalized social conventions' cumulative historical force.

While we argue later that there are alternative conceptions of race as group solidarity that do not risk reinforcing the inverted causality the

Fieldses criticize, *Racecraft* raises the question of how such erroneous beliefs have persisted over time. The Fieldses propose that because the concept possesses no coherent biological referent, it should be abandoned—an argument that critics have dubbed "racial skepticism."[36] "Identifying race as a social construction," they continue, "does nothing to solidify the intellectual ground on which it totters."[37] The book maintains that ritualistic social conventions explain race's historical persistence as an explanatory category long after the discrediting of a scientific discourse of biologically distinct groups of "unequal rank."[38] The critique of race that *Racecraft* stages is thus premised upon an understanding of the concept as entirely the byproduct of racist practices or rituals in an era when earlier scientific theories of racial hierarchies of innate intelligence, ability, and worth have been rigorously disproven. This opening definitional move has profound normative implications for the eliminativist conclusions they ultimately draw from their analysis.

For the Fieldses, social constructionist accounts of race continue to conceal the social forces that constitute and recreate racial distinctions by continually displacing critical attention away from how racist practices are justified through reference to the ascribed characteristics of racial groups. Race mystifies not only class inequality but racism itself by translating the practices and rituals of racial domination into a language of inherent racial group differences. "*Racism* is first and foremost a social practice," the Fieldses contend, "which means that it is an action and a rationale for action, or both at once":

> *Racism* always takes for granted the objective reality of *race*, as just defined, so it is important to register their distinctness. The shorthand transforms *racism*, something an aggressor *does*, into *race*, something the target *is*, in a sleight of hand that is easy to miss. Consider the statement "black Southerners were segregated because of their skin color"—a perfectly natural sentence to the ears of most Americans, who tend to overlook its weird causality. But in that sentence, segregation disappears as the doing of segregationists, and then, in a puff of smoke—*paff*—reappears as a trait of only one part of the segregated whole. In similar fashion, enslavers disappear only to reappear, disguised, in stories that append physical traits defined as slave-like to those enslaved.[39]

Race and racism, in this account, thus belong to different orders of social construction. "Race belongs to the same family as the evil eye," the Fieldses assert. "Racism belongs to the same family as murder and genocide. Which is to say that racism, unlike race, is not a fiction, an illusion, a superstition, or a hoax. It is a crime against humanity."⁴⁰ From sumptuary codes to segregated housing, a range of social practices seem to confirm the objective existence of races while offering an ideological justification for racist civic/legal double standards, social policies, and worsening economic inequality.⁴¹ For the Fieldses, racism has a material basis in histories of genocide, slavery, and economic inequality. Race, on the other hand, has no "material existence" and therefore no "material causation."⁴² The concept for them instead resembles the conjuring of spirits. From this perspective, explaining racism through race conceals the concept's historical origins and the specific practices that recreate it over time. However, suggesting that this transformation occurs in a "puff of smoke" or through a "sleight of hand" is itself a kind of shorthand for a set of practices whose relationship to capitalist processes requires further elaboration.

Rather than remapping the historically shifting material practices that render acts of ideological mystification materially consequential, the Fieldses invent a concept, "racecraft," that describes a collective mental terrain or, in their words, a kind of "twilight zone" and shared racial imaginary, that drives the conversion of racism into race.⁴³ Governed by rules of public deference, descent, and appearance in the U.S. with origins in the "historical processes of enslavement that cast a long shadow on subsequent history," "racecraft" represents a set of institutionalized social conventions that continue to reproduce race in everyday interactions beyond whatever individuals may believe.⁴⁴ Instead of reformulating a more capacious definitional understanding of race, the book opts for a far narrower way of framing the concept as a kind of epistemic error whose origins ultimately lie in thought and language.⁴⁵ However, racism possesses a sort of social objectivity that, for the Fieldses, is sustained through ritual action and social conventions.

The stark definitional separation between race and racism draws inspiration from the work of Émile Durkheim, who, in *Elementary Forms of Religious Life*, translated from the French by Karen Fields, bases what one might anachronistically call a social constructionist account of religion on a fundamental distinction between the divine and the rituals of divination. Through Durkheim's theory of religion, the Fieldses liken race-making ritual action, or "racecraft," to witchcraft or divination. If races, like spirits, do not exist, racecraft continually recreates race through ritual practice. An exclusive focus on the divine, Durkheim suggests, would miss how the presence of the divine is manifested through the ritualized social activity of veneration. For the Fieldses, the analytical separation of race from racism enables a similar critique of the idea of racism as the misrecognition or misperception of the essence of racial groups. Rather, racism describes the production of a collective racial "common sense" that such groups possess an essence. The ultimate target of the Fieldses' eliminativist argument is not biology per se but what they take to be a collective practice of race-making. "To eliminate racecraft from the fabric of our lives," the Fieldses argue, "we must first unravel the threads from which it is woven."[46] This unraveling would not merely be limited to correcting erroneous beliefs but to practices that lend such beliefs material form.

RACE/PROFIT

The Durkheimian arguments the Fieldses advance to describe racecraft raise the question of why such ritual practices persist in light of the book's ambiguous assessment of race-making as a function of the production and reproduction of economic inequality. Having defined race as an intellectual error, *Racecraft* is caught in a kind of double-bind where the "twilight zone" of racializing rituals are detached from political economy while at the same time racism and class inequality "in the United States have always been part of the same phenomenon."[47] "Probably a majority of American historians think of slavery in the United States as primarily a system of race relations," Barbara Fields writes, "as though the chief business of slavery were the production of white supremacy rather than the production of cotton, sugar, rice and tobacco."[48] Here Fields powerfully condenses the argument at the core of *Racecraft*, warning about the causal inversion produced by taking race as an explanation for racist practices and by isolating a desire for racial domination as the cause rather than consequence of slavery as a profit-making enterprise. This oft-quoted observation draws attention to the dangers of explaining changing historical practices through categories of analysis that systematically transform consequences into causes or explain race-making as an end in itself. While we argue that the dangers of causal inversion need not exhaustively define race as a signifier, this passage reveals how the book represents racism as a set of ritual practices that are either wholly functional or nonfunctional to exploitation.

Here an analysis of the materiality of racism, or rather the structured practices that materially produce racial differentiation, does not extend deeper into the social organization of capitalist commodity production. Instead, a narrower set of questions around the functional or nonfunctional relationship to capitalist profit-making emerges as a primary way to conceptualize the linkage between race and accumulation and a new iteration of the race/class problematic. More broadly, the question of the functional or contingent relationship between race-making and successful profit realization continues to haunt contemporary Marxist and post-Marxist accounts of race as an essentially precapitalist phenomenon, as a set of institutionalized material practices that produce subjects of ideology, or as a form of difference that represent the colonial underside of liberal capitalist modernity.[49]

The Fieldses' subsequent description of race as an "anomalous class position," for example, is not an attempt to capture the concept's materiality but rather to expose its fundamental irrationality.[50] It is not simply race but racism that oscillates between rationality and irrationality in their account, alternately reducible to economic interest and the profit motive or arbitrary double standards and irrational rituals. An elaboration of the ritualized social conventions of "racecraft," in our view, does not capture how racial animus might be systematically reproduced precisely through a calculus of group-differentiated material interests.

In our view, the structure of racist ideology does not simply represent a set of incoherent and scientifically unsupportable beliefs about group capacities but also describes heterogeneous and historically changing interpretations of economic rationality itself. The articulation of the standard of living and competitiveness of U.S. labor with U.S. national sovereignty, for example, has historically reinforced an opposition between citizens and noncitizens while exacerbating the racialization of this divide. In the absence of a substantive internationalist anti-racist analysis, a range of state policies designed to expel or exclude racially marked populations from the nation, shield native-born workers from foreign competition, or invalidate and erode indigenous territorial claims to facilitate resource extraction, can easily present themselves as practical, common-sense solutions to crises of capitalist profitability. In other words, material interest itself remains a politically contested terrain of rival explanations for shifting economic conditions. Repeatedly emphasizing the unscientific and arbitrary character of racist ideology has proven ineffective in countering the resurgence of ethnonationalist anti-migrant movements, for example, driven by the perceived negative impact of immigration on the unemployment rates and wages of native-born workers.

To return to the basic terms of the race/class problematic, because *Racecraft* defines class and capitalism specifically in terms of inequality, racism is consequently understood as a constraint on the economic opportunity of individuals within an already existing economic structure where their potential "improved class position might any time be subject to a racist veto."[51] The choice of inequality as a measure of racial and economic injustice frames both racism and class formation mainly in terms of maldistribution, limiting the horizon of politics to redistributive measures aimed at closing the inequality gap between distinct groups occupying differential class positions.[52]

The race/class problematic thus reappears in *Racecraft* as an identity and inequality problematic. In the remainder of the essay, we build on recent scholarship to reimagine the terms of the problematic, situating the measure of inequality within a broader account of three elementary formative processes that define capitalist accumulation and race as historically marking boundaries between these processes. In conclusion, we briefly argue for moving beyond the concept of identity to reconceptualize specifically capitalist forms of race-making as split between dynamic processes of boundary formation on the one hand and a more relational and politically differentiated conception of "linked fate" and group solidarity on the other. Reimagining race in terms of "linked fate," we contend, avoids what the Fieldses identify as the fundamental problem of taking racial or cultural difference as the "cause" of racial oppression. At the same time, the concept of "linked fate" emphasizes how race represents a dynamic context for action that remains in principle compatible with the broad vision of economic justice that the Fieldses endorse.

Race and Value

EXPROPRIATION, EXPLOITATION, EXPULSION

In a recent exchange, Michael Dawson and Nancy Fraser have proposed understanding racialization in terms of an integral relation between capitalist exploitation and what they call racial "expropriation"—ranging from enslavement and territorial dispossession to the contemporary dispossessive effects of wagelessness and the targeted application of state violence.[53] The concept of expropriation here opens onto a broader set of debates about the conceptual reach of Marx's account of "so-called primitive accumulation" as either a violent historical stage of the development of capitalist relations of production or as a permanent feature of a later general law of accumulation.[54] For our purposes, "expropriation" (*Enteignung*) represents not a stage but a structural component of the ongoing reproduction of the capital relation through dispossessive processes conditioned by exploitation but not reducible to it.

Attempting to account for "capitalism's systemic entanglement with racial oppression," Fraser explores how "racial hierarchy and imperial predation are anchored in the depths of capitalist society" through systematic forms of expropriation that represent what the theorist calls naturalized and often seemingly non- or extra-economic "background condition[s]" for the economic exploitation of formally free wage labor.[55] Fraser sketches an approach to theorizing the relationship between racial oppression and capitalism that does not depend on arguing, as some Marxists have, that racism and hierarchical racial differentiation are epiphenomenal expressions of capitalist exploitation.[56] For us, Fraser's more expansive conception of capitalism captures the role of capitalist processes in forging value relations across racial populations and between racist practices.

She argues that if exploitation works by capital's purchase of "'labor power' in exchange for wages, then expropriation works by *confiscating* capacities and resources and *conscripting* them into capital's circuits of self-expansion."[57] "The racializing dynamics of capitalist society," Fraser continues, "are crystallized in the 'mark' that distinguishes *free subjects of exploitation* from *dependent subjects of expropriation*"—the latter category of persons, subpersons, and nonpersons including "chattel slaves, indentured servants, colonized subjects, 'native' members of 'domestic dependent nations,' debt peons, felons, and 'covered' beings, such as wives and children, who lack an independent legal personality."[58]

Expropriation does not merely refer to the theft of resources, land, and labor (unfree, unpaid, or unfairly paid) but rather describes the subsumption of these resources into circuits of production, circulation, and surplus extraction that lend expropriative mechanisms a specifically capitalist character. Thus, as Glen Coulthard and Robert Nichols have argued, expropriation differs from instances of simple theft and plunder that have marked the global history of precapitalist societies.[59] The historically shifting boundary between expropriation and exploitation continues to produce racializing effects and remains a site of political struggle.

If expropriation comes to be defined by exploitation, then the racializing effects of the production of what Marx calls "surplus population(s)" or the racialization of what Michael Denning calls "wageless life" renders "expulsion" (*Verjagung*) another essential category of anti-racist analysis.[60] For example, Saskia Sassen has argued that the contemporary growth of inequality or poverty conceals subterranean processes of expulsion occurring at a historically unprecedented scale. "Since the 1980s, there has been a strengthening of dynamics that expel people from the economy and from society," Sassen contends, "and these dynamics are now hardwired into the normal functioning of these spheres."[61] For Sassen, these dynamics also represent a dramatic historical shift from a previous Keynesian and state-communist period where "the systemic tendency was toward incorporating people, especially as workers, notwithstanding social exclusions of all sorts."[62] Like Sassen, we believe that the concept of expulsion is not simply reducible to the phenomenon of superfluization produced by capitalist production but also refers to the forced removal or displacement of populations. Finally, the concept of expulsion for us also refers to the environmentally toxic material byproducts of capitalist production processes themselves.[63] We can understand the dynamics of contemporary comparative racial formation then as inscribed within processes of expulsion and expropriation constituted in relation to economic exploitation. These internally related processes not only link together what otherwise appear as incommensurable political struggles, positioning racial groups and defining racial difference within a logic of accumulation, but they also constitute the material basis for potential anti-systemic interracial solidarity. Whether such linkages may eventually give rise to more deliberate coordination among contemporary movements is an open question. The logic of the "exes" constitutes a potential material basis for solidarity beyond moral prescriptions or symbolic analogies of "parallel" oppression that have been subject to extensive contemporary criticism.

It is crucial to note here that the three "exes" do not describe distinct moments in a linear progressive teleology of capital, ending with the proletarianization of dispossessed racialized populations, but refers to overlapping and contradictory ebbs and flows of accumulation. Despite initial attempts to enslave native populations, settler expropriation of indigenous territory did not ultimately aim to proletarianize native groups, for example, but to displace and genocidally eliminate them to allow for the possibility of exploiting *other* laboring populations.[64] The interplay between the "exes" enables us to ask how racial boundaries are drawn across and within them in a more precise manner than tracing patterns of group inequality or noting historically durable status hierarchies.

The images of groups positioned within historically durable racial hierarchies are often presented as a kind of historically unchanging and endlessly self-perpetuating Foucauldian *dispositif*. Here the language of "power relations" that reproduce such hierarchies typically limits antiracist critique to institutions and institutionality or historically unchanging forms of racial group consciousness while sidestepping the question of how capitalist imperatives have historically shaped the terrain of institutional policymaking and relations between institutions. The image of racial groups stacked in a hierarchical status order, we contend, does not capture the complex, shifting patterns of intergroup and intragroup global value relations that index racial "life chances." Clarifying the action of capitalist imperatives enables a more detailed mapping and historicization of the integral relations between specific practices that produce and reproduce such group-differentiated material circumstances within overall patterns of capitalist inequality.

Tracing how shifting racial boundaries form between and within the "exes" counters a tendency within liberal and Marxist historiography to explain the ongoing reproduction of racial hierarchies, or ontologized racial positionality, through reference to a narrative of precapitalist or "primitive" accumulation that extends without interruption or material reconfiguration into the present. This narrative of the origins of race "freeze[s] our vision of the gendered racial violence indispensable to [capitalism's] birth as something that is essentially static, nonhistorical, and nonreproductive," as Nikhil Singh writes, "a historical event that ended in time and whose remains or traces in the present are vestigial, marginal, or anachronistic."[65] As Singh goes on to argue, the reproduction of capital through a logic of racialization is constitutive not only of enslavement and the production of wageless life but also of capitalist state formation and varieties of securitization where the application of force extends the reach of the commodity form into new zones of human activity.[66]

Understanding the three "exes" as mutually entailing avoids staging a critique of capital entirely from the standpoint of labor, in favor of theorizing the historical specificity of the wage relation within the broader context of core processes that define the capitalist mode of production. Doing so will allow us to trace relations between movements that arise to challenge institutional practices and policies that shape the distributive effects of these mechanisms while registering how ameliorating the consequences of one dimension of accumulation may often entail the intensification of others.

Foregrounding how the "exes" construct capitalist value as a general measure and medium of social relations helps us avoid reductive, monocausal debates about the causal primacy of either race or class as principles of social organization and instead connect otherwise seemingly disparate racialization mechanisms: incarceration, im/migration policy, and land grabs, along with forms of waged and unwaged labor, debt, and other financial instruments.[67] Bringing the "exes" into focus does not require a claim of causal primacy but instead enables us to retheorize how capitalism produces relational interlinkages among different domains of social life through a general measure of capitalist value. Rendering discrepant forms of social activity and the products of that activity commensurable, the formation and accumulation of capitalist value systematically reproduces state and nonstate institutions in relation to each other in ways that Fred Moten and Stefano Harney describe in terms of a common capitalist "language": "The hospital talks to the prison which talks to the university which talks to the NGO which talks to the corporation through governance, and not just to each other but about each other."[68] This shared language of capitalist value, they argue, "is the perfection of democracy under the general equivalent. It is also the annunciation of governance as the realisation of universal exchange on the grounds of capitalism."[69]

Moten and Harney's description of the entanglement of governance and capitalist conditions raises the question of how to understand the state-capital nexus. Most analyses of the state often remain focused on its relative autonomy or its disciplinary institutionality. Theorizing the links between the exes and the state, a specifically capitalist state form comes into view that is far more dependent upon the accumulation processes and the active construction and reproduction of capitalist social forms. Here the state management of capitalist imperatives historically anchors "racial hierarchy and imperial predation . . . in the depths of capitalist society."[70]

Territorial expropriation, state violence, and the destruction of local forms of subsistence by global and local capital in conjunction with imperialist interests, for instance, expel entire populations into im/migration streams toward centers of global accumulation to secure waged work or other means of reproduction. Such populations are subsequently vulnerable to expulsion from those centers at the hands of, for example, the massive U.S. deportation regime. Whether populations in motion remain within state boundaries or cross state lines, they are grouped into various legal categories created and managed through a territorialized capital-state nexus. The categories of immigrant and "illegal," acquired upon crossing the border into the U.S., operate as racialized categories of labor, noncitizenship, and restructured work regimes, while at the same time referring to cross-border joint security operations and infrastructures of incarceration, securitization, and detention.

The ongoing production of the "illegality" of highly expropriable laboring populations illustrates how exploitation, expropriation, and expulsion combine to transform immigration policy within the U.S. into a robust structural mechanism of racialization. Extending Marxist-feminist theories of social reproduction to account for how such policies "simultaneously rationalize and institutionalize a racialized regime of cheap labor," Susan Ferguson and David McNally have noted how such policy systematically "separates sites of production from sites of social reproduction" in ways that systematically lower the cost of the latter."[71] "Capital and the state in North America," they continue, "regularly draw from a pool of effectively 'cost free' labour power on whose past social reproduction they have not spent a dime."[72] Here Ferguson and McNally attempt to delineate expropriation and expulsion with the same specificity that has characterized theories of exploitation in order to more precisely analyze racialization processes often grouped under broad categories of increased immiseration and privation. It is important to note that expulsion need not physically displace populations. The same forces that set groups in motion can also immobilize them within deteriorating, spatially segregated zones abandoned by capital.

Finally, expulsion describes the specifically capitalist imperatives governing the insertion of planetary resources into cycles of accumulation and the resulting "externalities" of waste and catastrophic, ramifying environmental degradation. Against theories of climate change that seize upon notions of nature's revenge against humanity for its sins, theorists like Andreas Malm, Jason Moore, John Bellamy Foster, and Alfred Crosby, among others, have helped to interrogate undifferentiated conceptions of human activity at the heart of contemporary mainstream writing on anthropogenic climate change where an often dehistoricized figure of the human stands in an antagonistic relationship to an equally dehistoricized concept of nature.[73] Recent critical scholarship in the area of environmental racism from theorists like Robert Bullard, Laura Pulido, David Pellow, and Lisa Sun-Hee Park draw further attention to how the byproducts of capitalist production processes come to constitute the literal infrastructure of racialization in places like Flint, Michigan.[74]

The global outbreak of COVID-19 has moved the discussions on race, health, climate change, and the economy to the center of public debates. Thus far, most of the effort to understand race and COVID-19 in the U.S. has primarily registered the pandemic's grossly disproportional impact on Black, Latinx, and indigenous groups. Explanations of who is more likely to suffer catastrophic losses are premised on social stratification theories that highlight a range of racial, economic, and gendered disparities—including identifying populations most likely assigned to public-facing essential service work. Through a kind of causal reversal that the Fieldses have so sharply diagnosed, such unequal conditions have often been translated into a discourse of comorbidities that paint racial bodies as inherently more susceptible to infection, illness, and death.

By foregrounding the self-expanding character of accumulation, we can begin to connect the "exes" to the origins of COVID-19 and a series of recent viral outbreaks. This system-level analysis can also help to fundamentally challenge narratives of COVID-19's racial origins, as a "China plague," that have provoked waves of anti-Asian violence within the U.S. and calls for a civilizational war with an emerging global hegemon.[75]

Although further discussion of the Asiatic racial form of the pandemic is beyond the scope of this essay, we want to argue that a systemic antiracist analysis must move beyond simply challenging anti-Asian rhetoric or stereotypes. This Sinophobic imaginary is premised upon the disavowal of the material conditions of possibility for U.S. consumption patterns premised upon global supply chains connecting sites of consumption to global frontiers of resource extraction.

As Mike Davis and evolutionary biologist Rob Wallace have recently argued, the increasing frequency of "zoonotic spillover" events at the boundaries of the human and nonhuman natural world is not a biological inevitability but a sociohistorical product of global capitalist agricultural production practices driven by systemic growth imperatives.[76] Recent outbreaks of pathogenic diseases such as SARS-CoV-2 can be understood as the results of the large-scale commodification of animal and plant life that has historically set into motion the extensive clearing of forests, land dispossession, and erasure of complex biodiversity, along with the restructuring of health and subsistence networks that powerfully reshape the infrastructural conditions of racial group formation.

SARS-CoV-2 has emerged from the core of the historically racialized infrastructure of the capitalist global production and supply chains through which global populations meet fundamental material needs. A critique of this system of resource extraction, distribution, and valuation is radically incomplete if limited to an analysis of racially unequal access to the means of subsistence. System-level capitalist imperatives direct human movement and activity and render the nonhuman natural world an infinitely fungible input into a process of recursive value accumulation across every nation on earth. How states deliver commodified food, housing, and healthcare cannot be understood apart from how such subsistence categories index the exponential growth of an unfolding planetary catastrophe.

If the action of the exes highlights the materially interconnected nature of different projects of race-making, then we believe that the concept of race needs to be reimagined beyond discourses of identity and its properties as causal explanations for racial domination and exploitation. This essay's conclusion briefly addresses how we might understand race in alternative terms as an experience of group solidarity or "linked fate" that shapes, and is in turn shaped, by a field of multiple, local, and sometimes conflicting political projects. Reconceptualizing race in terms of "linked fate," we believe, presents an alternative to earlier scholarly debates over essentialism and anti-essentialism, or the mediated or unmediated character of subjective experience and epistemic standpoint that have come to define "identity politics" as an amorphous object of critique. For us, "linked fate" serves as a point of entry into a broader conversation about how race synthesizes politically contested practices and relational forms that the exes continually translate into capitalist value relations.

Redefining Race

THE SPLIT CHARACTER OF THE CONCEPT OF RACE

As David Camfield has observed, Marxist approaches to race have typically understood the concept as a mark of super-exploitation, national oppression, or denial of democratic rights.[77] The core arguments of *Racecraft* can be situated squarely within a tradition in which the concept has been defined as primarily an ascriptive social phenomenon and primarily subsumed within the project of forging working-class solidarity.

This approach to race contrasts sharply with popular and scholarly accounts of race that understand the concept mainly in terms of group cultural difference. While culture routinely functions as a proxy for race in contemporary debates over the nature of the economic demands of contemporary postwar anti-racist and feminist movements, popular and scholarly understandings of the relationship between race and culture have been profoundly impacted by Cold War geopolitical imperatives.[78] Figures like anthropologist Franz Boas and international organizations like UNESCO played a significant role in consolidating a postwar liberal anti-racist consensus around a pluralistic language of group culture and consciousness as a substitute for an older racial discourse of biological kinds.[79] By the mid-twentieth century, the turn to culture was imagined as a means to discredit earlier forms of scientific racism and racial eugenics in the aftermath of the defeat of Nazi Germany. As a tool of U.S. Cold War governance, a politics of cultural recognition would constitute a basis for equal citizenship claims while also fundamentally severing domestic anti-racist politics from an anti-systemic critique of capitalism and anti-colonial opposition to U.S. foreign policy.[80] As Alana Lentin has pointed out, UNESCO's mid-century approach to race was premised upon an understanding that the drivers of racism and racial violence lay in both individual prejudice and cultural misunderstanding, and therefore the possibility of reducing racial animus lay in encouraging intercultural communication.[81] Such a narrow reframing of the sources of racial domination, however, worked to systematically dematerialize racial reference and obscure the role that political economy and state power play in racial group formation, transforming the race/class problematic into what we take to be a misleading opposition between culture and political economy.[82]

The Cold War's impact on academic knowledge production in the U.S. powerfully shaped dominant affirmative conceptions of race by refuting an earlier biological discourse of racial kinds but translating older racial distinctions into an anthropological discourse of group culture. This turn to what Charisse Burden-Stelly has called an institutionalized "culturalism" informs subsequent attempts to frame the race/class problematic in terms of culture and political economy, conflating race and culture in ways that have structured contemporary liberal and neoliberal multicultural pluralism.[83]

In response to a post-1960s cross-disciplinary "cultural turn" across the academic social sciences and humanities, some scholars have sought to retheorize the concept of race to better account for the diverse and sometimes contradictory ways it functions as an affirmative category of political struggle tied to determinate political perspectives and programs.[84] In the context of contemporary political movements, race does not only describe a process that translates "something an aggressor does into ... something the target is," to return to the language of the Fieldses, but also describes how targeted populations have coordinated their responses to "something an aggressor does."[85] While a fuller engagement with their arguments is beyond the scope of this essay, Michael Dawson and Tommie Shelby offer overlapping reformulations of an affirmative conception of race—as linked fate and group solidarity—that neither reduces race to culture nor understands racial belonging as a guarantee of what Paul Gilroy has called the "pseudo-solidarities" of a "given or automatic unanimity."[86] Dawson's and Shelby's work offers some suggestive insights into how we might begin to reimagine the concept not primarily as an epistemic error, index of relative group inequality, or ascribed civic status, but instead as a field of sometimes politically opposed projects of survival and self-defense in the face of racist terror and subordination.

In relation to contemporary postwar U.S. black politics, in particular, Dawson has proposed the notion of "linked fate" in order to describe political behavior in which racial and ethnic "group interests have served as a useful proxy for self-interest."[87] Dawson's theorization of "linked fate" refrains from representing interest convergence as a normative ideal and instead attempts to describe the conditions that contribute to a sense of shared group challenges and common political objectives. Careful to distinguish his sense of interest convergence from theories of "group consciousness," Dawson has attempted to identify the changing conjunctural circumstances that might alternately produce interest divergence among black Americans—in particular focusing on the impact of class status and perceptions of black economic subordination on a sense of racial group belonging.[88] For Dawson, how a sense of "linked fate" develops or fails to develop along racial lines and the specific political programs that come to be associated with racial group interests create a dynamic context for political action.

Similarly, political philosopher Tommie Shelby has attempted to reimagine the contours of post–Jim Crow black politics in terms of group solidarity—a politically contested solidarity distinct from discourses of "thick" cultural identities proposed by earlier '60s-era cultural nationalist and later liberal multiculturalist ideals. In Shelby's analysis, neither cultural assimilation nor a commitment to a politics of respectability can protect black Americans from contemporary racism and racist practices. The philosopher thus distinguishes the project of constructing a collective identity from the cultivation of a practical "emancipatory black solidarity" that for him remains less exclusionary than models of racial group belonging defined primarily through normative cultural criteria.[89]

For Shelby, what he calls "nested" solidarities hold out the possibility of forming broader political coalitions that can extend across lines of intraracial and interracial differences.[90] Requiring consensus on what group culture is and ought to be as a basis for political action, Shelby continues, may constrain the pursuit of racial justice. Such an argument may seem committed to a too-restrictive conception of culture, but Shelby's reimagining of black solidarity as a historically developing form of "collective self-defense" nevertheless offers a useful model for regrounding the concept of race while avoiding "unanimist fantasies" of group consciousness that have been subject to persistent contemporary critique.[91] Shelby's normative vision of racial solidarity nevertheless raises the question of how such group solidarities emerge, combine, subdivide, and dissolve in the face of interest divergence, intragroup conflict, and the atomizing and combinatory force of capitalist competition. Racial solidarity is not singular, we argue, but instead describes a field of discontinuous, institutional, or parainstitutional projects that articulate group interest with a range of political objectives.

Racial group solidarity and instances of interracial solidarity have taken shape not only within capitalist workplaces but also against capitalist mechanisms of expropriation and expulsion shaping the application of state violence, geography of resource extraction, and historically gendered organization of socially reproductive labor. Such solidarities have facilitated the formation of improvised networks of material support that not only enable political action but help to meet material needs in the face of dispossession, unequal access to what Marx calls a historically and regionally specific "average amount of the means of subsistence" like food and shelter, and ongoing state and civilian violence.[92]

In elaborating a more expansive "nested" conception of linked fate at different levels of social construction, we take inspiration from a recent relational turn in contemporary sociology and racial formation theory that has aimed to move beyond discourses of isolable racial group *identities* and conceptualizing "race as a 'thing' or a property," toward an understanding of racial distinctions as produced and reproduced within relational fields.[93] Capturing a crucial premise of this relational turn, Natalia Molina and Daniel HoSang argue that "race does not define the characteristics of a person; instead, it is better understood as the space and connections between people that structure and regulate their association."[94] Here Molina and HoSang describe a methodological intervention that moves beyond theorizing interactions between discrete groups to consider specific processes that generate relational structures. Within this paradigm, there is not a single form of racism, but a relational field of discrepant racisms created by institutional mechanisms that are both portable and adaptable across groups.

Despite the relational critique of comparative approaches to the study of racial group formation, we combine a relational critique of substantialist conceptions of race with an account of enforced racial comparison in order to emphasize degrees of hierarchical social closure that continue to define racial boundaries in the U.S., even if the incorporation of subjects within the U.S. racial order presents a considerably more complex picture than an image of racial groups simply stacked atop each other in a fixed status hierarchy. For us, a comparative methodology remains important for theorizing how a "logic of [racial] sorting, ranking, and comparison" is entangled with the fundamentally comparative measure of value at the heart of capitalist production and social reproduction.[95] Our account of relationality, in other words, emphasizes how racial formation passes through state-managed processes of capitalist commodification, production, and social reproduction that produce distinctive racializing effects and encode the results of ongoing racial conflict and economic competition into calculable value differentials of labor, land, risk, and relative disposability.

While we build on the premises of this relational scholarship, this work raises the question of how to theorize the co-constitutive character of these mechanisms and the multiplicity of social relations generated by them. Moving beyond acknowledging racism as always already relational, we build on contemporary Marxist feminist attempts to grapple with the question of what materially binds and structurally reproduces these relations together beyond how they are experienced in consciousness. For us, theories that posit racial group consciousness and transhistorical forms of racial affinity or animus can explain neither the eruption of historically specific instances of interracial conflict nor the material constraints on collective action that anti-racist, anti-colonial, and anti-imperialist movements have been forced to confront over time.

Within this scholarship, capitalist accumulation processes do not generate one set of relations among many but rather constitute a measure of value that materially binds together entire social formations. Here the measure and medium of capitalist value are "integral to the social reproduction of the whole"—though it is important to note that the "whole" in this case is a specifically capitalist totality of relations and not an exhaustive description of relational bonds or systems of oppression.[96] This critical Marxist feminist insight enables a rethinking of material relations *between* such systems mapped by the "trinity" of race, class, and gender categories. As Susan Ferguson and others have argued, such systems and categories remain extrinsically related despite the desire to treat them in a non-additive manner.

Foregrounding how the "exes" reproduce entire social formations over time provide one persuasive response to the question of how categories of racial, gender, and class categories and the relational processes and formations they synthesize are materially reproduced together over time.[97] At the same time, the Marxist feminist emphasis on capitalism as describing not only exploitation at the point of production but a system of integral social reproduction resolves persistent theoretical problems posed by framing the race/class problematic primarily at the level of categorical "identities."

The abstract categories of analysis that construct the opposition between particularity and universality have in recent scholarship been mapped on to the race/class problematic in ways that for us conflate the features of subjects and structures, reify materially ungrounded normative ideals, and remain trapped within the ambit of a politics of the subject.[98] As Denise Ferreira da Silva has argued, the "debate seems stuck in modernity's constitutive oppositions":

> Where is the alternative when all that is offered is an old account of domination, in which a self-described (abstract) universal precludes any transformative opposition through a founding exclusion of (concrete) local cultures and a new account of hegemony in which the political field is inhabited by already constituted culturally

different others of the West who are dominated because of the identification of a particular local [Western] culture with the Universal?[99]

Da Silva maintains that both particularity and universality are bound up with historical and scientific production of an absolutely "transparent," autonomous, and self-determining Enlightenment subject and a corresponding racialized non-European subject susceptible to the heteronomy of external determination and experience. "Transparent" subjects are not only defined against non-European populations but also capable of "rewriting racial difference as a signifier of cultural difference" and embedding those populations within a narrative of historical development where "the racial subaltern is always already inscribed as a historical subject who finally come representation as a *transparent 'I.'*"[100] Moving beyond by now formulaic critiques of universality as a disavowed particularism, da Silva contends that difference can be rendered "transparent"—with profound implications for contemporary movements for racial emancipation.

Race can only appear as a form of "particularity" in relation to a racially marked or unmarked normative whiteness. Conversely, universality appears as a floating and historically changing signifier that opens a metaphysical space of freedom precisely through the negation of race as particularity and other forms of social determination. For us, this frozen theoretical antinomy does not call for an affirmation of either universality or particularity, but instead an analysis of the historical constitution of these terms under capitalist conditions.

As Moishe Postone has argued, capitalism produces a historically specific version of the opposition between universality and particularity, where universality does not describe an attribute of the working class as a collective subject but instead the alienated form of capitalist value itself shaping liberal ideals of formal equality. For Postone, Marxist critique "does not simply—and affirmatively—oppose the universal to the particular, nor does it dismiss the former as a mere sham; rather, as a theory of social constitution, it examines critically and grounds socially the character of modern universality and equality."[101] "The universal is not a transcended idea but a historically constituted 'specific universal form,'" he continues, "related to other social forms that emerge with the development and consolidation of the commodity-determined form of social relations."[102] Anti-capitalist critique thus "calls neither for the implementation nor the abolition of the ideals of bourgeois society; it points neither to the realization of the abstract homogeneous universality of the existent formation nor to the abolition of universality."[103] "With overcoming of capitalism, the unity of society already constituted in alienated form," Postone argues, could be "effected differently by forms of political practice, in a way that need not negate qualitative specificity."[104] In other words, the universality/particularity dyad refers to real social processes whose overcoming will help to dereify the quasi-logical form of the opposition as a framework for intuiting the potential shape of post-capitalist social relations. When superimposed upon the race/class problematic, the mutually defining terms of the universality/particularity opposition remain tied to notions of identity that pit a class-based universal subject of history against the particularism of a range of other group identities and group-based demands.

While indebted to Dawson's initial formulation, we thus take "linked fate" as a reference not only to politicized racial belonging but also to a matrix of relations systematically reproduced by capitalist processes over time. The interplay between these two senses of "linkage" is key to reframing the race/class problematic as a relational form under capitalist conditions.

This definitional clarification can help to theorize how racial group formation is entangled with processes of capitalist value formation, elaborate a more politically differentiated account of racial experience, and reimagine the potential material basis of ever-widening solidarities. As Ashley Bohrer has recently argued, "Capitalism thus links us together, in a tie that binds us, often painfully, in relation to one another," within a system where "difference and sameness are produced constantly and in relationship to one another."[105]

Linked fate is not merely a description of what binds us together at different spatial scales, however, but also how we might reconceive emancipatory solidarity, not in terms of the birth of a global revolutionary subject from the developmental overcoming of racial particularism, but instead through the elaboration and potential coordination of political objectives. Within this relational web, solidarity for us is not reducible to an additive gathering of populations with incommensurable experiences and identities but the possibility of coordinating transformative anti-systemic action across a field of materially interlinked political objectives.[106] In arguing for the usefulness of politicized linked fate as a framework for re-embedding phenomenological accounts of racialization within relational structures and the material processes that reproduce such structures, we want to offer a few broad observations on how these three levels of analysis might recontextualize lived experience as a crucial category of political analysis.

Often taken to be synonymous with identity, lived experience registers and synthesizes the effects of an array of social forces, often within historically gendered domains of social life. As a fundamental aspect of racial group formation, lived experience becomes powerfully defined through both oppression and affirmative visions of racial belonging. Racial positioning powerfully constitutes lived experience at a pre-reflective, non-discursive level, impacting political subjects' sense of embodiment, agency, and basic psychic integrity in profound ways.[107] As a criterion of political judgment within activist spaces, reference to lived experience is often mobilized to answer questions of who racially belongs, who can determine the boundaries of racially representative political perspectives, and who is and is not authorized to make political movement demands.

The fact that subjects who might share similar experiences of oppression, for example, can come to radically different political conclusions about that experience reveals how experiential authority both contains and potentially conceals a struggle over political interpretation. The boundaries of what counts as lived experience are often established by bracketing the question of political ideology and perspective—a development that numerous scholars argue has been facilitated by the progressive absorption of 1960s-era insurgent political movements into academic institutions, electoral politics, and an emergent nonprofit sector that have all progressively worked to sever anti-racist from anti-capitalist analysis.[108] Neither shared social location nor experience possesses an automatic political valence. Appeals to lived experience can authorize political ideologies that are regressive, just as affirmative identities can challenge ascriptive racialization by promoting profoundly conservative political visions. In the present, such visions include the resurgence of ethnonationalist fantasies of precolonial peoplehood mobilized by political regimes in India and Turkey.[109]

However, the concept of linked fate captures a moment of political determination where experience is an object of struggle over the authorization of specific political commitments without assuming that normative political judgments are immanent to experience itself. For us, race describes a field of contending political projects that converge and diverge, not the actions of monolithic collective racial subjects with singular political wills. Assuming that shared identities indicate shared political perspectives has significant negative strategic consequences for contemporary anti-racist political movements. In the wake of the police murder of George Floyd, for example, Black-led multiracial mobilizations in major cities across the U.S. continue to confront broad state and non-state opposition to abolitionist demands—opposition that includes Black mayors, city council members, and police chiefs. As Keeanga-Yamahtta Taylor contends, since the 1960s, "governments and politicians widely promoted greater Black control of urban space as a preventative measure against urban uprisings" in a context of budget cuts, deepening inequality, and shrinking municipal coffers.[110] Under these conditions, deepening austerity has been managed by an increasingly multiracial layer of municipal politicians who have consistently moved to strengthen the punitive arm of state governance. "The conflict between the Black political establishment and ordinary Blacks, however, has been driven not only by budget constraints," Keeanga-Yamahtta Taylor continues, "but also by contempt for black poor and a dramatically narrowed vision for what constitutes Black liberation."[111]

As a core liberal anti-racist measure of racial progress, this logic of racial representation has been transformed into a vast counterinsurgent infrastructure that disrupts, delegitimizes, and demobilizes political insurgencies by both concealing deep intragroup conflicts over political ideology and stigmatizing emergent forms of interracial solidarity. The collapse of political ideology into racial positionality elides conflicts *within* contemporary social movements between politicians, nonprofit organizations, and heterogeneous political actors with significantly different political priorities, strategies, and tactical repertoires.[112] Retheorizing racial group formation under specifically capitalist conditions does not deny the importance of experience. Instead, such contextualization helps to situate richer accounts of lived contradictions, the material particularity of social locations, and the significance of determinate political commitments in framing and reframing the very meaning of racial experience in an era of resurgent mass movements.

Notes

1. E. San Juan Jr., "Marxism and the Race/Class Problematic: A Re-Articulation," *Cultural Logic* 10 (June 2003): 1–16, https://doi.org/10.14288/clogic.v10i0.191792.

2. Mustafa Emirbayer and Matthew Desmond, for example, have recently attempted to offer a comprehensive theory of race focused on the U.S. racial order in particular; see Emirbayer and Desmond, *The Racial Order* (Chicago: University of Chicago Press, 2015).

3. In future work we intend to track the historical evolution of the race/class problematic and changing definitions of its terms, from the writing of early- to mid-twentieth-century Black communists to the contemporary scholarship of Cedric Robinson and Stuart Hall.

4. Alexandra Minna Stern, *Proud Boys and the White Ethnostate: How the Alt-Right Is Warping the American Imagination* (Boston: Beacon Press, 2020), 45. See also José Pedro Zúquete, *The Identitarians: The Movement against Globalism and Islam in Europe* (Notre Dame, Ind.: University of Notre Dame Press, 2018).

5. For a brief overview of the shifting contemporary rhetoric of separatist, ethnonationalist, and ostensibly "multicultural" Anglo-European racial "identitarian" movements, see Matthew N. Lyons, "Ctrl-Alt-Delete: The Origins and Ideology of the Alternative Right," *Political Research Associates* (January 20, 2017): 1–16, https://www.politicalresearch.org/2017/01/20/ctrl-alt-delete-report-on-the-alternative-right. In the words of U.S. "Alt-Right" spokesperson Richard Spencer, "Identitarianism is fundamentally about difference, about culture as an expression of a certain people at a certain time. . . . Identitarianism acknowledges the incommensurable nature of different peoples and cultures—and thus looks forward to a world of true diversity and multiculturalism" (ibid., 6).

6. On the race/class problematic reconfigured as an opposition between class politics and "identity politics," see Robin D. G. Kelley, "Identity Politics and Class Struggle," *New Politics* 6, no. 2 (Winter 1997): 84–96, and Todd Gitlin, "The Rise of Identity Politics," *Dissent* (Spring 1997): 172–77. On the problematic reconfigured as an opposition between culture and political economy, see Janice Peck, "Why We Shouldn't Be Bored with the Political Economy versus Cultural Studies Debate," *Cultural Critique* 64, no. 1 (Fall 2006): 92–125. On the problematic understood in terms of an opposition between particularity and universality, see Judith Butler, Ernesto Laclau, and Slavoj Žižek, *Contingency, Hegemony, Universality: Contemporary Dialogues on the Left* (London: Verso, 2000). For a reading of the race/class problematic in terms of exploitation and oppression, see Ashley Bohrer, *Marxism and Intersectionality: Race, Gender, Class and Sexuality under Contemporary Capitalism* (London: Transcript, 2020). On racial ontology, see Frank Wilderson III, "Gramsci's Black Marx: Whither the Slave in Civil Society?," *Social Identities* 9, no. 2 (August 2003): 225–40. For recent critiques of readings of Marx that presuppose an ontology of labor, see Jacques Derrida, *Specters of Marx: The State of the Debt, The Work of Mourning & the New International* (New York: Routledge, 2011). For a defense of a nonontological reading of Marx and Marxist critique, see Moishe Postone, *Time, Labor, and Social Domination: A Reinterpretation of Marx's Critical Theory* (Cambridge: Cambridge University Press, 1993). On the opposition between logic and history or a structural logic of capitalist accumulation versus the nonstructural historicity of racial hierarchies, see the exchange between Ellen Meiksins Wood, "Class, Race, and Capitalism," *Political Power and Social Theory* 15 (2002): 275–84, and Adolph Reed, "Unraveling the Relation of Race and Class in American Politics," *Political Power and Social Theory* 15 (November 2002): 265–74.

7. We would broadly characterize what Srdjan Vucetic calls "substitutionist" orientations toward the concept, in the work of Robert Miles, for example, as eliminativist; Srdjan Vucetic, "Against Race Taboos," in *Race and Racism in International Relations: Confronting the Global Colour Line*, ed. Alexander Anievas, Nivi Manchanda, and Robbie Shilliam (New York: Routledge, 2014), 109. See, for example, Robert Miles, *Racism after "Race Relations"* (London: Routledge, 2004).

8. For an introductory overview of critical race philosophy, see Kathryn T. Gines, "Introduction: Critical Philosophy of Race beyond the Black/White Binary," *Critical Philosophy of Race* 1, no. 1 (2013): 28–37, https://muse.jhu.edu/article/501720.

9. Although we do not have the space in this essay for an extended engagement with the body of contemporary scholarship organized under the rubric of "racial capitalism," indebted to the writing of Cedric Robinson, we plan to take up this work in future writing. While the term "racial capitalism" is frequently attributed

to Robinson, the term "first emerged in the context of the anti-Apartheid and southern African liberation struggles in the 1970s. Racial capitalism was used by activists and writers, many aligned with the Black Consciousness Movement"; Charisse Burden-Stelly, Peter James Hudson, and Jemima Pierre, "Racial Capitalism, Black Liberation, and South Africa," *Black Agenda Report*, December 16, 2020, https://www.blackagendareport.com/racial-capitalism-black-liberation-and-south-africa.

10. Karen E. Fields and Barbara J. Fields, *Racecraft: The Soul of Inequality in American Life* (London: Verso, 2012).

11. Michael C. Dawson, *Behind the Mule: Race and Class in African-American Politics* (Princeton, N.J.: Princeton University Press, 1995), 77. While initially developed as a measure of Black racial group solidarity and explanation for aggregate political behavior, Michael Dawson's concept of "linked fate" has been taken up by subsequent scholars to gauge degrees of group consciousness for a range of racial, ethnic, gendered, national, religious, and class populations; see Natalie Masuoka and Gabriel R. Sanchez, "Brown-Utility Heuristic? The Presence and Contributing Factors of Latino Linked Fate," *Hispanic Journal of Behavioral Sciences* 32, no. 4 (October 2010): 519–31, https://doi.org/10.1177/0739986310383129; Evelyn Simien, "Race, Gender, and Linked Fate," *Journal of Black Studies* 35, no. 5 (May 2005): 529–50; and Michael J. Donnelly, "Material Interests, Identity and Linked Fate in Three Countries," *British Journal of Political Science* (March 2020): 1–19.

12. We develop a more detailed analysis of these three levels of analysis in an upcoming book-length study.

13. While we focus on theorizing the relationship between capitalism and racial group formation, the framework we develop enables further inquiry into the material referent of other integrally related categories of analysis, such as gender and sexuality. Our analysis of the conceptual constitution of categories of analysis and of capitalist value formation as a relational logic reproduced across a range of social sites beyond the workplace is indebted to the wide-ranging Marxist feminist approaches to gender that include the work of Susan Ferguson, Lise Vogel, and Cinzia Arruzza.

14. Theodore Allen, "Summary of the Argument of *The Invention of the White Race*," *Cultural Logic* 1, no. 2 (Spring 1998): 3, https://doi.org/10.14288/clogic.v2i0.191851.

15. W. E. B. Du Bois, *Black Reconstruction in America 1860–1880* (New York: Simon and Schuster, 1999), 28.

16. Stefano Harney and Fred Moten, *Undercommons: Fugitive Planning and Black Study* (New York: Minor Compositions, 2013), 42.

17. Paul Gilroy extends eliminativist arguments to include a critique of what the theorist takes to be ultimately negative strategic consequences of race-based organizing for anti-colonial and anti-racist movements. Such movements, Gilroy contends, were and continue to be constrained by "unanimist fantasies" that turn ontologized conceptions of race into a "precondition for various versions of determinism: biological, nationalistic, cultural, and now, genomic"; Gilroy, *Against Race: Imagining Political Culture beyond the Color Line* (Cambridge, Mass.: Harvard University Press, 2001), 52.

18. Cedric J. Robinson, *Black Marxism: The Making of the Black Radical Tradition* (Chapel Hill: University of North Carolina Press), 66.

19. See Joshua Glasgow, "A Third Way in the Race Debate," *Journal of Political Philosophy* 14, no. 2 (April 2006): 163–85.

20. Commenting upon approaches to the problem of arriving at any single definitive definition of the concept of race, Ron Mallon has argued that what he describes as the "semantic strategy" of resolving debates over the referent of the concept are not only unproductive but obscure an underlying consensus among a broad range of scholars. "The semantic strategy seems to offer an avenue by which to settle disputes. . . . Nonetheless, pursuing racial phenomena from this direction is obfuscating and ineffective. It is obfuscating because, as we have seen, it makes a philosophical debate over the reference of racial terms and concepts appear as a genuine metaphysical disagreement about what is in the world. It is ineffective because it is unlikely to be fruitful in resolving the question of how we ought to use 'race' talk"; Mallon, "'Race': Normative, Not Metaphysical or Semantic," *Ethics* 116, no. 3 (2006): 548. While we concur with Mallon that false debates over the concept are often traceable back to unshared definitional presuppositions, we maintain that significant disagreements over how "we ought to use 'race talk'" are inseparable from the problem of definition.

21. Stuart Hall, *The Fateful Triangle: Race, Ethnicity, Nation* (Cambridge, Mass.: Harvard University Press, 2017), 31, 68. Due to space constraints, we cannot offer an extended engagement with the complex and changing ways in which concept of race, routed through a neo-Gramscian and Althusserian theory of ideology, develops in Stuart Hall's writings from the 1950s through the 2000s—especially its relationship to cultural representation and hybridity. We hope to take up this topic in the future. Here we would like to echo Hall's insistence, in his influential early essay "Race, Articulation, and Societies Structured in Dominance," that "the analysis of political and ideological structures must be grounded in their material conditions of existence; and the historical premise—that the specific forms of those relations cannot be deduced, a priori, from this level but must be made historically specific 'by supplying these further delineations which explain their *differentiae specificae*'"; in *Black British Cultural Studies*, ed. Houston Baker Jr., Manthia Diawara, and Ruth Lindeborg (Chicago: University of Chicago Press, 1996), 35.

22. Combahee River Collective, "The Combahee River Collective Statement," in *Home Girls: A Black Feminist Anthology*, ed. Barbara Smith (New Brunswick, N.J.: Rutgers University Press, 2000), 264–74. For an early critique of "identity politics" as fragmenting broader emancipatory social movements and leading to the decline of the U.S. New Left, see Gitlin, "Rise of Identity Politics," 172–77.

23. For a recent overview of contemporary scholarship looking to both retain and refine identity as a broad comparative concept, see Margaret Wetherell and Chandra Talpade Mohanty, eds., *The Sage Handbook of Identities* (Thousand Oaks, Calif.: Sage, 2013).

24. We draw our definition of the New Left from Van Gosse, "A Movement of Movements: The Definition and Periodization of the New Left," in *A Companion to Post-1945 America*, ed. Jean-Christophe Agnew and Roy Rosenzweig (Hoboken, N.J.: John Wiley & Sons, 2008), 277–302.

25. Linda Martin Alcoff, *Visible Identities: Race, Gender, and the Self* (Oxford: Oxford University Press, 2006), 42–43.

26. Zeus Leonardo, "After the Glow: Race Ambivalence and Other Educational Prognoses," *Educational Philosophy and Theory* 43, no. 6 (January 2011): 675–98.

27. Paul C. Taylor, *Race: A Philosophical Introduction*, 2nd ed (Cambridge, Mass.: Polity, 2013), 89–90.

28. Taylor's focus on the link between racial ideology and practice echoes both the notion of "racial projects" elaborated by Michael Omi and Howard Winant and Stuart Hall's deployment of the concept of articulation, though Taylor's arguments are not explicitly premised upon an Althusserian understanding of social formations as composed of economic, ideological, and political dimensions of social formations. "A racial project is simultaneously an interpretation, representation, or explanation of racial identities and meanings," Omi and Winant write, "and an effort to organize and distribute resources (economic, political, cultural) along particular racial lines"; Michael Omi and Howard Winant, *Racial Formation in the United States* (New York: Routledge, 2015), 125.

29. The anthropologist Patrick Wolfe has characterized these two orders as marking the difference between "race as doctrine" and "race in action," or racialization. For Wolfe, racialization processes are made up of "an assortment of local attempts to impose classificatory grids on a variety of colonised populations, to particular though coordinated ends." Racialization is thus an ensemble of social practices that are "prior to and not limited to racial doctrine"—an observation that highlights how the increasing systematization of racial doctrine is not only distinct from but also has historically lagged behind changing material practices; Wolfe, *Traces of History: Elementary Structures of Race* (London: Verso, 2016), 10. The ascriptive cast of the concept of racialization and its implicit normative focus on the imposition rather than assertion of racial identity has led critic David Theo Goldberg, for example, to abandon the term; Goldberg, "Racial Americanization," in *Racialization: Studies in Theory and Practice*, ed. Karim Murji and John Solomos (Oxford: Oxford University Press, 2005), 87–102.

30. The forensic verification and measurability of individual racist intent limit further investigation into how histories of racial domination can become institutionalized background conditions that are no longer measurable but a condition of measurement; see Lily Hu, "Disparate Causes, Pt. I," *Phenomenal World*, October 11, 2019, https://phenomenalworld.org/analysis/disparate-causes-i, and "Disparate Causes, Pt. II," *Phenomenal World*, October 17, 2019, https://phenomenal world.org/analysis/disparate-causes-pt-ii.

31. Taylor, *Race: A Philosophical Introduction*, 2nd ed. (Cambridge: Polity, 2013), 119.

32. Fields and Fields, *Racecraft*, collects together essays written during the period of 1988–2012.

33. Hall, *Fateful Triangle*, 31. A number of recent historical monographs on civil rights movement–building foreground questions of self-defense and survival. On the historical role of communal survival and self-protection strategies in the context of civil rights struggles, for example, see Christopher Strain, *Pure Fire: Self-Defense as Activism in the Civil Rights Era* (Athens: University of Georgia Press, 2005); Akinyele Umoja, *We Will Shoot Back* (New York: New York University Press, 2013); and Charles E. Cobb, *This Nonviolent Stuff'll Get You Killed: How Guns Made the Civil Rights Movement Possible* (New York: Basic Books, 2014). For historical studies of subsistence-based planning around food, housing, schooling, and health care as key aspects of a broader conception of community self-defense, see Monica M. White, "'A Pig and a Garden': Fannie Lou Hamer and the Freedom Farms Cooperative,"

Food and Foodways 25, no. 1 (February 2017): 20–39, and David Hilliard, ed., *The Black Panther Party: Service to the People Programs* (Albuquerque: University of New Mexico Press, 2010). White draws attention to how Mary Lou Hamer's Freedom Farm Cooperative in 1960s Sunflower County, Mississippi, directly connected land ownership with an ongoing voting rights campaign, allowing local community members to pool resources and weather job loss as the result of their political activity.

34. Fields and Fields, *Racecraft*, 101.

35. While we do not undertake this work in this essay, the concept of racism is itself in need of historization and semantic disaggregation not only because it defines race but because it also structures distinctive and changing U.S. postwar anti-racist political objectives—from representation to reparations. The term describes a range of policies, practices, and ideologies—from early debates over proto-racial distinctions like *limpieza de sangre* and the Christianization of indigenous populations to the biological determinism of nineteenth- and early twentieth-century "race science" and contemporary antidiscrimination law's concern with establishing causal linkages between intentions and racially disproportional impacts on legally protected populations. The general framework through which we retheorize the race/class problematic can also help to identify how references to racism are often implicitly tied to specific levels of analysis—identities, institutionally mediated group relations, and more rarely, processes of accumulation. Bringing capitalist processes into focus within this discussion can help to denaturalize the often-implicit capitalist background conditions that structure contemporary discussions of racial inequality, distributive justice, and "universal" social policies.

36. The Fieldses' eliminativism is not reducible to racial skepticism, however—a move that drastically narrows the concept of race to a peculiar self-perpetuating form of ideological projection cloaked in the language of biology. For a brief elaboration of the central arguments of racial skepticism, see Mallon, "'Race': Normative, Not Metaphysical or Semantic," 525–51.

37. Fields and Fields, *Racecraft*, 100.

38. Ibid., 16.

39. Ibid., 17.

40. Ibid., 101.

41. Ibid., 17.

42. Ibid., 22.

43. Ibid., 27.

44. Ibid., 111.

45. Ibid., 22.

46. Ibid., 25.

47. Ibid., 266.

48. Barbara Fields, "Slavery, Race and Ideology in the United States of America," *New Left Review* 1, no. 181 (May–June 1990): 99.

49. For us, the conceptualization of race as either functional or nonfunctional to profit-making often relies on reductive conceptions of capitalism that ignore how a range of economic forms, from property to interest, can be racially organized and differentiating. Just as there can be nonprofitable practices and industries that remain thoroughly structured by a capitalist logic of accumulation, racist practices

can either ensure or hinder successful profit realization for individual capitals while in both cases being thoroughly structured by capitalist imperatives and value relations.

50. Fields and Fields, *Racecraft*, 267.

51. Ibid., 267.

52. Critics like Walter Benn Michaels and Adolph Reed have mounted a series of critiques of anti-racism as a categorically neoliberal political program focused exclusively on amelioration of horizontal group inequality. For Reed and Michaels, a primary focus on racial group inequality redirects attention away from worsening general inequality and ignores the problem of how to build broader coalitions of support for universal social democratic policies like universal healthcare. As Michaels and Reed contend in a recent article, "Racism isn't what principally produces our inequality and antiracism won't eliminate it. And because racism is not the principal source of inequality today, antiracism functions more as a misdirection that justifies inequality than a strategy for eliminating it"; Reed and Michaels, "The Trouble with Disparity," *nonsite.org* 32 (October 2020), https://nonsite.org/the-trouble-with-disparity/. In an effort to answer critics who characterize this argument as an example of class reductionism, Reed has recently argued that the latter charge is designed to preemptively end political debate over policy and strategy and to obscure political histories in which the anti-capitalist left "understood the battles for racial and gender equity as constitutive elements of the struggle for working-class power. Class reductive leftism is a figment of the political imagination roused by those who have made their peace with neoliberalism"; Adolf Reed, "The Myth of Class Reductionism," *New Republic*, September 25, 2019, https://newrepublic.com/article/154996/myth-class-reductionism. Reed's rejection of a narrowly defined politics of anti-racism, however, largely accepts the polarized terms of the race/class problematic embraced by his critics. As Asad Haider has noted in a recent critique of Reed's position, "Reed sets out to refute the myth of class reductionism, he starts by pointing out there's actually no incompatibility between addressing racial inequality and economic inequality. But then when he proceeds to reject racism as an analytic category, and dismisses the politics of antiracism, he ends up mirroring the liberal separation between race and class"; Haider, "How Calling Someone a 'Class Reductionist' Became a Lefty Insult," *Salon*, July 25, 2020, https://www.salon.com/2020/07/25/how-calling-someone-a-class-reductionist-became-a-lefty-insult/. While others have engaged with these arguments at greater length, we would like to note that the argument advanced by Reed and Michaels depends upon a definitional association with anti-racism and "horizontal" group inequality rather than a range of other historical examples of how such a politics has been defined through an anti-colonial, anti-imperialist, and/or anti-capitalist analysis. Second, the argument defines capitalism primarily in terms of the concept of economic inequality and the alternative to neoliberal antiracism in terms of the social democratic management of the distributive consequences of capitalist production. For us, distributionist critiques of capitalism offer a limited explanation of the differentiated mechanisms that produce inequality while ignoring the self-expanding ecocidal character of capitalist imperatives, systemic constraints on redistributive policy, existing critiques of full employment as a normative ideal, and the historical trajectory of actually existing social democracies. For a critique of Marxist attempts to define capitalist exploitation as primarily a form of

maldistribution rather than a historically specific structure of production, see Guglielmo Carchedi, "Classes and Class Analysis," in *The Debate on Classes* (London: Verso, 1998), 105–25.

53. Although we concur with Jodi Byrd's contention that the logic of racialization and settler colonization are analytically distinct, the concept of expropriation and expropriability, we believe, can illuminate the specifically capitalist features of the ongoing racialization of indigeneity. Expropriation, of course, presents the continuous historical possibility of the emergence of what Patrick Wolfe has called a genocidal "logic of elimination"; Wolfe, "Settler Colonialism and the Elimination of the Native," *Journal of Genocide Research* 8, no. 4 (December 2006): 387. See also Jodi Byrd, *The Transit of Empire: Indigenous Critiques of Colonialism* (Minneapolis: University of Minnesota Press, 2011).

54. Karl Marx, *Capital: A Critique of Political Economy*, trans. Ben Fowkes (London: Penguin Classics, 1990), 1:873. For Marx, primitive accumulation, of course, gives way to "mature" capitalist social formations where the "silent compulsion of economic relations sets the seal on the domination of the capitalist over the worker. Direct extra-economic force is still of course used, but only in exceptional cases"; Marx, *Capital*, 1:899. For a nonteleological reconstruction of the concept of primitive accumulation as a descriptor of the systematic ongoing "separation of the bulk of humanity from the productive power of nature," see Robert Nichols, "Disaggregating Primitive Accumulation," *Radical Philosophy* 194 (November–December 2015): 18–28. For Nichols, the decidedly nonexceptional character of "extra-economic" force, dispossession, and expropriation that remains a structural feature of accumulation "comes to name a distinct logic of capitalist development grounded in the appropriation and monopolization of the productive powers of the natural world in a manner that orders (but does not directly determine) social pathologies related to dislocation, class stratification, and/or exploitation, while simultaneously converting the planet into a homogeneous and universal means of production"; Nichols, "Disaggregating Primitive Accumulation," 27. This logic of territorial appropriation and possession becomes for Nichols a key theoretical framework for understanding indigenous dispossession, sovereignty, and movements for decolonization.

55. Nancy Fraser, "Expropriation and Exploitation in Racialized Capitalism: A Reply to Michael Dawson," *Critical Historical Studies* 3, no. 1 (March 20, 2016): 164, 170, 168.

56. In their response to Nancy Fraser's 2018 presidential address to the American Philosophical Association, Jordan T. Camp, Christina Heatherton, and Manu Karuka argue for adopting the analytic of racism over that of race; Camp, Heatherton, and Karuka, "A Response to Nancy Fraser," *Politics Letters*, May 20, 2019, http://quarterly .politicsslashletters.org/a-response-to-nancy-fraser/). Following critics such as Cedric Robinson and the Fieldses, they define race as an "invention or conceit" and argue that Fraser's focus on race keeps her analysis grounded in a framework of disproportional effects and representations of purported group differences. They suggest that a missing engagement in Fraser's address with Marxist critical thinkers such as W. E. B. Du Bois, Oliver Cox, and Angela Davis on the racism/capitalism nexus prevents her from conceptualizing how Marxist theories of imperialism and colonialism provide the basis for theorizing racism. We agree with Camp, Heatherton, and Karuka about the crucial importance of developing frameworks in broader conversation with preexisting theoretical analyses of race/racism—analyses

that are either absent or mislabeled in Fraser's presidential address. However, we maintain that retheorizing race remains imperative for describing the contours of existing anti-racist politics. As our analysis of *Racecraft* has demonstrated, a normative eliminativist orientation toward race in favor of a focus on racism does not necessarily resolve the theoretical questions raised by the interplay of oppressive and affirmative group representation or dispense with disproportionality as a measure of relations of exploitation. Without further definitional clarification of the meaning and material referent of race, racial eliminativism forecloses inquiry into how capitalism continues to historically organize group formation, rework racial categories, and restructure the relations between populations. While definitions of race and racial oppression remain relatively undertheorized in Fraser's address, her recent writing has come to insist on the importance of defining capitalism as integral to the reproduction of racist ideology and practices. Fraser has attempted to move beyond "formal" approaches premised on ideal-typical definitions of market activity, in which capitalist logic appears to be race-neutral, to consider how basic state-mediated capitalist processes, such as exploitation and expropriation, are structurally related and historically racially organized. While within this essay we can't offer a more detailed evaluation of how Fraser maps and periodizes the connection between the "exes" and how she draws racial boundaries between the "exes," we understand her recent writing as a direct challenge to contemporary Marxist analyses that tend to counterpose a structural logic of accumulation to a contingent, nonstructural, and essentially epiphenomenal history of racial group formation.

    57. Fraser, "Expropriation and Exploitation," 166.

    58. Ibid., 169, 165.

    59. See Glen Sean Coulthard, *Red Skin, White Masks: Rejecting the Colonial Politics of Recognition; Indigenous Americas* (Minneapolis: University of Minnesota Press, 2014), and Nichols, "Disaggregating Primitive Accumulation," 18–28.

    60. Marx, *Capital*, 1:781, and Michael Denning, "Wageless Life," *New Left Review*, no. 66 (December 2010): 79. Marx uses the terms *Enteignung* (expropriation) and *Verjagung* (expulsion) to describe processes of expropriation and expulsion of fifteenth-century English agricultural laboring populations in the later chapters of volume 1 of *Capital*. Our use of these terms, while indebted to this initial formulation, is more elastic—including a broad range of capitalist processes that are not bound to the stadial trajectory of Marx's conception of primitive accumulation. For a remarkably prescient and understudied mid-century discussion of racialization and superfluization in the U.S. brought on by automation in particular, see James Boggs, *The American Revolution: Pages from a Negro Worker's Notebook* (New York: Monthly Review, 1963). For recent scholarship on automation that argues that rather than labor-saving technologies causing mass unemployment, low and slow growth rates in the U.S., along with the massive expansion of a low-wage service work sector, have been the main driver of employment precarity, see Aaron Benanav, *Automation and the Future of Work* (New York: Verso, 2020), and Jason E. Smith, *Smart Machines and Service Work: Automation in an Age of Stagnation* (New York: Reaktion, 2020). For a contemporary discussion of the global spatial politics of the production of racialized "stagnant" surplus populations, see Michael McIntyre and Heidi J. Nast, "Bio(Necro)Polis: Marx, Surplus Populations, and the Spatial Dialectics of Reproduction and 'Race,'" *Antipode* 43, no. 5 (June 2011): 1,465–88.

61. Saskia Sassen, *Expulsions: Brutality and Complexity in the Global Economy* (Cambridge, Mass.: Harvard University Press, 2014), 76.

62. Sassen, *Expulsions*, 76.

63. On territorial dispossession and capital formation, see Nichols, "Disaggregating Primitive Accumulation." For a comparative analysis of contemporary deportation regimes in relation to other historical forms of expulsion, see William Walters, "Deportation, Expulsion, and the International Police of Aliens," *Citizenship Studies* 6, no. 3 (July 2002): 265–92.

64. For a history of the colonial enslavement of indigenous groups in America, see Andrés Reséndez, *The Other Slavery the Uncovered Story of Indian Enslavement in America* (Boston: Mariner, 2017).

65. Nikhil Pal Singh, "On Race, Violence, and So-Called Primitive Accumulation," *Social Text* 34, no. 3 (September 2016): 37.

66. Singh, "On Race," 39.

67. We deviate slightly from Fraser's positing of exchange as the first of three "exes," and instead subsume the commodity form's abstract exchange value as a constitutive feature of capitalist exploitation.

68. Stefano Harney and Fred Moten, *Undercommons: Fugitive Planning and Black Study* (New York: Minor Compositions, 2013), 57.

69. Harney and Moten, *Undercommons*, 57. In Marx's analysis, the "general equivalent," or the money form, arises out of the system of exchange of commodities wherein the value of commodities is expressed in relation to one another. In its simple form, the value of a definite quantity of one commodity (relative form of value) is expressed in relation to a definite quantity of another commodity (equivalent form of value). In a society where the commodity form dominates, the money form becomes the general equivalent through which the value of all other commodities finds expression. For a substantive discussion of the value form, see Marx, *Capital*, vol. 1.

70. Fraser, "Expropriation and Exploitation," 170.

71. Susan Ferguson and David McNally, "Precarious Migrants: Gender, Race and the Social Reproduction of a Global Working Class," *Socialist Register* 51 (October 2014): 12, https://socialistregister.com/index.php/srv/article/view/22092.

72. Ferguson and McNally, "Precarious Migrants," 12.

73. Andreas Malm, *Fossil Capital: The Rise of Steam-Power and the Roots of Global Warming* (New York: Verso, 2016); Jason W. Moore, *Capitalism in the Web of Life: Ecology and the Accumulation of Capital* (New York: Verso, 2015); John Bellamy Foster, *Marx's Ecology: Materialism and Nature* (New York: Monthly Review Press, 2000); and Alfred W. Crosby, *Ecological Imperialism* (Cambridge: Cambridge University Press, 2015).

74. In the case of the much-publicized water crisis in Flint, Pulido writes that the decision to switch the water source from Detroit to the Flint River, leading directly to the lead poisoning of the city's residents, became a way to solve an ongoing municipal financial crisis; see Laura Pulido, "Flint, Environmental Racism, and Racial Capitalism," *Capitalism Nature Socialism* 27, no. 3 (July 2016): 1–16. Similar to Detroit, Flint continues to serve as a laboratory for the state management of waves of devalorization of labor and subsequent degradation and privatization of infrastructure. The city's initial reason for securing its water supply from Detroit was the contamination of the Flint River from the general activity and

waste produced by General Motors over time proving corrosive even to car parts being manufactured at the plant. Nestle corporation continues to draw water from nearby Michigan aquifers that is then resold to Flint residents, who continue to be billed for contaminated city water; see Robert D. Bullard, *Dumping in Dixie: Race, Class, And Environmental Quality* (New York: Routledge, 2018), and Lisa Sun-Hee Park and David N. Pellow, *The Silicon Valley of Dreams: Environmental Injustice, Immigrant Workers, and the High-Tech Global Economy* (New York: New York University Press, 2002).

75. Kimmy Yam, "Donald Trump Touts Racial Equality While Referring to COVID-19 as 'China Plague,'" *NBC News*, June 5, 2020, https://www.nbcnews.com/news/asian-america/donald-trump-touts-racial-equality-while-referring-covid-19-china-n1226176.

76. Mike Davis, *The Monster Enters: COVID-19, Avian Flu and the Plagues of Capitalism* (New York: OR, 2020), and Rob Wallace, *Big Farms Make Big Flu: Dispatches on Influenza, Agribusiness, and the Nature of Science* (New York: Monthly Review, 2016).

77. David Camfield, "Elements of a Historical-Materialist Theory of Racism," *Historical Materialism* 24, no. 1 (April 2016): 31–70, https://doi.org/10.1163/1569206X-12341453.

78. See, for example, Judith Butler, "Merely Cultural," *Social Text* 52/53 (Autumn/Winter 1997): 265–77, and Nancy Fraser, "Heterosexism, Misrecognition, and Capitalism: A Response to Judith Butler," *Social Text* 52/53 (Autumn/Winter 1997): 279–89. For an overview of the "cultural studies versus political economy" debate within the context of British cultural studies, see Peck, "Why We Shouldn't Be Bored," 92–125.

79. For a discussion of the history of UNESCO's advocacy for this shift in terminology as a means to delegitimize scientific racism, see Perrin Selcer, "Beyond the Cephalic Index," *Current Anthropology* 53, no. S5 (April 2012): 173–84.

80. See Penny von Eschen, *Race against Empire: Black Americans and Anticolonialism, 1937–1957* (Ithaca, N.Y.: Cornell University Press, 2014); Anthony Hazard, *Postwar Anti-Racism: The United States, UNESCO, and Race, 1945–1968* (New York: Palgrave Macmillan, 2016); and Jodi Melamed, "The Spirit of Neoliberalism: From Racial Liberalism to Neoliberal Multiculturalism," *Social Text* 24, no. 4 (Winter 2006): 1–24.

81. See Alana Lentin, "Replacing 'Race,' Historicizing 'Culture' in Multiculturalism," *Patterns of Prejudice* 39, no. 4 (August 2005): 379–96. UNESCO's intervention, Lentin argues, represents a significant milestone in a "history of how culturalist explanations came to dominate understandings of human difference and be posed as the solution to persistent racism, interpreted as an irrational prejudice between groups of culturally different human beings" (385). For a history of the mid-century social-scientific retreat from structural and political economic analysis of the sources of U.S. racial conflict and the subsequent popularity of theories that instead posited individual prejudice as the primary driver of racism and racial inequality, see Leah N. Gordon, *From Power to Prejudice: The Rise of Racial Individualism in Midcentury America* (Chicago: University of Chicago Press, 2016).

82. See Peck, "Why We Shouldn't Be Bored."

83. Charisse Burden-Stelly, "Cold War Culturalism and African Diaspora Theory: Some Theoretical Sketches," *Souls: A Critical Journal of Black Politics, Culture, and

Society 19, no. 2 (February 2017): 213. The postwar conflation of race and culture promoted through the language of state policy as well as academic knowledge production, Burden-Stelly contends, fortified a broader Cold War counterinsurgent political project developed in part to contain explicitly anti-capitalist forms of Black political analysis and organizing. "Culturalism can be understood as a regime of meaning-making, or an epistemology," Burden-Stelly writes, "in which Blackness is culturally specified and abstracted from material, political economic, and structural conditions of dispossession. Culturalism institutionalized the erasure of political economic critique in the theorizing of the global Black condition, the disciplining of Black militancy, and the cultural specification of Black connectivity. Culturalism supports the constitution and maintenance of Blackness as a category of economic exploitation and dispossession and racialized abjection in three fundamental ways. First, it reinscribes the Black on the margins of the state by accommodating Blackness in a way that maintains their subordination and subjection on cultural grounds. The foregrounding of the culture, behavior, and performance of Black people leaves the effects of inequality, increased poverty, unemployment, and the global mode of production on Black people largely undertheorized. Thus, on the one hand, deteriorating conditions of Black people globally are understood as innate cultural lack or pathology. On the other hand, it is assumed that Black empowerment and equality can be achieved in the struggle over cultural representation. Both of these positions reproduce cultural specifications of Blackness that negate the role of state and capitalist structures in its production and maintenance. Second, Culturalism asserts a particular outlook, behavior, and set of goals for Black people, and those who deviate from these norms that are ostensibly shared by the entire group are cast out. Third, Culturalism has the dual function of erasing political economy as a means of understanding and critiquing the Black condition and of specifying Black articulations of freedom and equality in terms of culture. Because it frames connections among African descendants in terms of abstract culture; asserts Black modernity and claims to equality on cultural grounds; and constructs culture and representation as the domain of struggle, it has resulted in the divorce of African Diaspora Theory from the Black radical tradition" (216–17).

84. For an overview of the social science scholarship on the "cultural turn" that displaced resurgent '60s-era forms of analysis that emphasized the causal primacy of class as a central axis of social conflict, see Barry Eidlin and Michael McCarthy, "Introducing Rethinking Class and Social Difference: A Dynamic Asymmetry Approach," *Political Power and Social Theory* 37 (2020): 1–23. "The cultural turn at its core was a challenge to the causal primacy of class," Eidlin and McCarthy observe, "which in many respects reversed the causal arrow and elevated the status of culture to that of causal primacy in its place" (8). Powerfully rewriting the concept of race in terms of culture, this post-sixties cross-disciplinary turn to culture reconfigured group cultural difference as a central *cause* of racial oppression and pluralistic cultural inclusion as an effective anti-racist political strategy. This turn thus often explicitly or implicitly framed racial difference as the origin of racial domination—a causal reversal that Barbara and Karen Fields subject to extended criticism in *Racecraft*. The cultural turn not only reinforced the social scientific translation of race into a post-Boasian language of group culture, but also reformulated class in cultural terms. In its most extreme iterations, the turn to culture led some critics to assert that "structures such as class and capitalism do not precede culture, they

themselves are culturally produced"; Eidlin and McCarthy, "Introducing Rethinking," 8. The cultural turn also marked a transition from singular to multicausal models of sociological explanation that took center stage in the context of waning scholarly attention to capitalism and a general "decline in class-based political organization(s)"; Eidlin and McCarthy, "Introducing Rethinking," ibid., 3.

85. Fields and Fields, *Racecraft*, 17.
86. Gilroy, *Against Race*, 41, 24.
87. Dawson, *Behind the Mule*, 77.
88. Dawson, *Behind the Mule*, 76.
89. Tommie Shelby, *We Who Are Dark: The Philosophical Foundations of Black Solidarity* (Cambridge, Mass.: Harvard University Press, 2009), 263.
90. Tommie Shelby, "Foundations of Black Solidarity: Collective Identity or Common Oppression?," *Ethics* 112, no. 2 (January 2002): 262.
91. Shelby, "Foundations," 245, and Gilroy, *Against Race*, 7. Within the context of post–Black Power politics in the U.S., Cedric Johnson has drawn a useful distinction between racial solidarity "as a spontaneous form of consciousness emerging from racial stratification" and "racial unitarianism" as a specific political aspiration that repeatedly confronts the problem that "racial affinity does not translate into common political interests"; Johnson, *Revolutionaries to Race Leaders: Black Power and the Making of African American Politics* (Minneapolis: University of Minnesota Press, 2007), 88).
92. Marx, *Capital*, 1:275, 172.
93. Daniel HoSang and Natalia Molina, "Introduction: Toward a Relational Consciousness of Race," in *Relational Formations of Race: Theory, Method, and Practice*, ed. Natalia Molina, Daniel HoSang, and Ramón A. Gutiérrez (Oakland: University of California Press, 2019), 6. On the relational turn in contemporary sociology, see Mustafa Emirbayer, "Manifesto for a Relational Sociology," *American Journal of Sociology* 103, no. 2 (September 1997): 281–317, and Matthew Desmond, "Relational Ethnography," *Theory and Society* 43, no. 5 (2014): 547–79, https://doi.org/10.1007/s11186-014-9232-5. In the recent edited volume *Relational Formations of Race*, Daniel HoSang and Natalia Molina argue for a relational conception of racial formation that moves beyond the limits of existing scholarship that assumes that racial groups are "autonomous and distinct social, political, and cultural spheres and within isolated, self-contained worlds"; HoSang and Molina, "Introduction," 8. The approach adopted by critics in this collection moves toward a much-needed critique of "substantialist" premises of disparate groups, where even theories' comparative racialization continue to posit racialized groups "as discrete and atomized entities that possess internally determined essences and characteristics" that can be subsequently compared. Writing in the same volume, Michael Rodríguez-Muñiz contends that comparative "group-centric analyses are often rooted in a 'substantialist' ontology that treats social phenomena as intrinsic and bounded"; Rodríguez-Muñiz, "Racial Arithmetic," 279.
94. HoSang and Molina, "Introduction," 6–7.
95. Ibid., 3.
96. Susan Ferguson, "Intersectionality and Social-Reproduction Feminisms: Toward an Integrative Ontology," *Historical Materialism* 24, no. 2 (June 2016): 47.
97. For a theoretical reframing of how such categories can variously refer to identities, concrete social relations, processes, outcomes, boundaries, hierarchies,

and systems of oppression, see Floya Anthias, "Intersectional What? Social Divisions, Intersectionality and Levels of Analysis," *Ethnicities* 13, no. 1 (October 2012): 3–19, https://doi.org/10.1177/1468796812463547.

98. For an influential example of how the race/class problematic can be recoded as a conceptual opposition between universality and particularity, see Butler, Laclau, and Žižek, *Contingency*. In this collection of essays, the universality/particularity dyad is often situated within a broadly neo-Gramscian problematic of group struggles for hegemony that describes group conflict over political representation within capitalist democracies. While critiques of the implicit racial exclusions that structure claims of universality are ubiquitous in contemporary scholarship on race, what has drawn less critical scrutiny is how this opposition conceptualizes the "particularism" of race itself primarily in terms of identities and a problematic of identification rather than a materialist account of the practices and policies that produce race as a relative material location. As Nicholas Thoburn has recently argued, "Freed-up from a theory of economic determination, the hegemony thesis configures race and class as signifiers of group identities where subjects must rid themselves of one form of identification in order to assume another"; Nicholas Thoburn, "Patterns of Production: Cultural Studies after Hegemony," *Theory, Culture & Society* 24, no. 3 (May 2007): 80. The race/class problematic can thus be restaged as the confrontation between "particularistic" non-class "identities" and a putatively "universal" working-class subject.

99. Denise Ferreira da Silva, *Toward a Global Idea of Race* (Minneapolis: University of Minnesota Press, 2007), 6, xxiv.

100. Ibid., xxiv.

101. Moishe Postone, *Time, Labor, and Social Domination: A Reinterpretation of Marx's Critical Theory* (Cambridge: Cambridge University Press, 1993), 162.

102. Postone, *Time*, 164. Postone insists that the "opposition between the abstract universality of the Enlightenment and particularistic specificity should not be understood in a decontextualized fashion; it is a historically constituted opposition, rooted in the determinate social forms of capitalism. To regard abstract universality, in its opposition to concrete specificity, as an ideal that can only be realized in a postcapitalist society is to remain bound within the framework of an opposition characteristic of that society. The form of domination related to this abstract form of the universal is not merely a class relation concealed by a universalistic facade. Rather, the domination Marx analyzes is that of a specific, historically constituted form of universalism itself, which he tries to grasp with his categories of value and capital" (163).

103. Ibid., 164.

104. Ibid.

105. Bohrer, *Marxism and Intersectionality*, 259, 252.

106. In *the Meaning of Freedom*, Angela Davis offers a critical assessment of the limits of a politics of racial unity and the urgency of orienting movements toward specific political objectives in relation to postwar black political history. "Many decades after the fiction of black unity was exposed, the most popular assumption within black communities continues to be that unity alone will bring progress.... What would be the purpose of uniting the entire black community? How would one possibly bring people together across all the complicated lines of politics and class? It would be futile to try to create a single black community today. But it does make sense . . . 'to think about organizing communities, organizing communities not simply

around their blackness, but primarily around political goals. Political struggle has never been so much a question about how it is identified or chooses to identify as it has been a question of how one thinks race, gender, class, sexuality affect the way human relations are constructed in the world'"; Davis, *The Meaning of Freedom: And Other Difficult Dialogues* (San Francisco: City Lights, 2012), 118–19.

107. There is a rich tradition of feminist affect theory and Fanonian/post-Fanonian scholarship that explores phenomenological investigations of the experience of racialization. There is a significant body of feminist scholarship, in particular, that has taken up the question of how experience is shaped by gender, sexuality, race, and colonial history. Critics such as Sara Ahmed, Joan Scott, Linda Alcoff, and Chandra Talpade Mohanty have attempted to counter essentialist representations of the category of women and women's experience as homogeneous and universal and to defend the category of socially situated experience from poststructuralist anti-essentialist critiques. Scott, for example, warns against understanding the lived experience of women as directly leading to a singular mode of resistance to "oppression, that is, to feminism"; Scott, "The Evidence of Experience," *Critical Inquiry* 17, no. 4 (Summer 1991): 787. For Scott, an analysis of experience requires further investigation of the conditions that produce experience and experiential knowledge, not a simple affirmation of the "knowledge said to be arrived at through experience" (787); see Linda Alcoff, "The Problem of Speaking for Others," *Cultural Critique* 20 (Winter 1991): 5–32, https://doi.org/10.2307/1354221; Chandra Talpade Mohanty, "Transnational Feminist Crossings: On Neoliberalism and Radical Critique," *Signs* 38, no. 4 (Summer 2013): 967–91; and Scott, "Evidence of Experience," 773–97.

108. In "The Architects of Abolitionism: George Jackson, Angela Davis, and the Deradicalization of Prison Struggles," a talk delivered at Brown University in 2019, Joy James identifies one of the central problems in organizing against the carceral state to be the presumption of a direct link between political beliefs and identity. For James, the excision of discussions of political ideology from discussions of identity marks the ascendance of a competitive and thoroughly commodified elite representational politics that claims individual exceptionality as collective racial progress and protection (www.youtube.com/watch?v=z9rvRsWKDxo). For James, this political deradicalization marks the institutional victory of a class-blind anti-racism over class-conscious revolutionary abolitionist and anti-capitalist political objectives. Because political "blueprints" clarified by political struggle do not flow automatically from a shared experience of oppression or precarity, references to the latter are not for James a reliable or sufficient basis for forging coalitional solidarity. Instead, she argues, "If I don't know your ideological marker [liberal or radical] we're not going to work together just because we have precarity. Because the material conditions are not going to be changed just by precarity. They're going to be changed by people who have blueprints. And that's what we're missing." On the impact of the nonprofit sector on post-1960s anti-racist politics, see Karen Ferguson, *Top Down: The Ford Foundation, Black Power, and the Reinvention of Racial Liberalism* (Philadelphia: University of Pennsylvania Press, 2013), and Dylan Rodriguez, "The Political Logic of the Non-Profit Industrial Complex," in *The Revolution Will Not Be Funded beyond the Non-Profit Industrial Complex*, ed. Incite! Women of Color Against Violence (Durham, N.C.: Duke University Press; 2017), 21–40.

109. See Aslı Çırakman, "Flags and Traitors: The Advance of Ethno-Nationalism in the Turkish Self-Image," *Ethnic and Racial Studies* 34, no. 119 (March 2011): 1,894–1,912, and Achin Vanaik, "India's Two Hegemonies," *New Left Review* 112 (July 2018): 29–59, https://newleftreview.org/issues/ii112/articles/achin-vanaik-india-s-two-hegemonies.

110. Keeanga-Yamahtta Taylor, *From #BlackLivesMatter to Black Liberation* (Chicago: Haymarket, 2016), 85.

111. Taylor, *#BlackLivesMatter*, 106.

112. There is a growing body of movement-participant writing that directly addresses such ideological conflicts over political objectives and tactical means—and in particular how intra-racial conflicts have been historically settled by displacing political disagreements onto outsiders or outside influence. On political schisms within the Black Lives Matter movement, for example, see George Weddington, "The Fall of 2014: Recovering the Roots of The Black Lives Movement," *Race, Politics, Justice*, September 1, 2018, https://www.ssc.wisc.edu/soc/racepoliticsjustice/2018/09/01/the-fall-of-2014-recovering-the-roots-of-the-black-lives-movement; We Still Outside Collective, "On the Black Leadership and Other White Myths," *Ill Will Editions*, November 9, 2020, https://illwilleditions.com/on-the-black-leadership-and-other-white-myths/; Idris Robinson, "How It Might Should Be Done," *YouTube*, August 4, 2020, https://www.youtube.com/watch?v=cQeW7RPkCZQ; and Yannick Giovanni Marshall, "Black Liberal, Your Time Is Up," *Al Jazeera*, June 1, 2020, https://www.aljazeera.com/opinions/2020/6/1/black-liberal-your-time-is-up. On interracial solidarity and the figure of the "outside agitator," see Jacey Fortin, "The Long History of the 'Outside Agitator,'" *New York Times*, June 8, 2020, https://www.nytimes.com/2020/06/08/us/outside-agitators-history-civil-rights.html. For a historical study of how intragroup political conflicts—in this case 1960s and post-1960s Chicana feminism—have been attributed to "outside influence," see Cristina Beltrán, *The Trouble with Unity: Latino Politics and the Creation of Identity* (Oxford: Oxford University Press, 2010).

Works Cited

Ahmed, Sara. *The Cultural Politics of Emotion*. London: Routledge, 2004

Alcoff, Linda Martin. "The Problem of Speaking for Others." *Cultural Critique* 20 (Winter 1991): 5–32. https://doi.org/10.2307/1354221.

———. *Visible Identities: Race, Gender, and the Self*. Oxford: Oxford University Press, 2006.

Allen, Theodore. "Summary of the Argument of *The Invention of the White Race*." *Cultural Logic* 1, no. 2 (Spring 1998): 1–33. https://doi.org/10.14288/clogic.v2i0.191851.

Anthias, Floya. "Intersectional What? Social Divisions, Intersectionality and Levels of Analysis." *Ethnicities* 13, no. 1 (October 2012): 3–19. https://doi.org/10.1177/1468796812463547.

Arruzza, Cinzia. *Dangerous Liaisons: The Marriages and Divorces of Marxism and Feminism*. Pontypool: Merlin, 2013.

———. "Remarks on Gender." *Viewpoint Magazine*, September 2, 2014. https://www.viewpointmag.com/2014/09/02/remarks-on-gender/.

Beltrán, Cristina. *The Trouble with Unity: Latino Politics and the Creation of Identity*. Oxford: Oxford University Press, 2010.

Benanav, Aaron. *Automation and the Future of Work*. New York: Verso, 2020.

Boggs, James. *The American Revolution: Pages from a Negro Worker's Notebook*. New York: Monthly Review, 1963.

Bohrer, Ashley J. *Marxism and Intersectionality: Race, Gender, Class and Sexuality under Contemporary Capitalism*. London: Transcript, 2020.

Bullard, Robert D. *Dumping in Dixie: Race, Class, And Environmental Quality*. New York: Routledge, 2018.

Burden-Stelly, Charisse. "Cold War Culturalism and African Diaspora Theory: Some Theoretical Sketches." *Souls: A Critical Journal of Black Politics, Culture, and Society* 19, no. 2 (February 2017): 213–37. https://doi.org/10.1080/10999949.2016.1239169.

Burden-Stelly, Charisse, Peter James Hudson, and Jemima Pierre. "Racial Capitalism, Black Liberation, and South Africa." *Black Agenda Report*, December 16, 2020. https://www.blackagendareport.com/racial-capitalism-black-liberation-and-south-africa.

Butler, Judith. "Merely Cultural." *Social Text* 52/53 (Autumn/Winter 1997): 265–77.

Butler, Judith, Ernesto Laclau, and Slavoj Žižek. *Contingency, Hegemony, Universality: Contemporary Dialogues on the Left*. London: Verso, 2000.

Byrd, Jodi A. *The Transit of Empire: Indigenous Critiques of Colonialism*. Minneapolis: University of Minnesota Press, 2011.

Camfield, David. "Elements of a Historical-Materialist Theory of Racism." *Historical Materialism* 24, no. 1 (April 2016): 31–70. https://doi.org/10.1163/1569206X-12341453.

Camp, Jordan T., Christina Heatherton, and Manu Karuka. "A Response to Nancy Fraser." *Politics Letters*, May 20, 2019. http://quarterly.politicsslashletters.org/a-response-to-nancy-fraser/.

Carchedi, Guglielmo. "Classes and Class Analysis." In *The Debate on Classes*, 105–25. London: Verso, 1998.

Çırakman, Aslı. "Flags and Traitors: The Advance of Ethno-Nationalism in the Turkish Self-Image." *Ethnic and Racial Studies* 34, no. 119 (March 2011): 1,894–912. https://doi.org/10.1080/01419870.2011.556746.

Cobb, Charles E. *This Nonviolent Stuff'll Get You Killed: How Guns Made the Civil Rights Movement Possible*. New York: Basic Books, 2014.

Combahee River Collective. "The Combahee River Collective Statement." In *Home Girls: A Black Feminist Anthology*, edited by Barbara Smith, 264–74. New Brunswick, N.J.: Rutgers University Press, 2000.

Coulthard, Glen Sean. *Red Skin, White Masks: Rejecting the Colonial Politics of Recognition; Indigenous Americas*. Minneapolis: University of Minnesota Press, 2014.

Crosby, Alfred W. *Ecological Imperialism*. Cambridge: Cambridge University Press, 2015.

Darder, Antonia, and Rodolfo D. Torres. *After Race: Racism After Multiculturalism*. New York: New York University Press, 2004.

Davis, Angela Y. *The Meaning of Freedom: And Other Difficult Dialogues*. San Francisco: City Lights, 2012.

Davis, Mike. *The Monster Enters: COVID-19, Avian Flu and the Plagues of Capitalism*. New York: OR, 2020.

Dawson, Michael C. *Behind the Mule: Race and Class in African-American Politics*. Princeton, N.J.: Princeton University Press, 1995.

———. "Hidden in Plain Sight: A Note on Legitimation Crises and the Racial Order." *Critical Historical Studies* 3, no. 1 (March 2016): 143–61.

Denning, Michael. "Wageless Life." *New Left Review*, no. 66 (December 2010): 79–97.

Derrida, Jacques. *Specters of Marx: The State of the Debt, The Work of Mourning & the New International*. New York: Routledge, 2011

Desmond, Matthew. "Relational Ethnography." *Theory and Society* 43, no. 5 (September 2014): 547–79. https://doi.org/10.1007/s11186-014-9232-5.

Donnelly, Michael J. "Material Interests, Identity and Linked Fate in Three Countries." *British Journal of Political Science* (March 2020): 1–19.

Du Bois, W. E. B. *Black Reconstruction in America 1860–1880*. New York: Simon and Schuster, 1999.

Eidlin, Barry, and Mike McCarthy. "Introducing Rethinking Class and Social Difference: A Dynamic Asymmetry Approach." *Political Power and Social Theory* 37 (2020): 1–23.

Emirbayer, Mustafa. "Manifesto for a Relational Sociology." *American Journal of Sociology* 103, no. 2 (September 1997): 281–317.

Emirbayer, Mustafa, and Matthew Desmond. *The Racial Order*. Chicago: University of Chicago Press, 2015.

Ferguson, Karen. *Top Down: The Ford Foundation, Black Power, and the Reinvention of Racial Liberalism*. Philadelphia: University of Pennsylvania Press, 2013.

Ferguson, Susan. "Intersectionality and Social-Reproduction Feminisms: Toward an Integrative Ontology." *Historical Materialism* 24, no. 2 (June 2016): 38–60.

Ferguson, Susan, and David McNally. "Precarious Migrants: Gender, Race and the Social Reproduction of a Global Working Class." *Socialist Register* 51 (October 2014): 1–23. https://socialistregister.com/index.php/srv/article/view/22092.

Ferreira da Silva, Denise. *Toward a Global Idea of Race*. Minneapolis: University of Minnesota Press, 2007.

Fields, Barbara. "Slavery, Race and Ideology in the United States of America." *New Left Review* 1, no. 181 (May–June 1990): 95–118.

Fields, Karen E., and Barbara J. Fields. *Racecraft: The Soul of Inequality in American Life*. London: Verso, 2012.

Fortin, Jacey. "The Long History of the 'Outside Agitator.'" *New York Times*, June 8, 2020. https://www.nytimes.com/2020/06/08/us/outside-agitators-history-civil-rights.html.

Foster, John Bellamy. *Marx's Ecology: Materialism and Nature*. New York: Monthly Review, 2000.

Fraser, Nancy. "Expropriation and Exploitation in Racialized Capitalism: A Reply to Michael Dawson." *Critical Historical Studies* 3, no. 1 (March 2016): 163–78.

———. "Heterosexism, Misrecognition, and Capitalism: A Response to Judith Butler." *Social Text* 52/53 (Autumn/Winter 1997): 279–89.

Gilmore, Ruth Wilson. "Globalisation and US Prison Growth: from Military Keynesianism to Post-Keynesian Militarism." *Race & Class* 40, no. 2–3 (March 1999): 171–88.

Gilroy, Paul. *Against Race: Imagining Political Culture Beyond the Color Line*. Cambridge, Mass.: Harvard University Press, 2001.

Gines, Kathryn T. "Introduction: Critical Philosophy of Race Beyond the Black/White Binary." *Critical Philosophy of Race* 1, no. 1 (2013): 28–37. https://muse.jhu.edu/article/501720.

Gitlin, Todd. "The Rise of Identity Politics." *Dissent* (Spring 1997): 172–77.

Glasgow, Joshua. "A Third Way in the Race Debate." *Journal of Political Philosophy* 14, no. 2 (April 2006): 163–85.

Goldberg, David Theo. "Racial Americanization." In *Racialization: Studies in Theory and Practice*, edited by Karim Murji and John Solomos, 87–102. Oxford: Oxford University Press, 2005.

Gordon, Leah N. *From Power to Prejudice: The Rise of Racial Individualism in Midcentury America*. Chicago: University of Chicago Press, 2016.

Gosse, Van. "A Movement of Movements: The Definition and Periodization of the New Left." In *A Companion to Post-1945 America*, edited by Jean-Christophe Agnew and Roy Rosenzweig, 277–302. Hoboken, N.J.: John Wiley & Sons, 2008.

Haider, Asad. "How Calling Someone a 'Class Reductionist' Became a Lefty Insult." *Salon*, July 25, 2020. https://www.salon.com/2020/07/25/how-calling-someone-a-class-reductionist-became-a-lefty-insult/.

Hall, Stuart. *The Fateful Triangle: Race, Ethnicity, Nation*. Cambridge, Mass.: Harvard University Press, 2017.

———. "Race, Articulation, and Societies Structured in Dominance." In *Black British Cultural Studies*, edited by Houston Baker Jr., Manthia Diawara, and Ruth Lindeborg, 16–60. Chicago: University of Chicago Press, 1996.

———. "The University and the Undercommons: Seven Theses." *Social Text* 22, no. 2 (Summer 2004): 101–15.

Harney, Stefano, and Fred Moten. *Undercommons: Fugitive Planning and Black Study*. New York: Minor Compositions, 2013.

Hazard, Anthony. *Postwar Anti-Racism: The United States, UNESCO, and Race, 1945–1968*. New York: Palgrave Macmillan, 2016.

Hu, Lily. "Disparate Causes, Pt. I." *Phenomenal World*, October 11, 2019. https://phenomenalworld.org/analysis/disparate-causes-i.

———. "Disparate Causes, Pt. II." *Phenomenal World*. October 17, 2019. https://phenomenalworld.org/analysis/disparate-causes-pt-ii.

Hilliard, David, ed. *The Black Panther Party: Service to the People Programs*. Albuquerque: University of New Mexico Press, 2010.

HoSang, Daniel, and Natalia Molina. "Introduction: Toward a Relational Consciousness of Race." In *Relational Formations of Race: Theory, Method, and Practice*, edited by Natalia Molina, Daniel HoSang, and Ramón A. Gutiérrez, 1–18. Oakland: University of California Press, 2019.

James, Joy. "Joy James: The Architects of Abolitionism." *YouTube*, May 6, 2019. Video. www.youtube.com/watch?v=z9rvRsWKDxo.

Johnson, Cedric. *Revolutionaries to Race Leaders: Black Power and the Making of African American Politics*. Minneapolis: University of Minnesota Press, 2007.

Kelley, Robin D. G. "Identity Politics and Class Struggle." *New Politics* 6, no. 2 (Winter 1997): 84–96.

Lentin, Alana. "Replacing 'Race,' Historicizing 'Culture' in Multiculturalism." *Patterns of Prejudice* 39, no. 4 (August 2005): 379–96.

Leonardo, Zeus. "After the Glow: Race Ambivalence and Other Educational Prognoses." *Educational Philosophy and Theory* 43, no. 6 (January 2011): 675–98.

Lyons, Matthew N. "Ctrl-Alt-Delete: The Origins and Ideology of the Alternative Right." *Political Research Associates*, January 20, 2017. https://www.politicalresearch.org/2017/01/20/ctrl-alt-delete-report-on-the-alternative-right.

Mallon, Ron. "'Race': Normative, Not Metaphysical or Semantic." *Ethics* 116, no. 3 (2006): 525–51.

Malm, Andreas. *Fossil Capital: The Rise of Steam-Power and the Roots of Global Warming*. New York: Verso, 2016.

Marshall, Yannick Giovanni. "Black Liberal, Your Time Is Up." *Al Jazeera*, June 1, 2020. https://www.aljazeera.com/opinions/2020/6/1/black-liberal-your-time-is-up.

Marx, Karl. *Capital: A Critique of Political Economy*. Vol. 1. Translated by Ben Fowkes. London: Penguin Classics, 1990.

Masuoka, Natalie, and Gabriel R. Sanchez. "Brown-Utility Heuristic? The Presence and Contributing Factors of Latino Linked Fate." *Hispanic Journal of Behavioral Sciences* 32, no. 4 (October 2010): 519–31. https://doi.org/10.1177/0739986310383129.

McIntyre, Michael, and Heidi J. Nast. "Bio(Necro)Polis: Marx, Surplus Populations, and the Spatial Dialectics of Reproduction and 'Race.'" *Antipode* 43, no. 5 (June 2011): 1,465–88.

Melamed, Jodi. "The Spirit of Neoliberalism: From Racial Liberalism to Neoliberal Multiculturalism." *Social Text* 24, no. 4 (Winter 2006): 1–24.

Miles, Robert. *Racism after "Race Relations."* London: Routledge, 2004.
Mohanty, Chandra Talpade. "Transnational Feminist Crossings: On Neoliberalism and Radical Critique." *Signs* 38, no. 4 (Summer 2013): 967–91.
Moore, Jason W. *Capitalism in the Web of Life: Ecology and the Accumulation of Capital.* New York: Verso, 2015.
Ndebele, Nhlanhla. "The African National Congress and the Policy of Non-Racialism: A Study of the Membership Issue." *Politikon: South African Journal of Political Studies* 29, no. 2 (August 2002): 133–46.
Nichols, Robert. "Disaggregating Primitive Accumulation." *Radical Philosophy* 194 (November–December 2915): 18–28.
Omi, Michael, and Howard Winant. *Racial Formation in the United States.* New York: Routledge, 2015.
Park, Lisa Sun-Hee, and David N. Pellow. *The Silicon Valley of Dreams: Environmental Injustice, Immigrant Workers, and the High-Tech Global Economy.* New York: New York University Press, 2002.
Peck, Janice. "Why We Shouldn't Be Bored with the Political Economy versus Cultural Studies Debate." *Cultural Critique* 64, no. 1 (Fall 2006): 92–125.
Postone, Moishe. *Time, Labor, and Social Domination: A Reinterpretation of Marx's Critical Theory.* Cambridge: Cambridge University Press, 1993.
Pulido, Laura. "Flint, Environmental Racism, and Racial Capitalism." *Capitalism Nature Socialism* 27, no. 3 (July 2016): 1–16.
Reed, Adolph. "The Myth of Class Reductionism." *New Republic*, September 25, 2019. https://newrepublic.com/article/154996/myth-class-reductionism.
———. "Rejoinder." *Political Power and Social Theory* 15 (November 2002): 301–15.
———. "Unraveling the Relation of Race and Class in American Politics." *Political Power and Social Theory* 15 (November 2002): 265–74.
Reed, Adolph, and Walter Benn Michaels. "The Trouble with Disparity." *nonsite.org* 32, (October 2020). https://nonsite.org/the-trouble-with-disparity/.
Reséndez, Andrés. *The Other Slavery: The Uncovered Story of Indian Enslavement in America.* Boston: Mariner, 2017.
Robinson, Cedric J. *Black Marxism: The Making of the Black Radical Tradition.* Chapel Hill: University of North Carolina Press, 2000.
Robinson, Idris. "How It Might Should Be Done." *YouTube*, August 4, 2020. https://www.youtube.com/watch?v=cQeW7RPkCZQ.
Rodriguez, Dylan. "The Political Logic of the Non-Profit Industrial Complex." In *The Revolution Will Not Be Funded beyond the Non-Profit Industrial Complex*, edited by Incite! Women of Color Against Violence, 21–40. Durham, N.C.: Duke University Press.
Rodriguez-Muniz, Michael. "Racial Arithmetic: Ethnoracial Politics in a Relational Key." In *Relational Formations of Race: Theory, Method, and Practice*, edited by Ramón A. Gutiérrez, Daniel HoSang, and Natalia Molina, 278–95. Oakland: University of California Press, 2019.

Roediger, David R. *Class, Race and Marxism*. London: Verso, 2017.
———. *Towards the Abolition of Whiteness: Essays on Race, Politics, and Working-Class History*. London: Verso, 2004.
San Juan, E. Jr. "Marxism and the Race/Class Problematic: A Re-Articulation." *Cultural Logic* 10 (June 2003): 1–16. https://doi.org/10.14288/clogic.v10i0.191792.
Sassen, Saskia. *Expulsions: Brutality and Complexity in the Global Economy*. Cambridge, Mass.: Harvard University Press, 2014.
Scott, Joan Wallach. "The Evidence of Experience." *Critical Inquiry* 17, no. 4 (Summer 1991): 773–97.
Selcer, Perrin. "Beyond the Cephalic Index." *Current Anthropology* 53, no. S5 (April 2012): S173–84.
Seymour, Richard. "Does David Roediger Disagree with Ellen Meiksins Wood?" *Verso Books*, July 24, 2017. https://www.versobooks.com/blogs/3321-does-david-roediger-disagree-with-ellen-meiksins-wood.
Shelby, Tommie. "Foundations of Black Solidarity: Collective Identity or Common Oppression?" *Ethics* 112, no. 2 (January 2002): 231–66.
———. *We Who Are Dark: The Philosophical Foundations of Black Solidarity*. Cambridge, Mass. Harvard University Press, 2009.
Simien, Evelyn M. "Race, Gender, and Linked Fate." *Journal of Black Studies* 35, no. 5 (May 2005): 529–50.
Singh, Nikhil Pal. "On Race, Violence, and So-Called Primitive Accumulation." *Social Text* 34, no. 3 (September 2016): 27–50.
Smith, Jason E. *Smart Machines and Service Work: Automation in an Age of Stagnation*. New York: Reaktion, 2020.
Stern, Alexandra Minna. *Proud Boys and the White Ethnostate: How the Alt-Right Is Warping the American Imagination*. Boston: Beacon Press, 2020.
Strain, Christopher. *Pure Fire: Self-Defense as Activism in the Civil Rights Era*. Athens: University of Georgia Press, 2005.
Taylor, Keeanga-Yamahtta. *From #BlackLivesMatter to Black Liberation*. Chicago: Haymarket, 2016.
Taylor, Paul C. *Race: A Philosophical Introduction*. 2nd ed. Cambridge, Mass.: Polity, 2013.
Thoburn, Nicholas. "Patterns of Production: Cultural Studies after Hegemony." *Theory, Culture & Society* 24, no. 3 (May 2007): 79–94.
Umoja, Akinyele. *We Will Shoot Back*. New York: New York University Press, 2013.
Vanaik, Achin. "India's Two Hegemonies." *New Left Review* 112 (July 2018): 29–59. https://newleftreview.org/issues/ii112/articles/achin-vanaik-india-s-two-hegemonies.
von Eschen, Penny. *Race Against Empire: Black Americans and Anticolonialism, 1937–1957*. Ithaca, N.Y.: Cornell University Press, 2014.

Vucetic, Srdjan. "Against Race Taboos." In *Race and Racism in International Relations: Confronting the Global Colour Line*, edited by Alexander Anievas, Nivi Manchanda, and Robbie Shilliam, 98–114. New York: Routledge, 2014.

Wallace, Rob. *Big Farms Make Big Flu: Dispatches on Influenza, Agribusiness, and the Nature of Science*. New York: Monthly Review, 2016.

Walters, William. "Deportation, Expulsion, and the International Police of Aliens." *Citizenship Studies* 6, no. 3 (July 2002): 265–92.

We Still Outside Collective. "On the Black Leadership and Other White Myths." *Ill Will Editions*, June 4, 2020. https://illwilleditions.com/on-the-black-leadership-and-other-white-myths/.

Weddington, George. "The Fall of 2014: Recovering the Roots of The Black Lives Movement." *Race, Politics, Justice*, September 1, 2018. https://www.ssc.wisc.edu/soc/racepoliticsjustice/2018/09/01/the-fall-of-2014-recovering-the-roots-of-the-black-lives-movement.

Wetherell, Margaret, and Chandra Talpade Mohanty, eds. *The Sage Handbook of Identities*. Thousand Oaks, Calif.: Sage, 2013.

White, Monica M. "'A Pig and a Farden': Fannie Lou Hamer and the Freedom Farms Cooperative." *Food and Foodways* 25, no. 1 (February 2017): 20–39.

Wilderson, Frank III. "Gramsci's Black Marx: Whither the Slave in Civil Society?" *Social Identities* 9, no. 2 (August 2003): 225–40.

Wolfe, Patrick. "Settler Colonialism and the Elimination of the Native." *Journal of Genocide Research* 8, no. 4 (December 2006): 387–409.

———. *Traces of History: Elementary Structures of Race*. London: Verso, 2016.

Wood, Emma Meiksins. "Class, Race, and Capitalism." *Political Power and Social Theory* 15 (2002): 275–84.

Yam, Kimmy. "Donald Trump Touts Racial Equality While Referring to COVID-19 as 'China Plague.'" *NBC News*, June 5, 2020.

Zúquete, José Pedro. *The Identitarians: The Movement against Globalism and Islam in Europe*. Notre Dame, Ind.: University of Notre Dame Press, 2018.

5 /   On Artistic Autonomy as a Bourgeois Fetish
SARAH BROUILLETTE AND JOSHUA CLOVER

Neoliberalism has become a popular term for characterizing "now," or life after the 1960s or 1970s or 1980s—an era thought to be plagued, uniquely or with a historically new intensity, by marketization, deregulation, privatization, and withdrawal of state-based social services. It is also often used to describe a particular subjectivization—the "neoliberal subject"—suited to these conditions: the profit-maximizing individual, possessed of self-managing "human capital," or the flexible, contract-based "creative" worker who embraces chaos and flux as liberating emancipation.

This familiar cluster of ideas about how we live now runs through the thinking and championing of autonomous art. Neoliberalism's individualizing drive is bemoaned in a critique of the narcissistic "subjective" interpretation of the artwork; the very importance of art's autonomy is said to be heightened by the growing rationalization of the artmaking process, the "real subsumption" of art under a creeping marketization. But like much scholarship whose self-understanding requires the terminology of neoliberalism, work about the unique power of autonomous art to oppose the neoliberal order is inattentive to the nature of the very economic phenomena that states have sought to offset through the policies that scholars characterize as neoliberal. We are left with a description of our social dispensation that is treated as self-evident—*it's the neoliberalism, stupid*—while in fact rendering the character, operation, and trajectory of post-Boom capitalism, already cloudy, even more opaque. And because neoliberalism now provides a framework not simply for contemporary political thought but for many accounts of contemporary art, including many arrogating for themselves a sort of anti-capitalist stature, it is worth endeavoring to clarify this foundational confusion in brief, as well as to provide some examples of its consequences for both political thought and cultural analysis.

The conventional critique of neoliberalism dramatically misrecognizes and thereby obscures historical causality. We might accept that the term "neoliberalism," at least in one of its many conflicting deployments, describes an extant concatenation of ideological suppositions—concerning the virtues and necessities of self-management and individualization more broadly, the inarguability of market forces and their ceaseless extension into all regions of life, and so on. However, the moment we suspect that these beliefs exist as a set of coherent policy prescriptions imposed by state and quasi-state actors to remake the world around us, we fall into error. This idea, even as implication, has the basic character of a theodicy, an explanation of the gods' ways to humans. Like a theodicy, it treats the gods as real, a conspiratorial committee perched on the Olympus of Mt. Pelerin that now causes the winds to blow in one direction rather than another because it suits them and their petty wills.

Materialism contra Neoliberalism

But the gods have no material existence; they are every bit as airy as their theodicy. There simply are no neoliberals (or "globalists," in the crude parallel fantasy of political theory in the time of Trump) sitting around figuring out how best to be neoliberal today, and there could not be, given the profound incoherence of the concept. It is more properly the case that a broad set of experiments were assayed to restore to capital adequate profitability as it began to soften and then decline in the 1960s. One might narrate neoliberalism as a project to restore class power by concentrating wealth upward, as does David Harvey, for example, in *A Brief History of Neoliberalism*—as long as one grasps that this is simply a different way of describing a struggle to restore profit rates, profit being by definition the transfer of wealth from one class to another. Many and varied schemes were tried toward this restoration. These experimental solutions both required and conjured an ideological supplement. "Neoliberalism" is the name for this supplement. It is not the material substrate and has almost no causal force or explanatory power regarding the political-economic transformations of nations and world-systems, which we grasp far better as addressed to the specific problematic of profitability, articulated differently in different regions of the world political-economic system, with at its core a situation of increasing productivity that hollows out both industrial expansion and the regularly waged employment that accompanied it.

This perhaps begins to explain the ineradicable discontinuities within the common knowledge about neoliberalism. In an example that would be farcical were its effects not so far-reaching, we might consider the Plaza Accord (1985), which endeavored to devalue the U.S. dollar against the yen and deutsche mark to restore U.S. manufacturing competitiveness; and the Reverse Plaza Accord one decade later, revaluing the dollar relative to those currencies to increase U.S. consumption power. Somehow both adjustments are part of neoliberalism—which is to say, the neoliberal project simply cannot be grasped as a set of policy prescriptions or as a worldview unless we stipulate that it is subject to mercurial reversals at any time, leaving its usefulness as an analytical category in grave doubt.

Or we might consider the coexistence of intransigent opposition to debt, particularly in certain national ledgers via analogy to the household budget, and simultaneously the strong preference for proceeding via the production of debt, both for individuals confronting the scission of wages from productivity post-1973 and for nations driven into structural adjustment programs by the Bretton Woods institutions. How would an agent bent on imposing "neoliberalism" know how to proceed? At the same time, from the perspective of profitability, the fact that different circumstances might suggest different solutions allows a coherent account of why one might assay this strategy here and that strategy there, might try debt financing and debt reduction both, without any recourse to ideological explanations.

In a final example of counterproductive ambiguity, one that will lead us toward the more specific and extended inquiry that follows, neoliberalism is commonly understood to prefer a logic of "horizontality" in the administration of firms, wherein workers are expected to be flexible, self-managing agents linked peer to peer and charged with producing and maximizing their own utility to justify their value to the firm, rather than requiring direction from above. This example illuminates how peculiarly effective the conventional critique of neoliberalism has been at allowing the transposition of economic content to cultural and political forms with little or no mediation. In *Contemporary Cinema and Neoliberal Ideology*, we are asked to "think carefully about the horizontality of the contemporary tracking shot in social realism as a potential mediation of neoliberal dynamics."[1] Similarly, some political theorists have suggested that the leaderless movements arising after the global crisis of 2007–8, proclaiming themselves as organizationally horizonalist (commonly sourced to the idea of *horizontalidad* within Argentina's social organizing around the turn of the millennium alongside contemporaneous alter-globalization movements, reappearing within the movement of the squares and the Occupy movement), were themselves therefore in thrall to the ideology of neoliberalism, unable to deploy the necessary hierarchies for effective organization.

It is entirely unclear that these instances feature *the same horizontalisms* in anything but orthography. One might ask in the former example after the underlying relationship between the physical horizontality of the tracking shot, having everything to do with gravity, equilibrium, and sight, and the metaphorical horizontality of organizational charts, having only to do with nominal assignments of institutional authority. Or in the latter example one might inquire after the historical basis for the development of leaderless movements in the first place, particularly whether it is related to the restructuring of enterprise and, if so, how so.

One can see instantly the kinds of problems that arise when one *explains an ideological expression via an ideological expression*, aesthetic form according to political form (the best one can say regarding what kind of object neoliberalism is), abandoning the most basic precepts of materialist analysis. Explaining one political form according to another is even less plausible.

For the moment, however, it is enough to note that the received notions of neoliberalism as characterized by horizontality are at best half true. Certainly, firms such as Uber and similar "platform capitalism" operations bear some resemblance to this horizontal vision, having succeeded in automating away one technical-managerial layer—while requiring another, that of coders who in effect become a technical-managerial class conducting oversight by algorithm. Certainly, the shift to "teams" detailed by Luc Boltanski and Eve Chiapello in *The New Spirit of Capitalism* will be familiar to many as a generative account of workplace transformations in the service sector particularly. At the same time, during the span in question, various sectors—the "neoliberal university" wherein many of these theorists' labor is among the dramatic examples—have undergone an increase in both the mass of the management layer and, even more profoundly, in the ratio of managers to nonmanagerial employees. Here, behind the quotidian scrim of persuading faculty to make their own photocopies and the inarguable expansion of precarious or contract work, along with the devastating increases in workload left to remaining lower-paid staff as their numbers are slashed, hierarchy has been not reduced but redoubled. Again, this phenomenon is impossible to explain via neoliberal ideology without producing an ideological field lacking any internal consistency. However, it becomes substantively explicable if, for instance, one asks what kinds of labor can and cannot be efficiently automated at present or supposes that the willingness to provide benefits accompanying regular employment is conditioned by the profit rate.

One might argue in defense of the conventional critique of neoliberalism that it simply *means* this set of suggested solutions to an ensemble of practical but heterogeneous problems. However, this leaves us with certain intractable puzzles. In the first instance, it is unclear what we gain by presenting a political-economic phenomenon organized by material compulsions as a primarily political one oriented by various beliefs and accompanying policy prescriptions. Meanwhile, the consequential losses stemming from a divorce of the political and the economic are many. Let us offer two examples, one at the largest scale of social existence, one carefully focused on a specific debate within literary studies.

If we are indeed concerned with totality, we must be equally concerned with causality. It is characteristic of capitalism that these are inextricable. For Lukács, the organic mode of totality has been lost: the immanent relations of the elements and experiences of life once available are now broken by capitalism's separations, alienations, reifications, appearances. Capitalism, however, has its own totality; it is characterized by the inaccessibility of its immanent relations, a totality constituted by the development of the global market and in particular by the set of "definite human relations" that allow the measuring of one expenditure of labor power against another, despite the separation of the laborers. It is through these relations that the law of value is expressed throughout the social whole behind the back of consciousness, compelling efforts to increase productivity and to drive down wages in all quarters, leading to ongoing recomposition of the class relation at a global level. The capitalist totality exists only insofar as it develops over time, as the store of value must expand to preserve the stability of capitalist relations as a whole. Thus totality is constituted not simply by the ensemble of relations (the synchronic character of capital) but by the development of this ensemble over time (its diachronic character), a characteristic that distinguishes it from all previous regimes of power. In short, capitalism's existence as a totality is inseparable from the causality that gives it a historical directionality.

Given this *differentia specifica*, which insists on capital's totalizing character as both relation and trajectory, spatial and temporal, it would be curious indeed to argue that the subjection of every corner and moment of life to the discipline of the value form is peculiar to neoliberalism. Yet this is central to the conventional critique, even in its most thoughtful iterations. Annie McClanahan, having recorded the extent to which the imagined subject of neoliberalism in Wendy Brown's landmark study *Undoing the Demos* is a denizen of the U.S. university, raises "the possibility that neoliberalism is not the becoming-economic of the non-economic, but rather the introduction of economic exigencies into the lives of a group—white, educated, upper middle-class citizens of the developed world—formerly protected from them."[2]

The Fetish of Autonomy

This development, which we might describe as an atavistic encounter with the problem of subsistence, provides the mental landscape for our second and far more particular example of a consequence arising from the worldview that the conventional critique puts on offer. This is what we refer to as the *fetish of autonomy*: the ceaseless quest for and inevitable discovery of purportedly "unsubsumed" art, characterized as possessing and/or figuring autonomy from the disciplines of the marketplace, as bearer of value independent from and consistently opposed to political-economic value.[3] This figure of autonomous value, and of the value of autonomy, requires exactly the viewpoint we have been detailing, wherein the political is understood to exist as its own content, separated from the economic and thus able to stand in opposition to it. These ideological separations are treated as real conditions, as somehow producing the conditions of possibility for the figuring of emancipation. This is a complicated inversion. The desire, and who could refuse it, is for a figure of emancipation. This emancipatory figure, autonomy itself, can only appear *as* autonomous—as undetermined by the capitalist form of value—*by taking as actual capital's self-presentation*, its ideology, wherein there is no underlying unity in contradiction, no negative totality, but rather fragmented and independent domains such as the political, the aesthetic, the economic, and so forth. It is in this sense that we identify autonomy as a bourgeois fetish, for it has always been the necessary belief of the bourgeoisie that these matters can be disentangled and treated independently, a fantasmatic independence that is treated as common sense.

The best-known expression of this fetishistic idea is what we have come to know as "rights discourse," wherein freedom appears as a purely political matter defined by struggles over a given regime of rights without challenging productive relations, a conception that provides traditional liberalism one of its bases. In a well-known passage, Marx identifies this with the separation of production from its dialectical relation to the marketplace, "a very Eden of the innate rights of man. It is the exclusive realm of Freedom, Equality, Property and Bentham."[4]

If this is an idealization of the political as an independent domain, its complement is found in what we might call "inequality discourse." This idealization treats the economic as an independent domain, while also sequestering itself unreflectively in the marketplace, the "noisy sphere" of circulation. Because, in this liberal vision, the category of class is mistakenly derived from a static measure of wealth and/or income (rather than being understood as a social relation to capital founded on whether one reproduces oneself via wages, rents, or profits), the fundamental economic ill appears to be "inequality"—that is, a quantitative maldistribution of said wealth that can be addressed via redistributive measures. While this is a laudable goal, it neglects that character of capitalism itself, which not only ceaselessly produces inequal distribution but requires it to function. Because inequality is the equilibrium condition of capitalism, redistribution can always only be temporary. This respite from inequality is no doubt water to the parched. Nonetheless, to identify inequality as the problem to be solved is to accept such respites as the far horizon of social change, to accept market approaches as the only approaches, and to concede in the process that capitalism itself shall be left in place, eternal and unchallenged.

Such a perforce temporary redress presents itself as an actual solution to the social problem only after one has first separated out the economic from the political within the market where both political rights and economic distribution find their home; inequality discourse is economic liberalism just as rights discourse is political liberalism. It is this separation and sequestration that in turn allows a demand for full employment, *as if compulsory employment were not itself the social problem necessary to constitute capitalism.*

In short, it is from the position of the bourgeoisie that these separations appear as the premise for emancipation, now reduced to the escape from exigency. It would be more helpful for all accounts of art and of capitalism to recognize exploitation, and dispossession more broadly, of which exploitation is a species, as the problem to be solved, the phenomenon both quantitative and qualitative whose overcoming opens onto the realm of freedom. But, and here we return to the crux of the confusion, this would involve recognizing the unity of the political and the economic and the concomitant necessity to transform both if one is to transform either.

All of this subtends the nature of Walter Benn Michaels's grasp of what he will refer to as the "objective" conditions of contemporary capitalism. The faith that there are meaningfully distinct realms of art, culture, politics, economics, and so on—realms that mustn't be confused if objective conditions are to be glimpsed—is one of the foundations of his investment in the fetish of autonomy, wherein art's formal properties afford it a unique vantage onto the economy. His basic idea is that objective conditions of capitalism are strictly delimited by one's respective level of employment or wealth (mistakenly identified as class), with everything else being just appearance and identity-political affect. For Benn Michaels, any attention to or placement of struggle within the realm of the identity-political partakes of neoliberalism, a phenomenon largely characterized for him precisely as the triumph of identity politics, because under the cover of more race and gender diversity at the highest ranks, the lowest ranks have, without our noticing, grown considerably. In turning then to art, he argues that select cultural elites, whose race and wealth are incidental rather than a force determining their ideas, are uniquely aware of the sheer objectivity of objective relations. They uniquely know that "the problem is capitalism." They know this because they embrace the idealization of the individual artist who has complete control over the sensuous formal expression of the work, work whose essential nature, value, and meaning have by strict necessity nothing to do with the particulars of any consuming viewer.

Benn Michaels insists that "no one argues, for example, that we need a certain amount of racism or sexism to make the economy work. Just the opposite." Yet many scholars have persuasively shown that racism, sexism, and capitalism are precisely inextricably imbricated—from "race is the modality through which class is lived," to racialization as disproportionate exposure to superfluity and early death, to the gendered and racialized division of reproductive labor, and on and on. Nothing is gained analytically by the denial of these imbrications. In the face of irreversible superfluity that is unevenly racially distributed, historical depredations of and accommodations to the wage nexus, intensification of expropriation of unwaged or informal work (again, racialized and gendered), those with faith in the power of autonomous art talk of "good jobs" and of art helping "us" to envision better "policy."

Consider as an indicative case Benn Michaels's appreciation of Viktoria Binschtok's photograph "Wand #1." The piece depicts scuff marks on the wall made by people waiting in line in an unemployment office. Benn Michaels argues that "since the bodies appear only by way of the marks on the wall, the question of what kind of bodies they are is as unanswerable (in effect, as unasked) as the question of what kind of character they have." He argues that the mark of the politics of the photograph is its refusal to show the victims of unemployment "by transforming the record of their presence into something that looks more like a Color Field painting than a documentary photograph."[5] And yet one could equally argue that the power of the photograph is in its representation of the very erasure of the unemployed, that its subject is their erasure, and that what should be emphasized is the meaning of the very fact that their representation has been reduced to scuffs on a wall—scuffs that may for some viewers evoke tallies, counting bodies, quantification, boredom, bureaucracy, state management of the unemployed population, and so on. While Benn Michaels claims that the absence of deliberate emphasis on race is part of what makes the piece particularly praiseworthy, we could just as well say that, regardless of what the photograph depicts, race is inextricably significant to the unemployment that occasioned the photograph. The people who did stand in line and whose bodies did make those marks are marked by race, just as race determines exposure to unemployment. We could argue that the work's apparent lack of emphasis on race is a failure or that the work provides a critical view on the very effacement that Benn Michaels celebrates. Or we could guess that the artist assumes that we would ourselves unavoidably imagine the bodies in that line and ascribe to them various features and that the way we imagine the nature of their presence would be powerful in its own right.

It is important to Benn Michaels's analysis, however, that we not conceive of artists as having any interest in the activity of their works' viewers. If they did, they would not be artists. He argues that, just as "the photograph establishes a distance from its subjects," it "seeks to mirror that distance with the one it establishes from its viewers." It does this by "making it impossible for us to identify by giving us no one to identify with, making the question of who its viewers are and how they feel as irrelevant as the question of who its subjects were and how they felt."[6] There can be no assumption of a viewer interacting with the work, attaching bodies to the scuff marks. This stands in distinction to a staple within our contemporary understanding of art: that it does (or should) entail interactive and participatory activities that are the only way that meaning can occur. For Benn Michaels, a proper embrace of the autonomy of the artwork is meant to undercut this by-now common idea that we participate in making the meaning of the art, that our participation is an integral part of art's artfulness rather than a gross distortion of the author's objective activity.

This is where a particular account of neoliberalism enters his analysis. For Benn Michaels, to embrace the viewer's role in the making of meaning is to affirm a neoliberal worldview, because neoliberalism is in his estimation a phenomenon that privileges personal, subjective perceptions and experiences over objective conditions. Hence the neoliberal's embrace of a politics that addresses inequality only at the level of representation (figured by, for example, the celebration of Barack Obama as the first black president), in turn neglecting the real battle against the conditions that cause the most harm to the most people.

In Benn Michaels's figuring, these conditions are by and large the depredations of inequality, particularly those associated with un-, under-, and precarious employment along with decimation of union membership. We have noted previously the degree to which these provide a straitened sense of capitalism's objective character. Nonetheless, claims to the status of art rest for him on the extent to which a work concerns these objective conditions *rather than* subjective experiences and perceptions—subjective experiences and perceptions that, importantly, include for him the experience of being racialized. He argues that, in looking at the scuff marks made by the unemployed in "Wand #1," "once we start worrying about whether . . . they're the victims of our racism or sexism and we're responsible for their plight, we've forgotten the real social problem—which is that if . . . there were no racism and sexism, there would still be (our economy would still need) unemployment."[7] His argument that the work counts as art *because* it does not focus on race is thus very clearly part of his ongoing project against identity politics as he conceives of them—as a powerful ruse created by people who benefit from its embrace, distracting us from the truths that we need to grasp if we are to effectively oppose contemporary conditions. To be sure, his is a common fantasy, centuries old, in which good art offers peculiarly acute evidence that one can create something irrespective of market desires, consumer desires.[8] What Benn Michaels adds to this tradition of thought is his insistence that art's autonomy is itself a powerful counter to identity politics and therefore to neoliberalism. A work that is too interested in engaging the viewer in some sort of emotive experience of sympathy or outrage around identity-political categories cannot be art because it fails this test. It fails to assert the ultimate truth of the objective conditions that exist regardless of our feelings about them. Such a work may be conscripted into the neoliberal political order with too much ease. It's "the very effort to produce something utterly self-contained," he argues, "that enables us to see in art not just a reflection of our current form of neoliberal capitalism but what Nick Brown has described as 'neoliberalism's other.'"[9]

Benn Michaels argues that "it's better to see the unemployed as marks on the wall than as people for whom we should feel compassion—our compassion is beside the point. . . . And that's why it's important for a picture like 'Wand 1'—in effect, a picture of the labor market—to imagine its own autonomy from that market."[10] Anyone who fails to experience the photograph as an occasion for an absence of compassion is thus doing something wrong—something neoliberal—and is truncating the artwork's political potential. The only way to make the art politically meaningful is to insist that it isn't interested in suffering or compassion. Correspondingly, no other kind of culture can afford anything like a similar political insight. It's "the formal perfection imaginable in works of art but *not in anything else*" that allows us to see "capitalism as itself the problem"[11]—capitalism, that is, as something itself autonomous from race, as well as any other ascribed subjective effect, because, as we recall, for Benn Michaels these are absolutely separable.

Not for nothing, these are works of art that one finds in museums and galleries, or perhaps in catalogues and magazines one might encounter during advanced training in art history. They by definition have a fairly limited reach in terms of audience, and exposure to them is more likely if one is relatively wealthy and white—a givenness that is in turn a characteristic of capitalism. These points of mundane sociology are never taken into Benn Michaels's account—indeed they cannot be, as considering them would mean reducing the work's political force by thinking about its social determinants.

Of course, if you do find yourself facing such a work of art, there is a good chance that you will make the mistake of imagining that it has something to do with people suffering and even have suspicions of who those people might be, *suspicions no less objective than the work itself,* and you will thus have ruined whatever political insight it might have afforded you, while also proving yourself a neoliberal subject (a condition that people can evidently escape through proper thinking). You may also in a parallel gesture fail to see that the only thing that matters about the work is its message—and it's always the same message. That because artists have market-independent intentions and the capacity to infuse the work with these, it is possible to resist neoliberal capitalism, which thrives precisely because we wrongly think that our subjective perceptions of things matter at all.

Not to worry, though, if you do miss the point. How you perceive the work is not relevant to its significance. The artwork's intentional form will, without you, serve as reassurance that the economy has objective conditions and that these objective conditions, which are race- and gender-indifferent, are to be opposed. Art's very freedom from the suffering of others allows for its apprehension of the "beauty" of the problem, and this narrow aesthetic apprehension will allow a true assault on capitalism. The effect is precisely magical, for there is no theory of mediation on offer here. Or rather, there is a mysteriously immediate theory of mediation: yes, the artwork's formal characteristics will be transformed into thought, but it will simply be the correct thought, immediately convertible to the correct action in the street below the gallery—though what such correct action is proposed to be, as we shall see, raises a further set of quandaries.

The supremacy of form is the only assertion necessary. Therein lies proof of a will capable of countering market demands—proof that protects the very idea of opposition to capitalism and the will to eradicate class-based inequalities. In Nicholas Brown's closely related claims (cited by Benn Michaels), the very foundations for a philosophy of art hinge on this idea that there is a distinction, not just makeable but decisive, between an artwork and a commodity—a distinction that art worries over but that cannot be traduced, lest we abandon the possibility for anything to exist beyond from capitalism and its preferences. Brown writes that art's meanings are "normative"; they are not a matter of consumer preference but of the artist's desired effect.[12] These meanings can be misapprehended but not erased. In Benn Michaels's account, to be sure somewhat different, art has intentional form that grants it an objectivity analogous to the economy's objective structures. Non-art commodities (and bad art, one gathers) are about the consumer's subjective point of view—what Brown designates, citing free-market theorists, as "consumer sovereignty."[13] For Benn Michaels, this subordination to the viewer-consumer functions as a subordination to neoliberalism *tout court*, it having a purportedly new, or newly intensified, relation to consumption.

Liberal Aesthetics as an Anti-Materialism

These are of course the fundamentals of post-Romantic aesthetic philosophy: intending artist; materials and tools for working with them; fickle public; market mechanisms for circulation that nonetheless do not impinge upon good art—indeed, to transcend the market is to attain the status of art. Adherence to this philosophy is positioned as political virtue because it affirms that there is something other than the marketplace. We are meant to suppose that the simple acknowledgment of the market would completely obscure the nature of the aesthetic act. The artist is either wholly intending or wholly subject to consumer demands; there is no middle ground. In turn the given artwork's consumers (or perhaps only those who suffer from being nonacademic or nonprofessional) are always both expressions and enforcers of a market logic. All this sums up to yet another fantasy of creation that transcends constraint and evinces instead the "intrinsic" drives of some genius.

For Benn Michaels a work is good, and so achieves the status of autonomous high art in the first place, to the extent that it asserts its own form as the product of an intentional "self-contained" will. It is political art to the extent that it "establish[es] a space of its own." He presents this as his radical departure from the usual approach to art's politics. What "we usually think," he writes, is that political art is art that "attach[es] itself to the world," by "showing us the victims of some dreadful abuse and reaching out to its viewers, inspiring in us the desire to correct that abuse."[14] But this derision directed toward purportedly neoliberal ideas of political art draws on the same set of presumptions that inform liberal understandings of art more broadly, wherein politics are "in" the work to the extent that the artist has decided to put them there. This understanding of the politics of art might gain from exposure to that of Walter Benjamin, to choose a particularly obvious and clarifying example, where the technique of lamenting human suffering is itself inadequate if the work arises from a solo producer who holds a copyright and circulates a property that is simply distinguished in the marketplace by its patina of political commitment. Or we might consider a definition of art's politics such as that of Raymond Williams, emphasizing the conditions of production and reception that shape any work's meaning, both within a moment of interpretation and at the level of general significance. Or we might continue on to Fredric Jameson's sense of art's politics, where the struggle between capitalism and its others is present at every stratum or horizon of every artistic activity, present in the contradictions that characterize every work. We might further consider the politics of art that we find in Pierre Bourdieu's sociology of culture, where autonomy is little more than art's self-conception, heteronomously determined by and indivisible from the development of a professional market-facing author function protected by copyright. There is no reason to stop there. We might next direct our attention to an approach derived from materialist feminism, which would encourage us to think about the roles that art and culture have played in helping people manage living through the historical unfolding of phases of capitalist development and attendant social relations. This might urge us to recognize art's belated insertion into people's lives as a form of reproduction of certain affects and evaluative norms that—in the case of high art—tend to reproduce the legitimacy of liberal bourgeois priority and authority. Or for that matter we might register Giovanni Arrighi's account of the way that investment in fine art provided a useful lodging place for surplus wealth in the Italian city-states, protecting the nascently capitalist economies from overinvestment.

All of which is to say that the conventional take on the politics of art that Benn Michaels identifies is not in fact all that common or generally accepted, at least not among Marxist critics and those broadly interested in a political economy of art, including fine art. It is common in mainstream liberal thought, to be sure, which as noted tends always to take the politics of the work as entirely present in the intention of the talent. Benn Michaels claims to be flipping the page from verso to recto, away from a standard celebration of a work that claims to represent suffering others, by instead preferring work that might appear to be too formal and "indifferent to suffering." He is still reading from the same paper.

It is standard-order idealism to argue that autonomous art will exist so long as we have faith in artists who understand their own work as entirely separable from the marketplace and from reception. And to stop at affirming what is in effect art's own faith in its distinct purview is to sideline what truncates and channels the nature of any given experience of the aesthetic. We take it that just as art exists in shifting but ever-present forms of relation to capital and just as artists often struggle in and against capitalist social relations, it is also the case that the nature of what art can do for its audience, including what it can mean, is dependent on audience members' own positions within the wider world of capitalist social relations: education, work, family, et cetera, all the things integral to inculcation in certain modes of aesthetic apprehension and all the things that make culture useful to us in a given moment or galvanizing or affirmative or what have you. Art's objectivity, such as it is, sets its relation to these matters; it does not nullify them. Moreover, we feel compelled to note once more, these matters—cavalierly dismissed as "subjective"—are themselves objective, not in the sense of their obduracy but of the ways they are produced by objective forces that sort lives according to the compulsions of capital's need for self-valorization.

Given this recognition, might we emphasize not the political power of autonomous art, but all culture's heteronomous prosaic determinations? These might include those determinations by and of "identity" that the aestheticist position deliberately brackets, even as participation in the European post-Romantic high art establishment is not a sign of universality but rather is determined by whiteness, relative wealth, access to higher education, and residence in one of the advanced capitalist nations. In what sense is it more auspiciously political to bracket these matters?

Heteronomy

Dave Beech has recently argued that the tendency to celebrate the singular genius artist at work can be grasped via a consideration of the history wherein the feudal guild system, supportive of various discrete artistic practices under one roof, began to give way to the dominance of the lone artist's workshop as the location where artistic production—but not materials fabrication, display, or sales—would occur. He writes that, with the displacement of the arts guilds, the "transition from the artisan to the artist . . . took place as an anomalous trajectory within the transition from feudalism to capitalism."[15] Art as a universal and elevated abstraction, that is to say, arises in tandem with the material reality of labor's abstraction, the work of producing art emerging as "distinct from both artisanal and industrial production" and even as, for some, "the cure for alienated labour." Artists have clearly continued to exist in this way, in fitful relation to the capitalist law of value. Their work is not "converted into capitalist commodity production," but neither is it unchanged by the dominance of capitalism.[16] It is subordinate to and interested in capitalist modes of production and circulation, in varying and contested but never exhausted degrees. In this light there is no real subsumption of art under capitalism—no neoliberalizing incorporation of art or of subjective mode of apprehension—but rather a complex set of changing relations among artists and audiences and capitalism as the dominant regime of organizing life and work.

The material foundations that make this somewhat unusual position possible are entirely hidden if we focus only on the relation between an autonomous artist and the artist's work. These foundations include, Beech notes, the displacement of apprenticeship models and guild systems, the tendency for direct fabrication of the work to become separate both from manufacture of materials like cameras and canvasses and film and paint and from the activity of displaying and curating and selling artworks. They also include a particular culture of prestige and a geographically and economically uneven distribution of access to the possibility of actually making a living by art, including making a living by appreciating, studying, teaching, or critiquing art.

A theory of art's autonomy from the perspective of totality thus cannot be an embrace of the ideal, but only an explanation of its conditions of its possibility. It must begin not from a focus on the private practice of the individual artist—this is more akin to an approach from liberal idealism—but from an account of the social conditions that make particular practices register importantly as "art" and that make the ideal of autonomy a relevant criterion for assessing art's quality or significance. It must extend also to a consideration of the investment in autonomous art in our present moment as a critical desire to explain not just what makes autonomy a defining feature of art's self-conception but what gives its idealization a new appeal among critics of neoliberal capitalism.

"Art" *is* these heteronomous prosaic determinations all the way down. The recent embrace of the autonomous-art nexus tells us not just that the more vocal theorists are influential professors who train many graduate students, but that we exist within these institutions where among the deepest fears is that our traditional objects of analysis are not doing the important work we need them to be doing. A feature of our current economic stagnation is the collapse of a certain tradition of formalism belonging to the postwar boom and Cold War preferences—an establishment founded on an educated and upwardly mobile cultural consumer and presupposing decent livelihoods for professionals in the high-cultural fields. We now confront diminishing institutional supports for ongoing cultivation of anything like a high-art sociolect. Part of the contemporary situation is thus found in transformed conditions of possibility for the making and consuming of the kinds of work that the autonomous-art nexus distinguishes for praise. These practices are increasingly restricted to wealthy elites who might move from expensive school to unpaid internship as preliminary donations to the shrinking arena of high culture they mean to staff, practices in turn implicated in gentrification that disproportionately affects racialized people, widening the gulf between artist and non-artist yet further. One can be forgiven some surprise then at finding scholarship still invested in the notion that elite art provides integrally effective resistance to the depredations of contemporary capitalism.

It is less surprising, though, when we grasp assertion of the priority of the aesthetic disposition as assertion of the priority of a bourgeois lifeworld whose foundations are collapsing. Scholars invested in the political potentials and affective rewards of art consumption are sorely tempted to raise bulwarks against the erosion of their positions within the remaining high-art establishments, university Humanities Departments foremost among them. Their fates are tied to the conditions that distinguish our times from the postwar period, when an expanding university sector eagerly trained people in embrace of civil society's liberal democratic values. What we have now instead is a diminishing component of well-paid fulltime workers and, as attendant phenomena, deficit-ridden legitimacy-deprived governments hesitant to spend anything more than a minimum on arts and culture funding or the university sector. Collapse of formal investment in the production of classical liberal democracy's rational educated citizen has been both a consequence of, and consequential for, these circumstances. The same is true of the decline of the classic high-cultural disposition—a disposition that flourished when state-funded educational institutions did not leave so many students indebted and anxious about pathways to meaningful job prospects in a market pushing people out of secure professional life. We must not allow ourselves to lapse into nostalgia for the earlier period—for a relatively robust welfare state and powerful labor force built on white supremacy and the patriarchal family home, U.S. industrial expansion in WWII and global reach during the Cold War years, alienating and resource-intensive suburbanization, ecologically devastating resource extraction, and political incorporation and pacification.

The popular left-academic critique of neoliberalism, which opposes more humane versions of capitalism to what we find around us now, reflects the vertiginous feeling that what once protected us from fates suffered by others—contingency, superfluity, austerity—is weak now, and that the bad stuff is seeping through the gates and into our lush enclaves. There are as we know fewer and fewer "good" academic jobs; tenure itself, the mark of the "good," is a somewhat weakened form of protection. In this context, the turn to concerted idealization of art's autonomy as an adequate response to capitalism's depredations is symptomatic. It is symptomatic of conditions in the contemporary university, the decline of which can only urge us to bolster our positions against the incursion of commercial forces from which we had sought refuge. The idealization of the self-legislating artist is in this way both a continuation of the Romantic-era idealization of artist as origin of creative articulation and meaning and a reflection of recent years' drives to fathom the humanities as a barricade against the closer and more explicit integration of the university and other elite enclaves within the circuits of profit.

Those who cling to the autonomous-art imaginary seem only to reckon with these institutional circumstances as phenomena that add urgency to their claims. It is not that the very matrices of power have made and continue to make "art" possible . . . for some. Instead, they claim, because the university is in ruins, we need autonomous art even more. Thus, the scholars affiliated with the autonomous-art nexus invest, adding a new intensity to an old tradition, in the universal validity, power, value, and insight of what is in fact and increasingly the manifestation of a particular sociolect: the artwork itself. They present as a radical and polemical intervention what in truth remains a generally embraced, if ever-more outmoded, narrative of Old World European culture, akin for instance to the logic of the Nobel Prize in Literature: art is more important when it disavows "causes"; formal experimentation is more important than "content"; culture is worthy of distinction when it separates itself from "mere" genre work or popular styles; art is not determined by a totality of social relations but instead takes those relations in and assesses them from on high.

This approach is not compatible with a materialist assessment of the contemporary condition of art, artist, art instruction, and art criticism or the history of the forms of relation between artists and their subsistence. Nor do its foundations in a particular vision of how contemporary capitalism works—one underpinned by an idealized, which is to say, ideological separation of the political and the economic—provide an adequate account of the totality of capitalist social relations as they are unfolding at present.

Notes

1. Paul Dave, "Bypass, Obscure Forces, and Ontological Anxiety," in *Contemporary Cinema and Neoliberal Ideology*, ed. Ewa Mazierska and Lars Kristensen (New York: Routledge 2017), 130.

2. Annie J. McClanahan, "Becoming Non-Economic: Human Capital Theory and Wendy Brown's *Undoing the Demos*," *Theory & Event* 20, no. 2 (April 2017): 512.

3. The technical category of *subsumption* (commonly understood to refer in particular to Marx's *real subsumption*, the transformation of the commodity production process toward greater productivity via automation and/or new organization) makes a regular appearance in autonomy discourse, though it is regularly the case that *commodification* or *marketization* would seem more apt; see Joshua Clover, "Subsumption," in *The Sage Handbook of Frankfurt School Critical Theory*, vol. 3, ed. Beverly Best, Werner Bonefeld, Chris O'Kane, and Neil Larsen (London: Sage, 2018).

4. Karl Marx, *Capital*, trans. Ben Fowkes (London: Penguin, 1992), 1:280.

5. Walter Benn Michaels, "The Beauty of a Social Problem," *The Brooklyn Rail*, October 3, 2011, https://brooklynrail.org/2011/10/art/the-beauty-of-a-social-problem.

6. Ibid.

7. Ibid.

8. See Martha Woodmansee's account of the origins of aesthetic philosophy in eighteenth-century Germany. The larger the market grew, the more it seemed that instrumentalist accounts that emphasized how people could be moved by a work ended up celebrating subpar products rather than those of trained experts. The theology of art that then arose—the work as self-sufficient, its value intrinsic and separate from consumers' pleasures—provided "not only a convenient but a very powerful set of concepts with which to address the predicament in which they found themselves—concepts by which (difficult, or 'fine') art's de facto loss of direct instrumentality could be recuperated as a (supreme) virtue"; Woodmansee, *The Author, Art, and the Market: Rereading the History of Aesthetics* (New York: Columbia University Press, 1994), 32.

9. Walter Benn Michaels, *The Beauty of a Social Problem: Photography, Autonomy, Economy* (Chicago: University of Chicago Press, 2015), 41.

10. Ibid., 41.

11. Ibid., 42; emphasis ours.

12. Nicholas Brown. "The Work of Art in the Age of Its Real Subsumption under Capital," nonsite.org, March 13, 2012: http://nonsite.org/editorial/the-work-of-art-in-the-age-of-its-real-subsumption-under-capital.
13. Nicholas Brown, *Autonomy: The Social Ontology of Art under Capitalism* (Durham, N.C.: Duke University Press, 2019).
14. Benn Michaels, "Beauty of a Social Problem."
15. Dave Beech, "Art and the Politics of Eliminating Handcraft," *Historical Materialism* 27, no. 1 (2019): 161.
16. Ibid., 178, 175.

Works Cited

Beech, Dave. "Art and the Politics of Eliminating Handcraft." *Historical Materialism* 27, no. 1 (2019): 155–81.

Brown, Nicholas. *Autonomy: The Social Ontology of Art under Capitalism.* Durham, N.C.: Duke University Press, 2019.

———. "The Work of Art in the Age of Its Real Subsumption under Capital." nonsite.org, March 13, 2012. http://nonsite.org/editorial/the-work-of-art-in-the-age-of-its-real-subsumption-under-capital.

Clover, Joshua. "Subsumption and Crisis." In *The Sage Handbook of Frankfurt School Critical Theory*, edited by Beverly Best, Werner Bonefeld, Chris O'Kane, and Neil Larsen, 3:1,567–83. London: Sage, 2018.

Dave, Paul. "Bypass, Obscure Forces, and Ontological Anxiety." In *Contemporary Cinema and Neoliberal Ideology*, edited by Ewa Mazierska and Lars Kristensen, 121–36. New York: Routledge, 2017.

Marx, Karl. *Capital*. Vol. 1, Translated by Ben Fowkes. London: Penguin, 1992.

McClanahan, Annie J. "Becoming Non-Economic: Human Capital Theory and Wendy Brown's *Undoing the Demos*." *Theory & Event* 20, no. 2 (April 2017): 510–19.

Michaels, Walter Benn. "The Beauty of a Social Problem." *The Brooklyn Rail*, October 3, 2011. https://brooklynrail.org/2011/10/art/the-beauty-of-a-social-problem.

———. *The Beauty of a Social Problem: Photography, Autonomy, Economy.* Chicago: University of Chicago Press, 2015.

Woodmansee, Martha. *The Author, Art, and the Market: Rereading the History of Aesthetics.* New York: Columbia University Press, 1994.

6 / Ecology with Totality: The Case of Morton's *Hyperobjects* and Klein's *This Changes Everything*

BRENT RYAN BELLAMY

> A large proportion of discourse on scale in ecological science writing grapples with [a] precise problem. It tries to represent something too large and distributed to be observed directly: the order that seems to persist at scales larger than those of individual organisms. Often referred to as the ecosystem, this order can't be observed in the same way that I can observe a bacterium through a microscope. Given this tension between visible and invisible objects of study, ecological science writing often relies on figurative language to represent the ecosystem as a whole.
>
> —DEREK WOODS,
> "SCALE IN ECOLOGICAL SCIENCE WRITING"

Twentieth-century ecological thought was founded with something like totality in mind. The most ready-to-hand example is Rachel Carson's 1962 breakthrough book *Silent Spring*. It intervened in the way government policy makers accepted industrial downplaying of the environmental impacts of chemicals, such as synthetic pesticides. To make its argument, *Silent Spring* describes the connections among chemicals, environments, and species, which it represents using the figure of the food chain.[1] Critical geographer Sara Holiday Nelson describes the role of totality thinking in *Silent Spring*, writing that in Carson's work "the global environment, rather than an inert collection of resources, came to be seen as a set of integrated complex systems whose dynamics defied prediction."[2] Ecology is the study of unpredictable and globally interconnected systems. Though

Carson does not name totality specifically, her focus on chemicals, environments, and species through the food chain offers the start of a model of ecological totality, and many ecological thinkers since have been working around the concept when they describe Earth systems.[3]

Food chains are only the beginning of the desire for large-scale representational figures in ecological thought. For instance, ecotechnology scholar Derek Woods tells an anecdote about the ecologist who coined the term *macroscope*. Fixated on studying "whole rather than individual parts," Howard T. Odum imagined that macroscopes might "observe things too large for the naked eye," revealing "wholes which exist at much larger scales than those of seemingly solid, unitary objects."[4] The problem here is that the macroscope does not exist, though it does provide a figure for understanding how ecological science writing uses tropes to express large-scale ideas.[5] Woods takes a second-order approach to ecological science writing to emphasize "the disjunctures that produce scale effects."[6] Woods's argument makes evident the rhetorical and conceptual strategies of ecological science writing, which I argue can be readily applied to popular environmentalist writing. Such a disjuncture in large-scale thinking might be bridged in at least two ways: moving beyond human sensation with figures of thought, on the one hand, and collecting data points to bootstrap a full sense of everything, on the other.

Recent popular environmentalist writing has grappled with what it might mean to think the connection between local ecosystems and the global earth system. For example, in a short essay titled, "It's Not Climate Change—It's Everything Change," literary author Margaret Atwood makes two entwined claims: the impacts of anthropogenic climate change are greater than those of global warming, and the response needed to address such transformations is not reduceable to fixing the environmental crisis but instead must overhaul fossil-fueled capitalism.[7] Atwood declares, "We are all joined together globally in ways we have never been joined before, so if we fail, we all fail together."[8] The necessity of such a political project and the outline of its stakes appeal to thinking totality. The necessity of "everything change" and that we stand to "fail together" are both essential truths of the current conjuncture. Atwood calls on readers to recognize how the totality of social and ecological relations will change should things continue as they have. She simultaneously calls for a collective subject to acknowledge the situation and do something proactive to stop it.

But there is something vacuous about this appeal to "everything" that suggests that a spurious theory of totality is at work here. "Everything change" skips tenses, bouncing from what will happen if we do nothing to what could happen if we act. Atwood's article recognizes the necessity of thinking big but rushes to contain such big thinking within the grammar of "everything." In a different context, Theodor W. Adorno wrote, "Everything must mean something, just what, however, must first be extracted."[9] This rhetoric imparts the gravity of the situation but does not do enough to outline the practical procedures and theoretical models that could possibly better approach the totality of nature-society relations. The question of totality for ecological thinking is both a conceptual and a representational problem. Atwood's argument appeals to totality thinking, but more, it asks its audience to equate big thinking with the immensity of the ecological catastrophe. Here, Atwood's everything emphasizes scale, yet interconnections remain abstract and assumed rather than detailed and legible. This simplistic generalization of "everything" needs care and, counterintuitively, slowing down. The challenge of thinking totality and the Earth system at once is that the scale of abstraction leaves little room for practical action. Conversely, an overemphasis on action focuses overmuch on the human register, which would concede the big picture. This chapter attempts to locate how the challenge of mediating ecological totality involves a struggle with figuration, the figure or the data, and with the subject, absent or multiplied.[10]

A gap separates two ecocritical versions of totality thinking from one another and from a satisfyingly accessible sense of totality thinking. Philosopher Timothy Morton and social activist Naomi Klein each use significant keywords to emphasize the scale and scope of their thinking. Morton coins the term "hyperobjects," and Klein writes about "everything change"; these words elicit a sense of large-scale entities and actions. Together they form what might be thought of as two modes for ecological totality thinking. Both aim for a large-scale figure, though they strike for this target in remarkably different ways. Morton emphasizes the incomprehensible interconnectedness of objects, while Klein engages with people and movements. Klein records multiple, ongoing struggles between resource extraction and the human and more-than-human actors caught in the fray, while Morton evacuates the subject.

Hyperobjects: Philosophy and Ecology after the End of the World (first published in 2013) and *This Changes Everything: Capitalism versus the Climate* (first published in 2014) are popular, generating interviews, speaking tours, reviews, essays, and further work.[11] They inhabit different registers of thought: Morton's is a theoretical, poetic elaboration of a concept; meanwhile, Klein's is a populist, justice-based accounting of environmental struggles. Yet both implicitly appeal to totality as a concept. By reading these two works, I develop a theory of totality thinking for environmental criticism in the negative. Put differently, I read their conceptual and representational strategies against the grain to detect the limits to totality thinking in these approaches. Morton's use of figures to elaborate hyperobjects and appeal to scientific language forms the basis of the first section. Klein's elaboration of the details of struggle is the focus of the second section. By the final section, I offer positive claims about ecological totality thinking.

Evacuating the Subject

The rhythms and durations of certain entities are not entirely legible, or conceivable, by human perception, in climate modeling or in aesthetic practice. Morton calls these entities "hyperobjects" and writes that such entities "occupy a high-dimensional phase space that results in their not being visible to humans for stretches of time."[12] For Morton, the hyperobject is "not a function of our knowledge"—hyperobjects are "real whether or not someone is thinking of them."[13] To be able to conceive of the challenge to representation that the modern world presents, some concept, such as the hyperobject, seems necessary. At first glance, Morton's claims seem compatible with a historical materialist sense of totality in that each aims at decentering human subjects and expanding a sense of a larger reality imperceptible by sight, smell, taste, or touch. But, in doing so, Morton in fact casts the subject adrift in a cosmic sea of objects.

Hyperobjects follows up on Morton's 2007 work *Ecology without Nature*. On Morton's account, both popular and philosophical definitions of nature forestall properly ecological thinking. Morton's major project here is to deracinate nature from ecological thought. Morton seeks to show how "the idea of nature" gets in the way "of properly ecological forms of culture, philosophy, politics, and art."[14] Morton's early work critiques the transcendental concept of nature, entrenched in ecocriticism most explicitly through the works of Ralph Waldo Emerson. Morton eschews ecstatic oneness for a stronger sense of the intricate relations of objects across a galactic expanse and an epochal timescale. Morton does this by devising exemplary lists, describing representational figures, and relying on particular rhetorical strategies.

Morton uses the grammar of ecological science writing at a cosmic scale. Morton's work pushes humans to think beyond the subjective frame of their own lives to imagine the forces and entities by which they are physically affected: the gravity of a distant black hole, the emanations of radionucleotides that drift in the surf of the world's oceans, and the untold impacts of microplastic fibers that fill our guts. Morton's list of hyperobjects includes objects of radically different orders and magnitudes—galactic forces, radioactive materials, petrocarbon polymers, and so on. Morton draws on the same figure of the chain that Woods identified in *Silent Spring*. Despite relying on such lists, Morton insists that "things are themselves, but we can't point to them directly," arguing that, for instance, one "can think and compute climate in this sense, but . . . can't directly see or touch it."[15] For Morton, an ontological gap disrupts human capacities to perceive climate. Put tautologically, we cannot see the thing that we cannot see. Though Morton gestures beyond the knowable to an idea just outside of human sensory capacity, the inclusion of listed examples flattens the entries grammatically and conceptually.

Beyond lists of examples, Morton uses figures to illustrate hyperobjects, asymptotically relating them to totality. By far the most compelling examples Morton relies on are the hologram and the Magic Eye picture. Morton privileges the visual and its access to the conceptual. I embellish each figure in turn as illustrative of Morton's project, and I argue that each uneasily gestures toward the place of totality in Morton's work.

One cannot look directly at a hologram. The perceivable mirage image on a credit card, for instance, is only the effect of light waves ricocheting off and passing through interference patterns. Holograms do not use a *gestalt* effect. As Morton explains, "Cut a little piece of hologram out . . . and you still see a (slightly more blurry) version of the whole object. Every piece of the hologram contains information about the whole."[16] In their fragmentation, holograms refuse to be fractured. Here the image of the hologram cut into pieces takes on explanatory power. Morton suggests that other things too might be nothing more than fragments containing a blurry image of the whole. The conceptual and poetic resonance of the image supersedes its material history. The use of holograms, in dollar-store toys or on credit cards, is hardly part of the point here. Rather, the qualities of the hologram offer Morton the figurative example to describe a relationship between the perception of a silvery, contained, three-dimensional image and the larger conceptual point about what might constitute a hyperobject. From Morton's rhetorical position, once the reader understands that a portion of the hologram escapes their field of vision even though that portion also produces visible effects, they can abandon it. The hologram hints at a conceptual relationship between the part and the whole, but on its own as an object, it is static. Unless one were to consider the viewer as an active part of the hologram, it remains unmediated. The figure of the hologram seems, in its physical nature, to deny the existence of a totality, yet in every piece of the hologram is information about the whole. Morton's argument relies on the figure of the hologram to provide clarity and illustrate the unillustratable.

Where the hologram illustrates the idea of something that one could not perceive directly, the Magic Eye shows the interference pattern itself. Known by the technical name *autostereogram*, Magic Eye images make it possible for a person to see a three-dimensional image in a two-dimensional pattern.[17] Unlike the hologram, autostereogram images are a sort of *gestalt*: the whole is greater than the sum of its parts. Through a practice of un-focusing and focusing one's vision, viewers diverge their eyes to perceive a hidden image. Unlike the hologram, where each fragment still contains the whole in a literal sense, with the Magic Eye any disruption to the pattern ruins the effect. In this model, the object is already there, but it is obscured from view—that is, it requires a particular way of looking to perceive it. The autostereogram contains an image only visible by careful relaxation of the eye, but once glimpsed and lost the viewer will insist that it must still be there. It produces a relationship between appearance and essence, yet essence here need not imply a model of depth; rather, it might be conceived of as something already apparent for those who know where to look. However fitting the metaphor may be, the autostereogram itself is preprogrammed. It has no history, nor is it capable of presenting anything other than the preselected image—be it a sea shell, a rhinoceros, or any other three-dimensionally rendered vision. Once again, the illustrative figure chosen by Morton seems to lack the possibility of mediation without the interaction of a viewer, and yet we might ask about the historicity of autostereogram images and the marketing of Magic Eye books as the way millennials have collectively come to know and think of such optical mysteries. The kernel of meaning Morton finds here speaks to the mysterious and wonderous character of such objects. I remember gathering around a Magic Eye book as a child in the 1990s. I remember straining to see the image. Anyone who claimed they could see it would be hailed with one imperative demand: "Prove it." The required effort of seeing the image, mundane though such an image may be, and the declaration that one could see it could only be confirmed by a social exchange.

The hologram and the autostereogram present images of representation without mediation. In both cases Morton develops the claim that such figures exist without human sensory observation. Morton uses the phrase "false immediacy" to critique other approaches to ecological thinking. The phrase aims to critique the human sense of locality, especially as rooted through material objects and the weather. It also mounts an attack on the intellectual practices of going meta, as Morton describes it. In decrying false immediacy, Morton posits the possibility of true immediacy.[18] I would prefer to omit the implication of true or false and simply call it "immediacy," following Adorno, who writes, "To speak immediately of the immediate is to behave much as those novelists who drape their marionettes in imitated bygone passions like cheap jewelry, and make people who are not more than component parts in machinery act as if they still had the capacity to act as subjects, and as if something depended on their actions."[19] Adorno makes Morton's point about the limitations of human experience, yet refutes Morton's underlying antipolitical premise.

Morton's dislike for false immediacy is a way of jettisoning mediation. It would be false to Morton if causal links could be found between seemingly discrete objects. For example, Morton writes about connections but in a manner that privileges connection without asking about the complex and indirect way the garden is connected, narratively or structurally, to the screen:

> Worlds need horizons and horizons need backgrounds, which need foregrounds. When we can see everywhere (when I can use Google Earth to see the fish in my mom's pond in her garden in London), the world—as a significant, bounded, horizoning entity—disappears. We have no world because the objects that functioned as invisible scenery have dissolved.[20]

Here the problem is an imagined immediacy of scale, which in truth is mediated by the survey work and servers of Google and the internet connection and screen of Morton's point of search.[21] Nothing has disappeared, and as with the hologram, one can know and remember the source of the mirage image even without seeing it directly. Moreover, Morton's description of the relation between horizons, backgrounds, and foregrounds presumes relationships from the perspective of a human observer (which is fine for me but seems to run against the posthuman aim of the project), and these snap-together connections between the limits of visibility (conceptual or material) and field of depth, as described here, are immediate relationships. No mediation is provided to situate horizon, foreground, and background in relation to one another or in relation to an abstract sense of the totality. As with the hologram and the autostereogram, such illustrations of the conceptual problem of hyperobjects proceeds with mimetic chains of examples. Moreover, in the example provided, the subject retains central importance to tracking the dissolution of a bounded world.

Hyperobjects attempts to think totality without the dialectical inflection of mediation. Morton alternates substituting metaphor (especially simile) and a certain form of scientific knowledge for the dialectical third term. For instance, rather than thinking the mediations of energy infrastructure and a planet's physical properties, Morton employs highly suggestive, comparative language instead: "Hyperobjects are agents. They are indeed more than a little demonic, in the sense that *they appear to* straddle worlds and times, *like fiber optic cables or electromagnetic fields*. And they are demonic in that through them causalities flow *like electricity*."[22] Setting aside the mixed metaphors here (a favorite rhetorical strategy of Morton's), the assertion that hyperobjects are agents gets confused because, according to the grammar, as agents hyperobjects "appear to straddle worlds and times." Does this imply that they only appear to do this? If so, to whom? I do not think these questions drive at Morton's intended meaning. While a certain reader might be compelled by the breakdown of the grammar of the book at a more granular level ("it holds true with Morton's explication of these concepts!"), such rhetorical imprecision emphasizes Morton's avoidance of subject inflected and emancipatory strands of materialist thought founded on the adage that *the abstract is material*.[23]

For Morton, there is no way out of thinking the general and particular at once. Take this sentence, for example: "When it comes to hyperobjects, nonlocality means that the general itself is compromised by the particular."[24] The passive being of the particular compromises totalizing thought, on Morton's account. A nineteenth-century word, *compromise* invokes arbitration, concession, the settling of differences, partial surrender of principals, or the risk of danger.[25] I can try to understand the point by rewriting the sentence: "When it comes to hyperobjects, nonlocality means that the particular compromises the general itself." Yet this rewriting does away with Morton's passive voice, with the relegating of agency to the material. This grammar confuses rather than clarifies. It is also symptomatic of the limits of thought for this philosophical register: passive constructions aim to move the burden of activity away from the human, without anthropomorphizing objects. The sentence, "The general itself is compromised by the particular" has a level of facticity to it, yet this too can be read as a figure that stands in for the place of a direct claim about hyperobjects.

Scientific language and concepts allow Morton to avoid mediation. For instance, a stated goal in *Hyperobjects* is to "incorporate contemporary science back into philosophy."[26] Morton discusses not only climate science, but also quantum states. Quantum theory becomes conceptually crucial for Morton to claim that the pieces of reality are more than the sum of the whole. Morton explains this reverse gestalt effect with a fractal logic, arguing that each named entity produces new objects, which proliferate the elements of a given world. Such systems approach the infinite. Though, "Objects entangle one another in a crisscrossing mesh of space-time fluctuations," there is no way, according to Morton, that these proliferating objects (and relationships between objects, as objects) could be totalized into overarching or subtending structures.[27] Morton insists on the parts being larger than, and uncollapsible into, the whole.

In each example from *Hyperobjects*, the subject is both missing and vital to understanding the argument. More than just evacuating the subject from the analysis, Morton evacuates social relations from the definition of capital. Though the opening salvo of the book includes "the sum of all the whirring machinery of capitalism," Morton pulls back from framing the book in terms of capitalism: "Hyperobjects pose numerous threats to individualism, nationalism, anti-intellectualism, racism, speciesism, anthropocentrism, you name it. *Possibly* even capitalism itself." Morton discusses "the metaphysical dimension of capital" as "the positing of value in some mystical, ethereal beyond," one that hyperobjects may threaten.[28] This sense of capital confuses metaphysics with abstraction. It insists that the abstract cannot be material. But how else are we to grapple with the effects of a volatile climate system? For Marx, value is not a thing but a social relation. Likewise, the weather itself does not comprise the climate; rather, the weather is a complex and indirect form of expression of the climate. When Morton does write about people or the weather, they are not subjects, but they are subjected to the effects of hyperobjects and objectified by this analysis.

Morton imagines the end of epistemology with the end of the world. As Morton argues in the introduction, one's sense of things comes from their outlook or position in relation to the thing (what a dialectical thinker might call "standpoint").[29] Even the hologram and the autostereogram are nothing without an observer, without a subject to witness the light bouncing off the interference pattern of the hologram or to unfocus their eye to see the image hidden in the Magic Eye image. For all its emphasis on the mesh of connection between objects, Morton's work evacuates the relations of the subject. It asks, "What if we considered the object as massively acting?" but does not look to the potential for humans to comprehend, let alone act in defiance of, the human-built world. Morton subtracts the human from ecological questions. Morton emphasizes ethics, in light of the argument, as in this passage:

> The ethical and political choices become much clearer and less divisive if we begin to think of pollution and global warming and radiation as effects of hyperobjects rather than as flows or processes that can be managed. These flows are often eventually shunted into some less powerful group's backyard. The Native American tribe must deal with the radioactive waste. The African American family must deal with the toxic chemical runoff. The Nigerian village must deal with the oil slick. . . . It is helpful to think of global warming as something like an ultra slow motion nuclear bomb. The incremental effects are almost invisible, until an island disappears underwater. Poor people—who include most of us on Earth at this point—perceive the ecological emergency not as degrading an aesthetic picture such as *world* but as an accumulation of violence that nibbles at them directly.[30]

Ultimately, though Morton appears to tackle one of the most vexing problems of the day—the relationship between capital and ecology—his work has no emancipatory project attached to it. It provides witty insights without thinking through how they might allow us to better understand human capacities to alter the course of history.

Hyperobjects follows a Heideggerian trajectory toward formulating a new ontology.[31] As I argue, Morton's work, and *Hyperobjects* in particular, might be read as an attempt to produce a theory of totality without mediation. Such a theory still looks to describe the enchainment of objects and seeks to understand the way they might influence and be influenced by other objects, yet the ultimate goal seems to be an epistemological one. Rather than tracing the lay lines of hyperobjects so that we, people, might better understand them and thus seek to redirect their sometimes malicious effects, Morton pushes the collective negotiation of social life aside. *Hyperobjects* produces a sense of the world where human capacities have diminished, despite the ongoing need for such capacities.

Multiplying the Subject

Echoing some of the challenges to thinking big outlined by Woods and Morton, *This Changes Everything* addresses the unwieldly conceptual scale of ecological catastrophe. Klein characterizes the elusiveness of climate change, writing, "It's hard to keep it in your head for very long."[32] Unlike Morton's collapsing of the ecology-capital problematic, Klein separates the Earth systems and capital systems; moreover, she describes their relationship explicitly, writing that "our economic system and our planetary system are now at war."[33] On Klein's account, forces of nature and forces of production work in opposing rhythms with mutually destructive effects: to stave off climate collapse, humanity needs to contract its use of Earth's resources, while to hold crisis at bay capitalism demands boundless expansion. As Klein puts it, "Only one of these sets of rules can be changed, and it's not the laws of nature."[34] This assessment restages a late twentieth-century environmental movement argument: the Earth has a certain carrying capacity, and economic development is pushing the boundaries of that capacity to sustain human life. These arguments aim at certain political ends. She writes, "We are left with a stark choice: allow climate disruption to change everything about our world, or change pretty much everything about our economy to avoid that fate."[35] This sentence offers a choice. Either humans continue to subsidize the fossil fuel industry and rampant commodity production and see what wild new catastrophes await us, or they make serious changes to human life activity. In each scenario, everything changes. In each case, everything is at stake.

This Changes Everything champions the emancipatory purpose of climate justice throughout. Within this political umbrella, its title plays with the sense of change and with what "everything" might mean. In writing *everything*, Klein considers totality, while maintaining a rallying point to enable politics. For Klein, *everything* seems to indicate both the effects of fossil capital on the Earth—its inhabitants and environments—that is, its ecosystems—and a proposal for how we might shift the meaning of "this"—a pronoun with an unclear antecedent, which allows the reader to imagine a collective path to changing everything. Klein's book transforms the pronoun *this* from a stand-in for capitalism—"*Capitalism* changes everything"—to a revelation—"This *book* changes everything"—and finally it might even be read in a third way: "This *movement* could change everything!"

Klein fills the space of *everything* with details and examples. Political movements are at the heart of the story of *This Changes Everything*. The book investigates the possibilities and limitations of acting against capital and for the climate. It characterizes the climate-capital problem, describes bad political approaches and celebrates good ones, and highlights the capacities of humans. Klein draws on the mutating climate system as a totality that forms the possibilities, imagined and real, for the future. In this way, she develops an explicit emancipatory project while working to refute the somewhat nihilistic claims of her contemporaries and capitalist ideologues. Klein's approach to describing the interwoven fate of the earth system and the capitalist world system begins with the panorama view, but it certainly does not stay here. *This Changes Everything* frames its contents through a vision of the social and ecological whole. It moves from such a foundation to process the particular contradictions that arise within this total frame: separation of capital and climate, recognition that does not equal action, and the impossibility of true testing of climate action.[36]

The first contradiction involves the treatment of plant growth, and forests in particular, as a mechanism for carbon storage. Polluting industries draw on the carbon-sequestering capacity of biotic life as an asset. The problem is that such natural carbon sequestration is treated as a reason to continue production and to continue emitting CO_2: "The trees, meadows, and mountains lose their intrinsic, place-based meaning and become deracinated, virtual commodities in a global trading system."[37] Drawing on the work of Geographer Bram Büscher, Klein uses this example as a starting point to map the totality of fossil capital:

> Once absorbed into this system, a pristine forest may look as lush and alive as ever, but it has actually become an extension of a dirty power plant on the other side of the planet, attached by invisible financial transactions. Polluting smoke may not be billowing from the tops of its trees but it may as well be, since the trees that have been designated as carbon offsets are now allowing that pollution to take place elsewhere.[38]

Here, we see hints of Morton's approach to hyperobjects, without the philosophical baggage. The integration of capital and climate is always, already total: their separation happens in representation and thought alone. Whether forests are recognized as carbon sinks or treated as crucial elements of fossil fuel infrastructure, they are a part of the capital-climate complex.

The second contradiction is that recognizing a problem does not equal acting on one. Though "corporate-partnered conservationists" may emphasize and repeat the mantra "everything is disconnected," the words of early ecologists, such as Carson, still ring true for Klein's "Everything is connected."[39] This distinction is political: capitalists can misrecognize the interconnectedness of life and have such mistakes still work to their advantage. The whole picture is that such mistakes affect human and non-human populations directly and indirectly.

The third contradiction involves other approaches to mitigating carbon output or impact moving beyond regulations. The problem of geoengineering solutions is a problem for systems thinking. Such an approach can only work at a large scale. Small-scale attempts at geoengineering make it difficult to gauge the results; moreover, there are no effective tests for geoengineering. For instance, Klein explains that "spraying sulfur in the Arctic or the tropics will impact rainfall in the Sahara or southern India. But that wouldn't be a test of geoengineering; it would actually be conducting geoengineering."[40] The Earth has a total climate, which expresses itself regionally in shifting patterns. As media scholar Wendy Hui Kyong Chun makes clear, thinking about climate poses several challenges to geoengineering models and to human experience:

1. many different factors affect climate/temperature;
2. these many different factors also affect each other;
3. it is difficult to exactly measure factors that affect climate;
4. much of the climate record precedes human-kept records and so we must use historical proxies;
5. climate is not something we immediately experience: we are affected by weather, not climate.[41]

The complexity of the capital-climate complex also means that geoengineering solutions undertaken in one area might have profoundly unpredictable effects elsewhere on the planet. Producing models for assessing climate change possibilities present related problems. Moreover, such models are only ever hypothetical insofar as they can never be disproven in the event of climate change mitigation: as Chun explains, "To wait for these models' calculations to be verified—for their accuracy to be proven—is to give up on the future by rewriting political problems as ones that science can (dis-)solve."[42] What falls under the name of geoengineering shares certain attributes: being based on large-scale operations, aiming to mitigate rather than reduce carbon emissions, challenging the capacity to model future ecosystems, and seeking nearly immediate results.

In the summer of 2012, Russ George, of Plakos Inc., and members of the Haida unloaded one hundred tons of iron sulphate into the Pacific Ocean just off the coast of British Columbia to encourage algae growth, which would thus act as a carbon sink.[43] The decision was made by George and the Haida. Haida Gwaii is part of the unceded territory of the Haida. Stephanie Pappas explains the implications for large-scale adoption of the technique: "Even widespread fertilization of the oceans would result in about 0.5 to 1 gigaton of carbon being shuttled out of the atmosphere annually.... That's about a third to a quarter of the carbon added to the atmosphere each year from man-made and other sources."[44] George and the Haida took the initiative to act. Others interested in finding ways to balance the carbon budget might similarly take geoengineering solutions into their own hands. In the case of this example, the Haida contributed over one million dollars to the project.

The challenges to geoengineering and climate modeling that Klein and Chun raise allow for ecological thinking to seek solutions under a different banner that take on global warming and fossil capital all at once. Principal among these are the redistribution of wealth and nationalization of energy infrastructures. Such alternatives might mean, in her words, "taking far larger shares of the profits from the rogue corporations most responsible for waging war on the climate and using those resources to clean up their mess" or "reversing energy privatizations to regain control over our grids."[45] But Klein highlights the work of the Indian author and activist Vandana Shiva. As Shiva's plan shows, the market becomes an enemy to realistic, humane solutions that produce jobs and food security in an environmentally responsible manner:

> Shifting to an agriculture model based on agro-ecological methods would not only sequester large amounts of carbon, it would reduce emissions and increase food security. And unlike geoengineering, "It's not a fifty-year experiment. It's an assured, guaranteed path that has been shown to work." Admittedly, such responses break all the free market rules. Then again, so did bailing out the banks and the auto companies. And they are still not close to as radical as breaking the primordial link between temperature and atmospheric carbon— all to meet our desire for planetary air-conditioning.[46]

Reaching an impasse in one project or on one register can be addressed by shifting to a different strategy elsewhere: *solutions* are not unthinkable, nor are they unrepresentable. People across the globe and from all manner of social classes are attempting to address the climate crisis.

Klein proposes some strategies for bringing about a socially just energy transition by looking to past moments of crisis and resolve. The book argues for a redistribution of wealth and a nationalization of energy infrastructures as part of the "unfinished business" of Civil Rights and the movements for Black lives, feminism, and Indigenous sovereignty and reconciliation. The level of practicality and clarity with which the way forward is gauged is one of the most remarkable components of Klein's approach to environmental politics. For instance, the proposed "Marshall Plan for the Earth" emphasizes a grand vision through reachable decisions and achievable policies. Such a plan "could deliver the equitable redistribution of agricultural lands that was supposed to follow independence from colonial rule and dictatorship; it could bring the jobs and homes that Martin Luther King dreamed of; it could bring jobs and clean water to Native communities," and "it could at last turn on the lights and running water in every South African township."[47] Here, the curious image described by Morton of the hologram recasts itself. Each part of the movement for justice contains a piece of the whole struggle for the climate. Similarly, the autostereogram image works as well: these struggles are already happening. You can see them if you know where and how to look.

Klein asks if an economic shift of the magnitude and impact necessary has occurred in history. She locates one example in the immense power of war measures undertaken in Canada, the United States, and elsewhere in the twentieth century when "presidents and prime ministers are the ones commanding the transformation from above."[48] Precedent of top-down change is not unexpected, but Klein also looks for records of change from below. Klein turns to the Civil Rights movement in the United States, the 1970s feminist demand of wages for housework, and the early twentieth-century labor victories that led to the New Deal in the United States; to the nationalization efforts of Mohammad Mosaddegh in Iran and Salvador Allende in Chile; to the struggle against apartheid in South Africa; and, further back, to abolition movements in late eighteenth-century and nineteenth-century Great Britain and the United States.[49] Klein is not the only thinker of ecological totality to offer solutions in this vein. Using similar language, Mark Jacobson has been arguing since 2013 that the United States could meet all its energy needs with renewables, which would be "a large-scale transformation": such a plan would "require an effort comparable to the Apollo moon project or constructing the interstate highway system. But it is possible, without even having to go to new technologies. We really need to just decide collectively that this is the direction we want to head as a society."[50] Klein and Jacobson are not alone in such calls for a return to social planning or full employment.

Marxist cultural theorist Fredric Jameson has recently made a similar call for a collective return to bureaucracy. In *An American Utopia* (2016), he suggests that we rehabilitate bureaucracy by beginning to acknowledge "the altruistic fervor and sacrifice such as we witness historically in the movements of social workers through the ages" (7). When both revolution and reform seem broken beyond repair, Jameson calls for a return to the concept of *dual power*. The phrase has its origins in the emerging Soviet Union and could be used to describe "the way organizations like the Black Panthers yesterday or Hamas today function to provide daily services—food kitchens, garbage collection, health care, water inspection, and the like—in areas neglected by some official central government" (4). For Jameson the bureaucratic force capable of welcoming the most into its ranks, of having the networks in place to provide housing, healthcare, and education, is the army. Bracketing any conscientious objections, there is already an ecologically minded component to this suggestion. As Jameson points out, "The army is also notoriously the source of manpower [sic] for disaster relief, infrastructural repair and construction and the like," and "the question of food supply would immediately place this institution (if it can still be called that) in charge of the ordering and supply of food production and therefore in a controlling position for that fundamental dietetic and agronomic activity as well" (29). One might combine what Jameson calls for with Klein's recommendations. There is a remarkable resonance between these visions. Klein writes, "Public dollars also need to go to the equally important, though less glamorous projects and services that will help us prepare for the coming heavy weather. That includes things like hiring more firefighters and improving storm barriers. And it means coming up with new, nonprofit disaster insurance programs so that people who have lost everything to a hurricane or a forest fire are not left at the mercy of a private insurance industry that is already adapting to climate change by avoiding payouts and slapping victims with massive rate increases" (109). Both suggestions feature an expansion of employment along the avenue of public service. Jameson's and Klein's visions share a certain elegance, too, throwing so many problems at one another to seek their mutual resolution: unemployment, climate crisis, and a waning state.[51] Electoral representation, the volunteerism of electoral politics, and the need for decisive action create a significant hurdle in desperate times, owing to climate crisis, economic downturn, and pandemic conditions.

    The difficulty with plans such as these, argues Marxist energy historian Andreas Malm in "Revolution in a Warming World," is that whereas when oil exploration "intrudes on a people's ancestral homeland to drill for fuel, the antagonism is in your face and resistance comes naturally"; global warming *writ large* "can slaughter millions from within a castle never seen, and, alas, hard to raid."[52] Put in other words, to paraphrase Alberto Toscano and Jeff Kinkle, "[climate change] as a totality is devoid of an easily grasped command-and-control-centre."[53] Crucially then, in addressing climate-justice movements, Klein opens up possibilities for staving off and preparing for a warming world. In light of these observations, it is striking that Malm describes Klein's book as the "most promising vision" for the "struggle against climate change," adding that "*all* struggles are struggles against fossil capital; the subjects only need to be made aware of it."[54] Inspired by Klein and the ongoing struggles for justice and self-determination around the world, Malm suggests an update to the list of ten starting points from the *Communist Manifesto*. Malm offers this list:

1. Enforce a complete moratorium on all new facilities for extracting coal, oil, or natural gas;
2. Close down all power plants running on such fuels;
3. Draw 100 percent of electricity from nonfossil sources, primarily wind and solar;
4. Terminate the expansion of air, sea, and road travel; convert road and sea travel to electricity and wind; ration remaining air travel to ensure a fair distribution until it can be completely replaced with other means of transport;
5. Expand mass transit systems on all scales, from subways to intercontinental high-speed trains;
6. Limit the shipping and flying of food and systematically promote local supplies;
7. End the burning of tropical forests and initiate massive programmes for reforestation;
8. Refurbish old buildings with insulation and require all new ones to generate their own zero-carbon power;
9. Dismantle the meat industry and move human protein requirements towards vegetable sources;
10. Pour public investment into the development and diffusion of the most efficient and sustainable renewable energy technologies, as well as technologies for carbon dioxide removal.[55]

This list mediates totality as a social and ecological whole. The world imagined by Malm's list is one of true technological solutions, of actual mitigations, and of committed politics. These points could each be described with those same labels given to strategies discussed by Klein, such as geoengineering, with the crucial distinction that Malm's list does not serve the interests of capital. Though few would count Klein as a Marxist, her enumeration of climate and social justice movements and trenchant critique of market fundamentalism generates a similar, and similarly imaginative, approach to the current conjuncture. Klein's attention to a critique of corporate and state climate-change approaches and conviction in movements shows the limits of abandoning the interests of subjects in favor of objects. Morton's approach to totality produces insights about the physical interconnections of energy and matter, yet in evacuating the mediation of social relations, it avoids the question of what to do in the face of this knowledge. Klein's approach provides solutions, difficult as the path to realize them may be. Klein bootstraps totality by centering emancipatory projects.

Ecology with Totality

We cannot think the climate crisis without a properly dialectical account of totality. Likewise, and this has been the implicit suggestion of this essay, we cannot produce a properly dialectical account of totality without considering climate crisis and the struggles already underway against it. The juxtaposition of Morton and Klein illustrates the problem of totality today. Klein's emphasis on politics, including the importance of human subjective agency that politics presupposes, contrasts with Morton's evacuation of subjectivity itself. This point is crucial to distinguish the implicitly political—that is to say, ideological—work of these two popular environmentalists. To put it emphatically, the hinge that connects Morton's work to Klein's has to do with the possibility of surmounting climate crisis. For the very impetus of both works is the same, save for one crucial feature. Yes, both writers address ecological catastrophe in the twenty-first century, but they are not writing from the same grounded purpose. Their results vary wildly. Morton, by focusing on the object, diminishes the subjective capacities of collective action, while Klein, at every turn, seeks to empower humanity's emancipatory forces. Moreover, the distinction between these two thinkers extends even further. Morton's writing solidifies the concept of time. The shift to hyperobjects produces a relativity effect: time seems to pass more slowly here than elsewhere, whereas for Klein the moment of resistance, the struggles at the blockade, and the small victories take on a punctual rhythm. Making clear such distinctions, however, has an effect of deadlocking the two thinkers.

Crisis makes structure apparent. Thinking totality is about thinking obscured options and finding unique ways to represent the unrepresentable. According to Klein, "disaster" can reveal "how dangerous it is to be dependent on centralized forms of energy that can be knocked out in one blow."[56] This Lukácsian take on crisis as a narrowing of mediation, as a moment of exposing contradictions, is true and yet, somehow, still inadequate to the task of rendering the warming world politically apprehensible. As Klein reports, "Over the course of the 1970s, there were 660 reported disasters around the world, including droughts, floods, extreme temperature events, wildfires, and storms. In the 2000s, there were 3,322—a fivefold boost."[57] How to square these circles? The dramatic uptick in extreme weather events ought to be a wake-up call, just as the ongoing stagnation of capital should set off alarm bells. Yet, capital's inertia pushes the Earth system toward the brink of collapse.

The whiplash caused as we leap back and forth between Morton's and Klein's explanatory systems reflects a sort of conceptual limit. Their irreconcilability begins to outline the impasse of their positions. Morton and Klein bring to the surface one of the contradictions of the climate-capital impasse. It is the very kernel that has prominent utopian leftists, such as Kim Stanley Robinson, calling for a reconsideration of geoengineering, while Alain Badiou suggests that what is needed is an "organization of societies on the scale of the whole world."[58] Intuitively, claims to massive scales, large projects, and big requests seem to be about reconfiguring human perceptions of daily life as one embedded in larger systems and structures. From the vantage of an individual living on the Earth, such claims offer a conceptual handle on social relations, on understanding the human journey as one with a collective destiny *whether or not we recognize it as such*. Ecological catastrophe and economic crisis are two expressions of the same capitalist dynamic. Some examples of this kind of overlay already exist. For instance, Nelson, who helped me open this chapter, draws explicitly on environmental and dialectical language to describe the crisis that early environmentalist texts identified: such a crisis was "ecological in the sense that it was not the production of a single cause or group of causes, but emergent from the totality of relations that made up modern society. The *problematique* was an apocalypse without cause, or whose cause was the totality itself."[59] Though they each emerge from the workings of capital, addressing one or the other directly tends to produce an intensification of the other. The language of a single line of causality breaks down when thinking about environmental systems because the health of ecosystems grows out of a multiplicity of emergent, contingent factors. Totality is thus a necessary, and necessarily inadequate, placeholder in systems thinking about both capitalism and climate change. Moreover, if capital proves a system that cannot be represented in its entirety, the Earth system surely poses similar problems of figuration. This problem itself defines what I mean when I use the word *totality*, just as it emphasizes the ultimate difference between the two thinkers I have considered. Put directly, totality names a problem for thought, a representation. At best, Morton seeks to remove the individual, human-focused actor from ecological questions; meanwhile Klein addresses the doubling and redoubling of climate injustice and social inequality that characterize the present. Ecology with totality can still be about you, me, us, and them, even as we seek to understand how to end the destructive habits of corporations, governments, institutions, and systems. The solution might rest in taking more of what we need instead of disappearing and in giving back according to our collective capacities, which can only grow as we extend and stretch such powers toward a new social and ecological whole.

Notes

1. Derek Woods, "Scale in Ecological Science Writing," in *The Routledge Handbook of Ecocriticism and Environmental Communication*, ed. Swarnalatha Rangarajan, Scott Slovic, and Vidya Sarweswaran (New York: Routledge, 2019), 121.

2. Sara Holiday Nelson, "Beyond the Limits to Growth: Ecology and the Neoliberal Counterrevolution," *Antipode* 47, no. 2 (2015): 466, https://doi.org/10.1111/anti.12125.

3. For instance, James Lovelock's 1972 Gaia hypothesis imagined the Earth and its inhabitants as a complete, integrated system. Similarly, sociologist Christian Parenti has argued the central thrust of the Club of Rome's 1972 report *Limits to Growth* was that it focused on "the interconnectedness of things"; Parenti, "'The Limits to Growth': A Book That Launched a Movement," *Nation*, December 5, 2012, https://www.thenation.com/article/limits-growth-book-launched-movement/.

4. Woods, "Scale in Ecological Science Writing," 118. For more on the macroscope, see Howard T. Odum, *Environment, Power, and Society* (New York: Wiley-Interscience, 1971), 11.

5. Woods focuses on superorganisms, chains, wheels, terraria and aquaria, and computers and networks.

6. Woods, "Scale in Ecological Science Writing."

7. "For everything to stay the same, everything has to change"—the source for Atwood's title is a character in Giuseppe di Lampedusa's novel *The Leopard* (London: Collins and Harvill Press, 1963), 149. This line of Lampedusa's emphasizes the constant transformation of the capitalist world-system that allows a certain portion of the population to experience a stable existence at the expense of immiseration and debt for everyone else.

8. Margaret Atwood, "It's not Climate Change—It's Everything Change," in *Energy Humanities: An Anthology*, ed. Dominic Boyer and Imre Szeman (Baltimore: John's Hopkins University Press, 2017), 147–48.

9. Theodor W. Adorno, "The Idea of Natural History," *Telos* 60 (1984): 118.

10. Some ecologists have made great work at forwarding a world-systems analysis approach; see Jason W. Moore, *Capitalism in the Web of Life: Ecology and the Accumulation of Capital* (New York: Verso, 2015), while others have taken up Marx's project of a critique of capitalist political economy; see Andreas Malm, *Fossil Capital: The Rise of Steam Power and the Roots of Global Warming* (New York: Verso, 2016). Other thinkers approach the question from a critique of colonialism or settler-colonialism; see Rob Nixon, *Slow Violence and the Environmentalism of the Poor* (Cambridge, Mass.: Harvard University Press, 2013), and Iyko Day, *Alien Capital: Asian Racialization and the Logic of Settler Colonial Capitalism* (Durham, N.C.: Duke University Press, 2016).

11. See the film *This Changes Everything*, dir. Avi Lewis (Abramorama, 2015).

12. Timothy Morton, *Hyperobjects: Philosophy after the End of the World* (Minneapolis: University of Minnesota Press, 2013), 1.

13. Ibid., 2

14. Timothy Morton, *Ecology without Nature* (Cambridge, Mass.: Harvard University Press, 2007), 1.

15. Ibid., 12

16. Ibid., 46.

17. Computer programmer Maureen Clark and neuroscientist Christopher Tyler produced the first black-and-white autostereogram in 1979. In 1993 N. E. Enterprises released *Magic Eye: A New Way of Looking at the World* (and subsequently, in 1996, changed the company name to Magic Eye Inc.).

18. Morton refers to false immediacy on pages 48, 62 103, 136, and 146 of *Hyperobjects*.

19. Theodor W. Adorno, *Minima Moralia: Reflections from a Damaged Life* (New York: Verso, 2005), 15.

20. Morton, *Hyperobjects*, 5.

21. Chris Tong argues that sliding-scale models make two related assumptions: they impose "a vertical hierarchy in which the astronomically vast hovers over the atomically tiny," and they imply "some entities are more fundamental than others by virtue of their size"; Tong, "Ecology without Scale: Unthinking the World Zoom," *Animation: An Interdisciplinary Journal* 9, no. 2 (2014): 198, https//doi.org/10.1177/1746847714527199. For work on the materiality of the digital, see Jeff Diamanti, "Energyscapes, Architecture, and the Expanded Field of Postindustrial Philosophy," *Postmodern Culture* 26, no. 2 (January 2016), https://doi.org/10.1353/pmc.2016.0006; Carolyn Elerding, "The Materiality of the Digital: Petro-Enlightenment and the Aesthetics of Invisibility," *Postmodern Culture* 26, no. 2 (January 2016), https://doi.org/10.1353/pmc.2016.0007; and Mél Hogan and Alix Johnson, eds., *Location and Dislocation: Global Geographies of Digital Data*, special issue of *Imaginations: A Journal of Cross-Cultural Image Studies* 8, no. 2 (September 6, 2017), https://doi.org/10.17742/IMAGE.LD.8.2.

22. Morton, *Hyperobjects*, 29; emphasis mine.

23. Anti-racism, critical animal studies, feminism, and Marxism, for instance.

24. Ibid., 54.

25. See "Compromise," OED Online, October 14, 2020. http://www.oed.com/view/Entry/37904?rskey=M7ONio&result=1&isAdvanced=false.

26. Ibid., 150.

27. Ibid., 65.

28. Ibid., 150.

29. See Neil Larsen, "Literature, Immanent Critique, and the Problem of Standpoint," *Mediations* 24, no. 2 (Spring 2009): 48–65.

30. Morton, *Hyperobjects*, 125.

31. For a useful discussion of Adorno and Heidegger, see Tom Whyman, "Understanding Adorno on 'Natural-History,'" *International Journal of Philosophical Studies* 24, no. 4 (2016): 452–72, https://doi.org/ 10.1080/09672559.2016.1206604.

32. Naomi Klein, *This Changes Everything: Capitalism versus the Climate* (Toronto: Vintage Canada, 2014), 4.

33. Ibid., 21. On the use and abuse of militarized metaphors for climate change, see Kate Yoder, "War of Words," *Grist*, December 5, 2018, https://grist.org/climate/the-war-on-climate-the-climate-fight-are-we-approaching-the-problem-all-wrong/.

34. Klein, *Everything*, 21.

35. Ibid., 22.

36. Klein's multinational approach moves beyond nationalistic approaches to understanding environmental struggles, especially in her discussion of environmental reparations, and she addresses what it means to be a settler activist from a settler-colonial state.

37. Ibid., 224.

38. Ibid.

39. Ibid., 193.

40. Klein, *Everything*, 269. Klein's arctic sulfur example has to do with the cooling effect produced as volcanoes spew gases into the atmosphere. Some scientists and geoengineers have worked on plans to pump sulfur into the atmosphere to combat the greenhouse gas effect and bounce some of the sun's rays spaceward.

41. Wendy Hui Kyong Chun, "On Hypo-Real Models or Global Climate Change: A Challenge for the Humanities," *Critical Inquiry* 41, no. 3 (March 2015): 690, https://doi.org/10.1086/680090.

42. Chun, "On Hypo-Real Models," 678. For another example of how ecological models produce conceptual challenges, see ecocriticism scholar Dana Phillips, who writes about the challenge of demonstrating the coherence and system-quality of ecosystems for even the best models. For instance, "significant numbers of the living creatures found in any given habitat are likely not to be integral participants in whatever large-scale phenomena may be occurring in their habitat day after day. They are, in effect, antisocial dropouts." Yet, Phillips adds that the challenge for ecologists is to determine which species are "redundant" and which are "vital" to the ongoing wellness of the habitat, adding, "What looks antisocial to one organism may be just another organism's way of biding its time"; Phillips, "Ecology Then and Now," in *The Truth of Ecology: Nature, Culture, Literature in America* (New York: Oxford University Press, 2003), 66, 67.

43. George Dvorsky of io9.com reported that "recent satellite images are now confirming [the iron sulphate's] effects—an artificial plankton bloom that's 10,000 square kilometers (3,861 square miles) in size. The intention of the project is for the plankton to absorb carbon dioxide and then sink to the bottom of the ocean"; "A Massive and Illegal Geoengineering Project has been Detected Off Canada's West Coast," *io9.com*, October 16, 2012, https://io9.gizmodo.com/5952101/a-massive-and-illegal-geoengineering-project-has-been-detected-off-canadas-west-coast.

44. Stephanie Pappas, "Iron Dumping in The Pacific Ocean Stirs Controversy over Geoengineering," *Huffington Post*, October 19, 2012, https://www.huffingtonpost.com/2012/10/19/pacific-ocean-iron-dumping-geoengineering_n_1986517.html.

45. Ibid., 284.

46. Ibid.

47. Ibid., 458.

48. Ibid., 452.

49. Many of these concessions were made through the burning of fossil fuels. Capitalists, men, and white people gave up less as fossil fuels cushioned the amortization of inequality, staving off any real accounting of reparations and equalization.

50. Pappas, "Iron Dumping in The Pacific Ocean," 102. See also Elisabeth Rosenthal, "Life After Oil and Gas," *New York Times*, March 23, 2013, http://www.nytimes.com/2013/03/24/sunday-review/life-after-oil-and-gas.html.

51. I would further illustrate the shared critical assessment and political vision, by making clear that while Jameson argues that the nationalization of banks is of the utmost import at present, even he adds that "what has come to seem more immediately urgent, particularly in the era of climate change now upon us, is the wholesale seizure of all energy sources, the appropriation of the oil wells and the coal mines and the destitution of the immense transnational companies that control them"; Fredric Jameson, *An American Utopia: Dual Power and the Universal Army* (New York: Verso, 2016), 7.

52. Andreas Malm, "Revolution in a Warming World: Lessons from the Russian to the Syrian Revolutions," *Socialist Register* 53 (2017): 136.

53. Alberto Toscano and Jeff Kinkle, *Cartographies of the Absolute* (London: Zero, 2015), 24.

54. Malm, "Revolution," 136.

55. Malm, "Revolution," 134–35. See also Kark Marx and Friedrich Engels, *The Communist Manifesto*, ed., trans. L. M. Findlay (Peterborough: Broadview, 2004), 82–83.

56. Klein, *Everything*, 105.

57. Ibid., 107. Here's another figure from Klein's book: there is so much oil being extracted and transported within the U.S. today that the number of railway cars shipping oil has increased "4111 percent in just five years, from 9,500 cars in 2008 to an estimated 400,000 in 2013." Klein adds a salient point in parenthesis following this statistic: "(Little wonder that significantly more oil spilled in U.S. rail incidents in 2013 than spilled in the previous forty years combined—or that trains engulfed in smoking fireballs have become increasingly frequent sights on the nightly news)" (311).

58. See Alexander C. Kaufman, "The King of Climate Fiction Makes the Left's Case for Geoengineering: Kim Stanley Robinson Argues That Blanket Opposition to Intervening in the Climate Is Wrongheaded," *Huffpost*, July 28, 2018, https://www.huffingtonpost.ca/entry/climate-geoengineering-kim-stanley-robinson_us_5b4e54bde4b0de86f487b0b9. Badiou's formulation is beautiful: "No privatisation of property which must be common, namely the production of all that is necessary for human life. No family of heirs, no concentrated inheritances. No separate state protecting the oligarchies. No hierarchy of work. No nations, no closed and hostile identities. Collective organization of everything that has a collective destiny"; Alain Badiou, "Capitalism, The Sole Culprit of the Destructive Exploitation of Nature," trans. Sam Warren Mie, *Le Monde*, July 26, 2018, http://theoryleaks.org/text/articles/alain-badiou/capitalism-the-sole-culprit-of-the-destructive-exploitation-of-nature/.

59. Nelson, "Beyond," 468.

Works Cited

Adorno, Theodor W. *Minima Moralia: Reflections from a Damaged Life*. New York: Verso, 2005.

———. "The Idea of Natural-History." *Telos* 60 (1984): 111–24.

Atwood, Margaret. "It's not Climate Change—It's Everything Change." *Energy Humanities: An Anthology*, edited by Dominic Boyer and Imre Szeman, 139–50. Baltimore: John's Hopkins University Press, 2017.

Badiou, Alain. "Capitalism, The Sole Culprit of the Destructive Exploitation of Nature." Translated by Sam Warren Mie. *Le Monde*, July 26, 2018. http://theoryleaks.org/text/articles/alain-badiou/capitalism-the-sole-culprit-of-the-destructive-exploitation-of-nature/.

"Compromise, v." OED Online. September 2020. Oxford University Press. www.oed.com/view/Entry/37904. Accessed October 14, 2020.

Chun, Wendy Hui Kyong. "On Hypo-Real Models or Global Climate Change: A Challenge for the Humanities." *Critical Inquiry* 41, no. 3 (March 2015): 675–703. https://doi.org/10.1086/680090.

Day, Iyko. *Alien Capital: Asian Racialization and the Logic of Settler Colonial Capitalism*. Durham, N.C.: Duke University Press, 2016.

Diamanti, Jeff. "Energyscapes, Architecture, and the Expanded Field of Postindustrial Philosophy." *Postmodern Culture* 26, no. 2 (January 2016). https://doi.org/10.1353/pmc.2016.0006.

Dvorsky, George. "A Massive and Illegal Geoengineering Project Has Been Detected Off Canada's West Coast." *io9.com*, October 16, 2012. https://io9.gizmodo.com/5952101/a-massive-and-illegal-geoengineering-project-has-been-detected-off-canadas-west-coast.

Elerding, Carolyn. "The Materiality of the Digital: Petro-Enlightenment and the Aesthetics of Invisibility." *Postmodern Culture* 26, no. 2, January 2016. https://doi.org/10.1353/pmc.2016.0007.

Hogan, Mél, and Alix Johnson, eds. *Location and Dislocation: Global Geographies of Digital Data*, in *Imaginations: A Journal of Cross-Cultural Image Studies* 8, no. 2 (September 6, 2017). https://doi.org/10.17742/IMAGE.LD.8.2.

Jameson, Fredric. *An American Utopia: Dual Power and the Universal Army*. New York: Verso, 2016.

Kaufman, Alexander C. "The King of Climate Fiction Makes the Left's Case for Geoengineering: Kim Stanley Robinson Argues That Blanket Opposition to Intervening in the Climate Is Wrongheaded." *Huffpost*, July 28, 2018. https://www.huffingtonpost.ca/entry/climate-geoengineering-kim-stanley-robinson_us_5b4e54bde4b0de86f487b0b9.

Klein, Naomi. *This Changes Everything: Capitalism versus the Climate*. Toronto: Vintage Canada, 2014.

Lampedusa, Giuseppe di. *The Leopard*. London: Collins and Harvill Press, 1963.

Larsen, Neil. "Literature, Immanent Critique, and the Problem of Standpoint." *Mediations* 24, no. 2 (Spring 2009): 48–65.

Lewis, Avi, dir. *This Changes Everything*. Abramorama, 2015.

Lovelock, James E. "Gaia as Seen through the Atmosphere." *Atmospheric Environment* 6, no. 8 (1972): 579–80. https://doi.org/10.1016/0004-6981(72)90076-5.

Malm, Andreas. *Fossil Capital: The Rise of Steam Power and the Roots of Global Warming*. New York: Verso, 2016.

———. "Revolution in a Warming World: Lessons from the Russian to the Syrian Revolutions." *Socialist Register* 53 (2017): 120–42.

Marx, Karl, and Friedrich Engels. *The Communist Manifesto*. Edited and translated by L. M. Findlay. Peterborough: Broadview, 2004.

Moore, Jason W. *Capitalism in the Web of Life: Ecology and the Accumulation of Capital*. New York: Verso, 2015.

Morton, Timothy. *Ecology without Nature: Rethinking Environmental Aesthetics*. Cambridge, Mass.: Harvard University Press, 2007.

———. *Hyperobjects: Philosophy and Ecology after the End of the World*. Minneapolis: University of Minnesota Press, 2013.

Nelson, Sara Holiday. "Beyond *The Limits to Growth*: Ecology and the Neoliberal Counterrevolution." *Antipode* 47, no. 2 (2015): 461–80. https://doi.org/10.1111/anti.12125.

Nixon, Rob. *Slow Violence and the Environmentalism of the Poor*. Cambridge, Mass.: Harvard University Press, 2013.

Odum, Howard T. *Environment, Power, and Society*. New York: Wiley-Interscience, 1971.

Pappas, Stephanie. "Iron Dumping in The Pacific Ocean Stirs Controversy over Geoengineering." *Huffington Post*, October 19, 2012. https://www.huffingtonpost.com/2012/10/19/pacific-ocean-iron-dumping-geoengineering_n_1986517.html.

Parenti, Christian. "'The Limits to Growth': A Book That Launched a Movement." *Nation*, December 5, 2012. https://www.thenation.com/article/limits-growth-book-launched-movement/.

Phillips, Dana. "Ecology Then and Now." In *The Truth of Ecology: Nature, Culture, Literature in America*, 42–82. New York: Oxford University Press, 2003.

Rosenthal, Elisabeth. "Life After Oil and Gas." *New York Times*, March 23, 2013. http://www.nytimes.com/2013/03/24/sunday-review/life-after-oil-and-gas.html

Tong, Chris. "Ecology without Scale: Unthinking the World Zoom." *Animation: An Interdisciplinary Journal* 9, no. 2 (2014): 196–211. https//doi.org/10.1177/1746847714527199.

Toscano, Alberto, and Jeff Kinkle. *Cartographies of the Absolute*. London: Zero, 2015.

Whyman, Tom. "Understanding Adorno on 'Natural-History.'" *International Journal of Philosophical Studies* 24, no. 4 (2016): 452–72. https://doi.org/10.1080/09672559.2016.1206604.

Woods, Derek. "Scale in Ecological Science Writing." In *The Routledge Handbook of Ecocriticism and Environmental Communication*, edited by Swarnalatha Rangarajan, Scott Slovic, and Vidya Sarweswaran, 118–28. New York: Routledge, 2019.

Yoder, Kate. "War of Words." *Grist* 5 December 5, 2018. https://grist.org/climate/the-war-on-climate-the-climate-fight-are-we-approaching-the-problem-all-wrong/.

Acknowledgments

This book would not exist without Kevin Floyd. We mean this in a more profound sense than the fact that he was co-conceiver and coeditor of the volume. We mean that the ideas in this book and labor that went into its making would not have been possible without Kevin. His brilliance runs through these essays, sometimes surfacing in quotations from his groundbreaking *The Reification of Desire* or his provocative "Automatic Subjects: Gendered Labour and Abstract Life," sometimes resting just under the page. Whether explicitly cited or not, Kevin and his commitment to thinking the hardest thoughts about the most pressing and complex issues—class, sexuality, race, gender, labor, capitalism, et cetera (aka, totality)—has in one way or another pushed everyone involved in this collection to think harder and better and more clearly. But to describe Kevin as brilliant is only to give half a sense of the person. Kevin was the most generous listener and conversation partner in whatever room he found himself in. At the annual Marxist Literary Group conferences, he attended every session, listened to every presentation with equal intensity and interest, and followed up with speakers to continue discussing their work. He was particularly attentive to graduate students; Kevin was as brilliant a teacher as he was a theorist, as enthusiastic a cheerleader as he was a questioner. And this still doesn't capture Kevin. You can't remember Kevin without remembering sometime or another laughing so hard you were both crying; you can't remember Kevin without remembering some meandering conversation that touched on books and movies and music and family and fears of flying. Even with all this, we fear we haven't quite described Kevin. He was, simply put, the best of us, and we all miss him terribly.

Our hope is that this book gets his ideas into more heads and hands, that maybe a phrase or an idea opens a new thought, or maybe it just reminds the reader of something particularly smart or funny or kind Kevin said or wrote.

Because of Kevin's too-soon death, when this book was barely assembled and the introduction only half-written, we have some important acknowledgments to make. To the press, particularly Richard Morrison, and to our peer readers: thank you for your encouragement and commitment. To Jerry Floyd and Tammy Clewell, thank you for helping us get this book across the finish line.

We have a few individual acknowledgments to make as well. Brent Ryan Bellamy would like to thank Barbara Bell, Alexandra Carruthers, and George, Kevin Floyd, and Jen Phillis. Sarika Chandra and Chris Chen want to thank Kevin Floyd, Jen Phillis, and Colleen Lye for reading and commenting on drafts of their essay, and Angie Sijun Lou for formatting work. They also want to express their tremendous gratitude for emancipatory global movements that continue to challenge existing theoretical maps of the conditions of political struggle. Jen Hedler Phillis would like to thank her mister, Richard, and her bestie, Lindsay.

Collectively, we would like to thank comrades, bourbon, coffee, and Kleenex, not always in that order.

We would also like to collectively situate this book in relation to the territories on which much of it was conceived and written, including the Mississaugas of the Credit, the Anishnabeg, the Chippewa, the Haudenosaunee, and the Wendat peoples, the Ojibwe, the Odawa, the Ohlone, the Potawatomi, the Miami, the Ho-Chunk, the Menominee, the Sac, and the Fox, among many others. We note the forces of ongoing settler colonization and recognize the resurgence of Indigenous lifeways, modes of relation, peoples, and relatives across the lands known as Turtle Island, North America, and by other names. The contributors have come by different paths to different territories. Long before the arrival of settlers and before treaties were made or disavowed, nations and peoples with many varied relations to the land abided here. As each of us acknowledges that our own history and relationship to the land are partial, so too do we recognize that this acknowledgment passes over kin, land, and people in silence. As much as our work here is incomplete (we think of it as ongoing), we also believe this status is fitting, given our self-appointed task in this collection to broaden the meaning of totality, which, among other things, stands against colonial infrastructures and mindsets.

Contributors

Brent Ryan Bellamy teaches courses on critical worldbuilding, graphic fiction, American petrocultures, and science fiction as a contract instructor at Trent University. He has recently published articles in the *Canadian Review of American Studies*, *Polygraph*, *Resilience*, and several edited collections. He has edited journal special issues on energy humanities, resource aesthetics, and science fiction and the climate crisis and two books, *Materialism and the Critique of Energy* (MCM', 2018) and *An Ecotopian Lexicon* (University of Minnesota Press, 2019). His book *Remainders of the American Century: Post-Apocalyptic Novels in the Age of US Decline* is available from Wesleyan University Press (2021).

Sarah Brouillette is a Professor in the Department of English at Carleton University in Ottawa, Canada. She is the author of three books: *Postcolonial Writers in the Global Literary Marketplace* (Palgrave, 2007); *Literature and the Creative Economy* (Stanford, 2014); and *UNESCO and the Fate of the Literary* (Stanford, 2019).

Sarika Chandra is an Associate Professor of English at Wayne State University. She researches and teaches in the areas of globalization studies, American Studies, and Race and Ethnic Studies. Theorizing the U.S. in a transnational frame, her work focuses on race, ethnicity, im/migration, and the environment. Chandra is the author of *Dislocalism: The Crisis of Globalization and the Remobilizing of Americanism* (Ohio State University Press, 2011). Her publications have appeared in various volumes and journals including *American Quarterly*, *Cultural Critique*, and *Modern*

Language Notes. With Chris Chen, she is finishing a book on capitalism and contemporary theories of racial group formation.

Chris Chen is an Associate Professor of Literature at the University of California at Santa Cruz. Chen has published poetry, essays, interviews, and reviews in *boundary 2*, the *South Atlantic Quarterly*, *The Routledge Companion to Literature and Economics*, the *New Inquiry*, *Crayon*, *1913: A Journal of Forms*, *Tripwire*, and the *Los Angeles Review of Books*. His book-length comparative study of contemporary Black and Asian North American experimental poetry, *Literature and Race in the Democracy of Goods*, is forthcoming from Bloomsbury. With Sarika Chandra, he is finishing a book on capitalism and contemporary theories of racial group formation.

Joshua Clover is the author of seven books, including *Roadrunner* (Duke University Press, 2021) as well as *Riot.Strike.Riot: the New Era of Uprisings* (Verso 2016), a political economy of social movements, with recent editions in French, German, Turkish, and Swedish. He is a currently Professor of English and Comparative Literature at University of California, Davis as well as Professor of Literature and Modern Culture at University of Copenhagen.

Tim Kreiner is a Lecturer in the Department of English at Yale University. He is completing a book of literary history titled *The Long Downturn and Its Discontents: Poetry, Culture Wars, and the New Left*. His writing on poetry and politics has appeared in or is forthcoming from *The Routledge Companion to Literature and Economics* (Routledge, 2018), *Contemporary Literature*, *Post-45*, *Los Angeles Review of Books*, *Viewpoint Magazine*, and *Lana Turner*.

Jen Hedler Phillis lives in Chicago. Her primary academic area of interest revolves around the intersection of poetics and politics; her primary political area of interest revolves around dismantling capitalism. Her first book, *Poems of the American Empire*, was published by the University of Iowa Press in 2019.

Arthur Scarritt is Professor and Chair of the Department of Sociology at Boise State University. He studies how people challenge and reproduce the multiple forms of inequality that make up their lives. His book *Racial Spoils from Native Soils* (Rowman and Littlefield, 2015) looks at how Peruvian neoliberal reforms exacerbate the racist coloniality that keeps indigenous Andeans oppressed. He is working to apply these insights to the U.S. and globally. Scarritt's 2019 article, "Selling Diversity, Promoting Racism," published in the *Journal for Critical Education Policy Studies*, explains how the diversity efforts of a commercially oriented university end up bolstering campus racism. This research comes out of the Intermountain Social Research Lab (IMSRL). The lab employs intensive undergraduate research training as part of its investigation into the privatization of public higher education. Research from the project has shown how the neoliberal university trains students to embrace the inequalities, limited learning, sexism, and racism that undermine the value of their educations. He earned his bachelor's at the Evergreen State College and his Ph.D. at the University of Wisconsin-Madison.

Zoe Sutherland is a writer based in Brighton. She is a Senior Lecturer in Humanities at the University of Brighton and writes on various aspects of feminist theory and history, as well as on contemporary art.

Marina Vishmidt is a writer and editor. She teaches at Goldsmiths, University of London. Her work has appeared in *South Atlantic Quarterly, Artforum, Afterall, Journal of Cultural Economy, e-flux journal, Australian Feminist Studies*, and *Radical Philosophy*, among others, as well as a number of edited volumes. She is the co-author of *Reproducing Autonomy* (with Kerstin Stakemeier) (Mute, 2016), and the author of *Speculation as a Mode of Production: Forms of Value Subjectivity in Art and Capital* (Brill 2018/Haymarket 2019). She is one of the organizers of the Centre for Philosophy and Critical Thought at Goldsmiths and a member of the Marxism in Culture collective and is on the board of the New Perspectives on the Critical Theory of Society series (Bloomsbury Academic).

Index

Adorno, Theodor, 5–6, 13, 213
Alcoff, Linda, 144
Allen, Theodore, 93, 105–6
Alquati, Romano, 36–37
Appiah, Kwame Anthony, 141
Arrighi, Giovanni, 204
Arruzza, Cinzia, 13, 76, 81–82, 84–85
art: and class, 20, 206–7; and identification, 200–3; interpretation of, 202–3; and the marketplace, 203–4; and politics, 19–20, 199–205; and the university, 207–9
Atwood, Margaret, 212–13
autonomia. *See* workers' movement: in Italy
autonomy, 19–20, 197; aesthetic, 198–99

Bacon's Rebellion, 103
Bannerji, Himani, 75
Beech, Dave, 205–6
Benjamin, Walter, 204
Bhandar, Brenna, 18
Bhattacharya, Tithi, 12, 74
Black Lives Matter, 84
Black Panthers, 39–40
Black Power, 30. *See also* race: liberatory movements
Boggs, James, 30, 41
Bourdieu, Pierre, 204
bourgeoisie, 33, 35
Brenner, Johanna, 73
Brenner, Robert, 10
Brown, Nicholas, 203
Butler, Judith, 43–44

capitalism: and art, 20–21, 205–6; and COVID-19, 159–60; and ecology, 156, 159, 220–21, 222, 224, 227, 228; and identity, 165; industrial, 92–93, 95, 107–10, 114; and race, 14, 108, 146, 167; and racialization, 136–39, 152–57; and the state, 158; and totality, 1–2, 81–82
carbon storage, 222
Carmichael, Stokely, 113
causality, 229; and class, 157; and race, 148–50, 152, 157
Chang, Harry, 40
Chun, Wendy Hui Kyong, 223
class: as economic inequality, 136, 152–54, 198, 199; as relation, 143
class composition, 135–36. *See also* proletariat
class struggle, 33–35; and identity, 7–8, 18–19, 70–71, 92, 109–10, 135–37, 143–44, 199; and inequality, 198–99; under neoliberalism, 118–20
Collins, Patricia Hill, 73
colonialism, 2, 16; Dutch, 98; and feudalism, 96–100; and industrialization, 110; internal, 38–39, 40; and racialization, 98, 99–107, 121; and renter class, 97–100; Spanish, 98–102; UK, 97–98
Combahee River Collective, 6–8, 8–9, 46, 70, 143
Crenshaw, Kimberlé, 71–73

da Silva, Denise Ferreira, 165–66
Dalla Costa, Mariarosa, 44–45

244 / INDEX

Darder, Antonia, 141
Dauvé, Gilles, 30
Davis, Angela, 72, 141
Davis, Mike, 160
Dawson, Michael, 18–19, 154, 162–63
de Sismondi, Simonde, 32
De'Ath, Amy, 69
Du Bois, W. E. B., 15, 140
Durkheim, Émile, 151, 152–53

energy transition, 224–26
exclusion, 16–17, 119–21. See also totality: negative
exploitation, 94–95, 138, 198; and expropriation, 154–55
expropriation, 138, 154–55, 156–60
expulsion, 138, 155–60

feminism: antagonisms within, 83–84; cultural, 42–43, 46; and law, 68, 72–73; materialist, 68–70, 73–74, 204; and race, 69–70; radical, 42–43, 46; second wave, 42; and sexuality, 69–70
Ferguson, Susan, 1–2, 10, 12, 73–75
feudalism, 96–100
Fields, Barbara 141, 159. See also *Racecraft*
Fields, Karen, 141, 159. See also *Racecraft*
financialization, 118
Firestone, Shulamith, 30–31, 44
Floyd, George, 168
Floyd, Kevin, 68, 70–71, 78, 80–81, 83
Fraser, Nancy, 2, 11, 18, 154–55

gender: classification of, 42, 47, 67–69; liberatory movements, 29–32. See also feminism
geoengineering, 222–24, 227
George, Russ, 223
Gilmore, Ruth Wilson, 17, 41, 141
Gilroy, Paul, 141
Gonzalez, Maya, 45, 79

Haider, Asad, 83, 85
Hall, Stuart, 142, 144
Hardt, Michael, 93–94
Harney, Stefano, 141, 157–59
Harris, Cheryl, 18
Harvey, David, 92, 116, 193
Hayden, Casey, 42
hologram. *See* hyperobjects
Horne, Gerald, 103
Hudson, Peter James, 15

hyperobjects, 225; and capitalism, 219; definition of, 214–15; examples of, 215–16; and subjectivity, 217–20; and totality, 214, 215, 218

identity, and rights, 197; classification of, 38, 47, 67–69, 73; and the law, 81; as sliding signifier, 144–45; as social relation, 144–45
identity politics, 2–3; and art, 19, 199; and class struggle, 7–8, 18–19, 29–32, 35, 46, 135–37, 143–44, 199; cultural, 38–40, 42–43, 137; and culture, 48–49; and heterogeneity, 140; history of, 6–8, 31, 69–70, 143–44; of labor, 76–77; and racialization, 139; and totality, 9
Ignatiev, Noel, 141
incarceration, 17, 41, 48, 120–21, 157
industrial workers. *See* proletariat
International Women's Strike, 49, 84
intersectionality, 10–11, 71–74; Marxist critique of, 73–74; and totality, 74, 77–79, 83

Jacobson, Mark, 225
Jameson, Fredric, 204, 225–26
Jones, Claudia, 72

Karenga, Maulana, 39–40
King, Mary, 42
Klein, Naomi, 213–14

liberalism, 197–98
Lorde, Audre, 84
Lukács, György, 3–5, 13, 196

Magic Eye. *See* hyperobjects
Malm, Andreas, 226–27
Manrique, Nelson, 112
Mascat, Jamila, 82
McNally, David, 11, 73–74
mediation, 202–3, 216–19, 220, 229
mestizo, 111–12
Michaels, Walter Benn: on autonomy, 198–99, 200; on interpretation, 202–3, 204–5; on neoliberalim, 200–2; on race, 201–2; on "Wand #1," 199–202
Mies, Maria, 79
migration, 157, 158–59
Miles, Robert, 141
Mohandesi, Salar, 6, 10–11
Mojab, Shahrzad, 46
Moore, Jason W., 79

Morton, Timothy, 213–14. *See also* hyperobjects
Moten, Fred, 141, 157–59

neoliberalism, 91–92, 95–96; and art, 192–93, 194–95, 200–2; definition of, 192–96; horizontalism of, 194–96; 197–98; and labor, 118; and race, 92, 115, 118; and rentier class, 93, 115–17, 119–21; and subjectivity, 192, 197, 200; and surplus populations, 117
Neton, Jeanne, 45, 79
New Deal, the, 108
New Left, the, 29–30, 69, 144
Newton, Huey, 39–40
Ni Una Menos, 84

Odum, Howard T., 212
O'Kane, Chris, 80
Organization for Black Power (OBP), 41
operaismo. *See* workers' movement: in Italy

Patterson, Orlando, 18
Peru: *encomienda* system of, 98–101; land reform, 110–11, 112; neoliberalism in, 119; Toledo reforms, 101–2, 103
Postone, Moishe, 5–6, 13, 166–67
proletarianization, 8–9, 34–35
proletariat, 4–5; and colonialism, 102; composition of, 48–49; definition of, 32–38, 47–48; divided, 45–48, 104–7, 108, 109–10, 114, 121; as identity, 36; as industrial workers, 6, 29, 37, 48; in Marx, 32, 33–35

race: abolition of, 137, 140–42; and capitalism, 14, 146, 167; classification of, 47, 135–36, 142–43; conservation of, 137, 140, 141, 147; and COVID-19, 159–60; and culture, 161–62; definition of, 145–47; eliminitavist accounts of, 137, 140–42, 147; as group solidarity, 3, 163–64; and hierarchy, 164; liberatory movements, 29–32, 38–41; as linked fate, 19, 162–63, 167; and lived experience, 168; in Marxism, 161; political economy of, 40–42; and racialization, 146; as relation, 140, 143, 164; and relative privilege, 113–14, 115, 121; as sliding signifier, 142–43; and social reproduction, 14–15, 158–59, 165; and universality, 166; and welfare state, 113–14
Racecraft, 137–38, 161; definition of race, 147–48; on economic inequality, 152–54; and eliminativist accounts of race, 149–52; race and economic inequality in, 148–49;

racialization, 149–51; on racism, 148–49, 150–51
racialization, 3, 15, 40, 142–43, 150–51; and capitalism, 136–39; deracialization, 109, 110; and identity, 139–40; and labor, 101–2; in North America, 102–6; in Peru, 100–2, 106, 111–12; and race, 146; and rentier class, 94, 100–7, 110–13. *See also* race: classification of
racism, 15–16, 92, 135–36, 145–46; global system of, 93–94, 110, 113, 122
Racism Research Project, 31
Rainbow Coalition, 39–40
Razack, Sherene, 73
Redstockings Manifesto, 30
rentier class, 16, 92–94; and class struggle, 118–20; and colonialism, 97–100; end of, 107; and industrialization, 114; and neoliberalism, 115–17, 119–21; and racialization, 94, 100–7, 110–13; in the UK, 97
reproduction: of gender, 3, 45, 48; of labor, 95; of race, 48. *See also* social reproduction
reproductive labor, 12–14, 48. *See also* social reproduction
revolutionary subject, 4–5, 10, 31, 44, 47–49; and race, 18. *See also* proletariat
Robinson, Cedric, 141
Roediger, David, 141

Samuelson, Paul, 116
Sassen, Saskia, 116, 155–56
Schor, Juliet, 116
Shelby, Tommie, 162–63
Shiva, Vandana, 224
Silent Spring, 211–12
Singh, Nikhil, 17, 157
Sisters Uncut, 84
slavery, 15, 18, 103–6
social reproduction, 44–45; and ecology, 21; and gender, 11–14, 17; and labor, 76–79; and race, 14–15, 158–59, 165; and racialization, 17–19; and surplus population, 17; theory, 74–79; and universality, 83; and value, 77–79
social whole, 1–2; and capitalism, 75, 82; and rights, 68. *See also* totality
surplus population, 4, 16–17, 78, 94; and colonialism, 97; and neoliberalism, 117. *See also* expulsion

Tadiar, Neferti, 15
Taylor, Keeanga-Yamahtta, 169

Taylor, Paul C., 145–47
Thompson Patterson, Louise, 71
Tomba, Massimiliano, 81
Torres, Rodolfo, 141
totality: aspiration toward, 1, 3–5, 10–11, 22, 76, 80–81, 211–12; and capitalism, 81–82, 196–97; and crisis, 229; and ecology, 211–14, 221, 226–30; and identity politics, 9; and intersectionality, 74, 77–79, 83; in Marx, 80; negative, 79–81, 82; as socioeconomic, 3–6, 11–12, 13; *versus* universality, 68–69, 81–82
Truth, Sojourner, 71

unemployment, 78, and race, 200
universality, 6–9, 165–67; and art, 205; politics of, 67–69, 79, 82–83; and race, 166; and totality, 68–69, 81–82
Us organization, 39–40

value form, 77–79, 196
Velasco, Juan, 110–11
Vogel, Lise, 14, 76
von Stein, Lorenz, 33

Wages for Housework, 44–45, 225
Wallace, Rob, 160
welfare state, 113
white supremacy. *See* racism
Wilderson, Frank, 18
Wilhelm, Sidney, 41
Williams, Eric, 15
Williams, Raymond, 21, 204
Women's Liberation Movement, 42–44
workers' movement, 10, 29–32, 34, 35; and identity, 8–9; in Italy, 36–37; and race, 107–8

Zack, Naomi, 141
Žižek, Slavoj, 121

www.ingramcontent.com/pod-product-compliance
Lightning Source LLC
Chambersburg PA
CBHW032032290426
44110CB00012B/771